Struggles over Difference

Struggles over Difference

Curriculum, Texts, and Pedagogy in the Asia-Pacific

Edited by

Yoshiko Nozaki, Roger Openshaw, and Allan Luke

State University of New York Press

Published by
State University of New York Press, Albany

For information, address State University of New York Press,
194 Washington Avenue, Suite 305, Albany, NY 12210-2384

Production by Michael Haggett
Marketing by Anne M. Valentine

Library of Congress Cataloging-in-Publication Data

Struggles over difference : curriculum, texts, and pedagogy in the Asia-Pacific /
edited by Yoshiko Nozaki, Roger Openshaw, and Allan Luke.
    p.cm.
Includes bibliographical references and index.
    ISBN 0-7914-6397-4 (alk. paper) — ISBN 0-7914-6398-2 (pbk. : alk. paper)
    1. Multicultural education—Curricula—East Asia. 2. Multicultural
education—Curricula—Pacific Area. 3. Critical pedagogy—East Asia.
4. Critical pedagogy—Pacific Area. 5. Textbook bias—East Asia.
6. Textbook bias—Pacific Area. I. Nozaki, Yoshiko, 1956– II. Openshaw, Roger.
III. Luke, Allan.

LC1099.5.E18S87   2005
370'.95—dc22   2004048222

Contents

Introduction   1
Yoshiko Nozaki, Roger Openshaw, and Allan Luke

Chapter 1   Curriculum, Ethics, Metanarrative: Teaching and
            Learning Beyond the Nation   11
            Allan Luke

Chapter 2   "… Nothing Objectionable or Controversial":
            The Image of Maori Ethnicity and "Difference"
            in New Zealand Social Studies   25
            Roger Openshaw

Chapter 3   State Formation, Hegemony, and Chinese School
            Curricula in Singapore and Hong Kong, 1945–1965   41
            Ting-Hong Wong

Chapter 4   Official Knowledge and Hegemony: The Politics
            of the Textbook Deregulation Policy in Taiwan   59
            Jyh-Jia Chen

Chapter 5   Thai English Language Textbooks, 1960–2000:
            Postwar Industrial and Global Changes   79
            Noparat Suaysuwan and Cushla Kapitzke

Chapter 6   The Construction of Culture Knowledge in
            Chinese Language Textbooks: A Critical
            Discourse Analysis   99
            Yongbing Liu

Chapter 7   New Ideologies of Everyday Life in South Korean
            Language Textbooks   117
            Dong Bae (Isaac) Lee

Chapter 8   Environmental Education and Development in
China   131
Darren M. O'Hern

Chapter 9   School Knowledge and Classed and Gendered
Subjectivities in South Korean Commercial
High Schools   147
Misook Kim

Chapter 10   Identity Conversion, Citizenship, and Social Studies:
Asian-Australian Perspectives on Indigenous
Reconciliation and Human Rights   163
Michael Singh

Chapter 11   Fastening and Unfastening Identities: Negotiating
Identity in Hawai'i   183
Gay Garland Reed

Chapter 12   The Question of Identity and Difference: The
Resident Korean Education in Japan   199
Hiromitsu Inokuchi and Yoshiko Nozaki

Chapter 13   History, Postmodern Discourse, and the Japanese
Textbook Controversy over "Comfort Women"   217
Yoshiko Nozaki

Contributors   235

Index   239

Introduction

Yoshiko Nozaki, Roger Openshaw, and Allan Luke

This volume is about education and schools, textbooks, and pedagogies in the countries of the Asia-Pacific. The chapters in this volume offer critical and reconceptualist curriculum studies and policy analyses of various national and regional educational systems. All of these systems face significantly complex challenges linked to new social and economic formations, cultural globalization, and emergent regional and international geopolitical instabilities and conflicts. The chapters in this volume offer empirical and theoretical insights on the issues of what counts as official knowledge, text, discourse, and discipline; how they should be shaped; who should shape them; and through which social, cultural, and institutional agencies they should be administered and practiced.

There are, of course, various possible approaches to such issues,—which focus on "identity," "hegemony," "nation," "gender," and "culture," no matter how unstable such concepts might be. Until recently, however, educational researchers have drawn principally from two limited approaches in the available literature and texts on the Asia-Pacific. The first approach consists of a general descriptive and comparative discussion of policy, history, and context, often with little specific documentation of the actual politics involved in teaching, learning, curriculum, and pedagogy at macro and/or micro levels. The second approach has tended to present comparative views of "Asia" from the standpoint and perspective of Western and Northern epistemologies and disciplines.

Both are, in part, the legacies of comparative education and Western "area studies." Both have their genesis in European and North American university studies of the "Other"—fields that were often supported by Western governments and their surveillance and intelligence arms, churches and religious organizations, and, later, nongovernment development and aid agencies. Much of this work has tended to position countries, systems, and educators of the Asia-Pacific within discourses of aid, "development," poverty amelioration, and, most recently, neoliberal discourses that call for the "modernization" of such systems through marketization, economic rationalization, and new managerial models (see also Stiglitz, 2001). Hence, there has been a de facto relegation of the Asia-Pacific to studies of education in "foreign" context and, however unintentionally, treatment of its communities

1

and systems as exotic or "exceptional" objects within the fields of curriculum studies and educational policy. These approaches have been destabilized, first by successive waves of postcolonial and indigenous epistemology and theory, as well as feminist and women's perspectives, and more recently by varied and complex analyses of the push/pull and local/global dynamics of globalization—with much of the most interesting and innovative cultural studies and social science work coming from scholars in Taiwan, Japan, Korea, Singapore, and Hong Kong.

The works contained in this volume present a diverse set of tools from social theory and critical educational studies for addressing a range of pedagogic contexts and curricular practices which many have increasingly found troubling and in need of attention. The chapters in this volume do not fall neatly and tidily into any of the overarching theoretical categories or standpoints (such as "postcolonial," "neo-Marxist," "feminist," "poststructuralist," and "postmodernist") that have become de facto grids for recent Western research on the issues of curriculum and pedagogy. They do, however, address scholarly fields and concerns, as well as developing and ongoing intellectual and political projects, and—as instances of grounded theory—they open up analyses and readings of the world and so make intervention possible.

The writings collected here disrupt many popular mythologies about education in Asia and the Pacific. These include base suppositions about the "Other": that Asian pedagogy is exclusively "rote learning"; that educational systems and governments in the Asia-Pacific are faced with classical "developing country" issues; and that institutional and state formation in the Asia-Pacific can be assessed on a North/South, West/East, or left/right continuum as moving inexorably towards neoliberal economic and social policy and Western "democracy" affiliated with the United States and Europe. Further, there is a broader supposition underlying most Western curriculum work: that issues of ideology and curriculum content are principally "developed country" concerns; that Western and Northern concepts and approaches of "multiculturalism," "cultural appropriateness," affirmative action, and so forth can be unproblematically generalized across national and regional contexts; that the educational systems of these countries are either anachronistic colonialist or authoritarian throwbacks; or that the teachers, administrators, scholars, and bureaucrats of the Asia-Pacific are simple ideological "dupes" of national governments, Western graduate schools, and multinational corporations.

The pieces in this book create a range of tensions around these circulating myths and stereotypes and attempt to respond to critical questions—some unresolved and some still preliminary. At the same time, we want to live and model the undoing of some truisms that no one has as yet been game enough to speak of: the assumptions that critical, theoretical, and metatheoretical work on teaching and curriculum is done solely in North America, the United Kingdom, and Australia, and that this work is "too hard" or suppressed among scholars and systems in the Asia-Pacific; that emerging scholars coming "out of Asia" are concerned principally with technical issues such as English as a second language and educational administration; and that only work done by sophisticated Western and Northern scholars and researchers can and should count in the critical analysis of education and globalization.

If Western/Northern readers are to have an understanding of, and engagement with, the complex push/pull forces of economic and cultural globalization, they must read and act beyond educational and social theorizing that, even where it attempts to be critical, can be celebratory and reinforcing of the power of American and Anglo-European educational economies and research. There is a serious need to move beyond research on globalization that takes for granted the efficacy of the center/periphery, inside/out force that emanates from the North and West. We need to engage with regional, local, and community-specific uptakes and contestations, transformations, and transliterations of the educational discourses and practices that now traverse borders and media (Luke & Luke, 2000).

Difference and the Ethics of Globalization

What is "Asia" or the "Pacific"? In the past, the answer might have been simple and transparent—for the colonizer and colonized, for the local community, for the revolutionist and nationalist, or, for that matter, for the neighboring tribes and states drawn together by common struggle or cause. Today, however, equipped at the dawn of the early twenty-first century with somewhat more substantial theoretical and empirical insights, the terms are much more risky and debatable. Whatever they might have been, peoples of Asia and the Pacific have been dispersed throughout the region, giving rise to hybrid cultures, histories, and discourses, and posing new, different, and highly volatile material conditions. It is vital, therefore, that we examine the diverse ways educational systems, school curricula, and pedagogies have responded to these changing and challenging realities.

If education is to be, or can be, about learning to live together across borders and within them, and in and through differences instead of against or in spite of them, then educators and educational systems must tackle matters of diversity and difference directly and explicitly. Across the Asia-Pacific, the Philippines, Thailand, Japan, Korea, Hawai'i, and elsewhere, struggles have arisen to develop a vocabulary and optics for seeing the heterogeneity of their student populations. The epistemological and cultural rights of indigenous peoples in countries such as Taiwan, New Zealand, and Australia (e.g., Smith, 1999) and the social and intellectual movements of

Third World women to represent their voices (e.g., Mohanty, 1991) have added a further dimension to the question of whose knowledge and standpoints should count in schools and universities. The events following September 11, 2001, including the U.S.-led war in Iraq, strongly suggest that nations should no longer direct educational systems as if difference (cultural and racial, religious and ideological, social and economic, gender and sexuality) were a momentary historical aberration. We share time, space, resources, and environment with others, and increasingly, one nation's problem has global connections and implications (e.g., China's environmental problems are those of Korea and the United States). The dangerous legacy and tendency of (neo)colonialism—a monocultural and masculine ethnonationalism—is an inadequate educational response.

If there is a new lesson facing educational systems everywhere, it is that teachers, students, teacher educators, and researchers in schools and classrooms must struggle with, argue over, and begin to deal with difference, both within and across nations, regions, and genders. The differences that we face and live take many shapes: student bodies that cross borders as migrants, refugees, and guest workers; minority communities that might have been written off as aberrant or deficient by mainstream educators; the gendered identity of nation (and its citizens and workforce) that is enacted by official educational policies and school textbooks; and ongoing tensions within educational systems over whose knowledges and ideologies, beliefs, and values should count in curriculum and pedagogy. These are not exclusively Western and Northern concerns. Education in Asia and the Pacific has struggled over these issues for years.

Peoples of the Asia-Pacific could argue that economic and cultural globalization began centuries ago—whether through the Macrossan traders who bridged established trading and cultural links between Southeast Asia and Australian Aboriginal peoples, or the Polynesian and Micronesian peoples who linked islands and cultures. Long before the processes of European, American, and Japanese colonization, processes of language and culture blending, hybridity, and exchange were common. At the same time, it is important not to romanticize the histories of cultural contact in the region. These were not benign processes (Miyoshi, 1994); they often involved cultural conflict and violence between tribal and geographic neighbors long before the coming of the missionaries, soldiers, bureaucrats, and teachers from the imperial countries.

Since World War II, the region as a whole has experienced uneven processes of decolonization (and globalization), with some European colonies still extant and some countries once colonized now colonizing the internal and/or external Others. For many countries, the process of "nation building" is as yet incomplete—and for many communities, there are substantial struggles involved in attempting to have their cultural and linguistic difference and forms of life recognized by governments, educational systems, dominant media, and multinational corporations. Nations and citizens have experienced not only the complexity and difficulty inherent in postcolonial identity formation, but its potentialities as well.

At the same time, transnational flows of people, capital, social movements, cultures, representations, and discourses have accelerated, creating new forms of expression and identity. For example, the international feminism entering the region—one encouraging women of various classes, races, ethnicities, and sexualities to form an alliance and take actions against multiple forms of oppression—marks the reworking of social relations and relationships. So does the spread and popularity of Western/American capitalist cultures throughout the region (e.g., Disneyland, McDonald's, and Starbucks). Such transformations, positive or negative, have been complicated by the emergence of new media and information technologies and the local impact of transnational consumer culture and youth identity. Across these nations, middle-class children are literally building and expanding youth cultures and gendered identities around, say, digital games. Hence, many nations in the region are sites of conflict not only between contending political, economic, social, and linguistic forces within nations, but also between traditional, modern, and postmodern cultures.

While much of the Asia-Pacific is changing, certain continuities remain across the time and space of modern-era educational systems. For example, textbooks have been a principal form of educational technology—grounded in particular narratives, languages and codes, and canons and values. Along with religious texts, they are often the principal means of building particular ideologies, cultures, and economies through languages and narratives of what has been termed "the Center." Textbooks represent modernist educational technologies par excellence in the countries of the region, including Australia, Thailand, Korea, China, and Japan. They have acted as the major mode of information, mediated and re-mediated through face-to-face social relations and language, for the "doing" of information. Surviving changes in government, natural disasters, and the elements, together with wide swings of ideology, the textbook has remained one of the constants of colonial and postcolonial education. Its economies of production remain focal, budget-line items in education departments and major industries in many countries of the Asia-Pacific. Their narratives, facts, and truths remain among the most contestable, controversial, and topical objects of legislative, academic, and popular scrutiny.

Important, as well, are the readers—including, but not limited to, students, teachers, and policymakers—and the meanings they make of these curriculum and pedagogical texts. It is essential for us to take a critical look at the relations between texts and readers from various perspectives within the Asia-Pacific. The geopolitics and culture of the region has historically been multicentered and multiperipheral. With a multitude of identity formations, the Asia-Pacific has been an exciting site for reading practices, but also one of the most problematic sites because of the differential powers operating throughout the region. While specific identities such as Asian Australians, "locals" in Hawai'i, "nativists" in Taiwan, and Resident Koreans in Japan have faced different struggles, they all suggest that the decentering of educational research paradigms preoccupied with Western and Northern perspectives is not only possible, but productive.

CONTRIBUTIONS

The vital question of which grand narratives should count in curriculum and pedagogy is one that all the contributors to this volume address as they critically examine the diverse regional and national systems of education found throughout the Asia-Pacific. In the first chapter, Allan Luke seeks to renegotiate the complex issues this core curriculum question raises in light of events post–September 11, 2001. In so doing, he frames a central challenge faced by those seeking to critically examine the connections between schooling and globalization. This challenge involves avoiding an uncritical adherence to curriculum grand narratives that lean towards totalization and essentialism. But he is also skeptical of the tendency toward a naïve cultural relativism that threatens to disrupt our ability, both as scholars and teachers, to make strong ethical claims about, around, and against dominant notions of schooling based on systematic efficiency and human capital.

The need to challenge existing metanarratives, and to supersede them with new theories that take into account both the fluidity of ethnic constructions and the contestability of state policies, runs across the works in this volume. They provide, collectively, through examples furnished from diverse sites and locations, a sustained focus on the challenges and contradictions of state formation, governmental curriculum, and textbook policies, along with ethnic responses to those policies today and in the past. In chapter 2, Roger Openshaw demonstrates, through his historical case study, that New Zealand's debates concerning ethnicity and difference have long been both controversial and contestable. This is especially the case in the social studies curriculum where, rhetoric not withstanding, both programs and texts have historically been shaped by political pragmatism, rather than educational concerns. Openshaw argues that portrayals of Maori culture and history have long been shaped by the need to project an image of ethnic harmony and social success, and that current versions of Maori culture in schools correspond with the emergence of a new Maori middle class that has learned to operate successfully within a neoliberal, corporate, and global environment, where ethnic marketing strategies are a significant component of capital expansion.

In chapter 3, Ting-Hong Wong takes his historical analysis of the struggle over difference in the Asia-Pacific to post–Second World War Singapore and Hong Kong, where complex relations between state formation and school curriculum policymaking have long been evident. The ruling group seeks to construct identity, attempting in the process to integrate society: it accommodates and wins the consent of subordinated groups, and it outmaneuvers political opponents. Wong concludes, however, that the state's capacity to include and then transform ethnic culture into a hegemonic curriculum depends on the complex relationships between the state and other racial groups in society. Similarly, in chapter 4, Jyh-Jia Chen seeks to challenge one-dimensional theories that focus solely on the imposition of the state's political ideology by examining the geopolitical process of deregulating national standardized textbooks within the context of Taiwanese state transformation over the last two decades. Chen illustrates how both the state and opposition forces constructed discourses and adopted methods of textbook reform, resulting in the gradual incorporation of reform processes into the official textbook deregulation project.

While the process through which a text is made available to students always requires critical examination, textbooks as products of culture and politics deserve scholarly attention in their own light. Textbooks are sites par excellence of ideological and cultural hegemony for children, who often have little input into the selection of curricular materials. Noparat Suaysuwan and Cushla Kapitzke in chapter 5, in examining three textbooks used by Thai children to learn English, illustrate the ways in which textbooks reflect a contemporary, transitional Thai society. That social transition includes the industrialization brought about by social changes, the increased productivity and improvements in living standards, the weakening of traditional kinship and family ties, and the decline in religious and spiritual beliefs. By representing particular ideologies, versions of childhood, and knowledge deemed appropriate for children, the authors argue, textbooks encourage the uncritical adoption of Western ideas and practices, including consumerism and middle-class lifestyles and values.

In chapter 6, Yongbing Liu utilizes the methods of critical discourse analysis to examine the construction of culture knowledge in Chinese language textbooks. He points out that after two decades of reform, Chinese society now displays many of the features of capitalist societies elsewhere, including structural inequalities. Many school texts, however, continue to promote patriotism and a modernist discourse of science and technology, while simultaneously excluding more problematic topics such as environmental damage, the growing gap between rich and poor, and various social problems. In a similar vein, chapter 7, authored by Dong Bae (Isaac) Lee, looks at selected narratives from textbooks used for teaching the Korean language to early primary school children. Lee focuses particularly on how texts represent contemporary ideologies based on three key themes: environmental issues, emerging Western lifestyles emphasizing leisure and consumption, and the complex question of reunification. He concludes that there are many silences and absences in textbook narratives, with the result that the social realities of contemporary South Korea, including poverty, crime, social problems, and structural inequalities of gender and class, are not represented or addressed.

While an inquiry into a curriculum text, be it a policy document or a textbook, is extremely important, how a text is used in school and the classroom—a pedagogical consideration—poses another important question to be examined. In chapter 8, Darren O'Hern illustrates the systemic and pedagogical constraints currently limiting the potential of environmental education in China. The goals and priorities of a society sometimes characterized as "the largest developing nation in the world" are emphatically reflected in a managerial view of education and a curriculum that emphasizes technological and economic superiority through teacher-centered instruction. Given current realities in China, O'Hern questions whether the perceived tensions between development and environment can be addressed in a way that might alleviate the nation's growing environmental crisis.

A critical study of education cannot end without asking questions concerning the struggle over identity—be it gendered, raced, or classed—that takes place in and through education. Although always ideologically called upon to form certain identities, students and teachers are "readers" of curriculum and pedagogical texts and practices, and as such they possess an ability to make their own meanings. In chapter 9, utilizing two South Korean commercial high schools as case studies, Misook Kim illustrates not only how vocational education functions to form students' subjectivities in terms of gender and class, but how students respond to such subjectivities. The two commercial high schools she examines had an active involvement in social differentiation. They were ideological in the sense that their regulatory practices and other practices were aimed at producing a gendered workforce among students. Kim also demonstrates, however, that, contrary to the views of earlier reproduction theorists, subordinated groups (the girls in vocational high schools in her case) contest that process of identity formation in a number of ways.

In chapter 10, Michael Singh focuses on the need to construct new, more responsive and dynamic multifaceted linguistic and cultural identities. Through interviews with Asian Australians, Singh demonstrates how the Australian colonialist legacy sustains a highly problematic relationship between Indigenous Australians and Asian Australians. As such, it is contested by those who suffer most from it. Accordingly, Singh argues that funds of community knowledge may supply social studies education with material to explore and dissolve the divisions that separate Indigenous and Asian

Australians, ultimately leading to social movements such as Reconciliation and Reparations. Through such innovative pedagogical strategies, Singh hopes that social studies educators can foster a new Australian cosmopolitics that will both actively challenge White Australia politics and make a useful contribution to Reconciliation between Indigenous and Asian Australians.

In a similar critical vein, but with reference to a much different ethnic and social context, chapter 11 focuses on the essentially fluid process of identity negotiation in Hawai'i. In Hawai'i, the cultural and ethnic identity is such that everyone is a minority, which leads to a distinct local identity. Author Gay Garland Reed argues that ethnic labels, as reflected in local, nonlocal, and *haole* terminologies, are historically situated and continuously contested. They depend as much on the cultivation of sensibilities and attitudes as they do on ethnic history and heritage. In Hawai'i, for instance, *hapa* (mixed ancestry) is more common and more accepted than on the U.S. mainland, and the rate of interracial marriage is increasing. In turn, changing demographics has led to a shift in identity construction, which facilitates a repositioning of Whiteness, making it less invisible, less privileged, and less central.

The question of identity and difference is a complex one. In chapter 12, Hiromitsu Inokuchi and Yoshiko Nozaki examine the education of Resident Koreans, the largest minority group in Japan. The chapter is particularly concerned with the way power is exercised to construct the category of Resident Koreans as "different," along with the approaches Resident Koreans have taken to challenge that construction by way of identity formations through Korean ethnic education. Inokuchi and Nozaki conclude that the educational struggle of Resident Koreans has now entered a new phase in which the often taken-for-granted binary categories of citizen versus noncitizen are being scrutinized and deconstructed; this provides significant challenges for both dominant and minority groups in Japan. The authors suggest the need to develop a new curriculum and pedagogy that allows the students of the dominant group to learn the history and experiences of minority groups—and that such an approach is essential to the creation of a national identity reflecting the multiplicity and fluidity of the nation.

In chapter 13, Yoshiko Nozaki examines the current Japanese history textbook controversy over the issues of "comfort women" in terms of scholarly debates over historical research, education, women's voices, and postmodern discourse. The existence of forced military prostitution and international traffic in women during Japan's Asia-Pacific War was no secret to many Japanese, above all to the several million Japanese men who fought in the war. What changed dramatically in the 1990s, however, was the emergence of the comfort women issue as a major Japanese war crime and human rights violation. A politically charged public and intellectual controversy over the nation's history and education ensued, one entailing the use of postmodern vocabularies. Nozaki argues that although postmodern discourse so far seems to have brought additional confusion to the controversy, such discourses can benefit historical research and education in significant ways if the fundamental questions posed are addressed in a productive manner.

Taken together, the pieces in this volume suggest the complexity of formations of educational policy, provision, and practice in the Asia-Pacific. These tend to stand in relation to quite diverse material conditions—differentially impacted by economic and cultural globalization—and in relation to ideologically varied institutional traditions and practices. The cases here are often not as readily amenable to Western educational, political, or social theory as they might appear. To understand and explain them in-depth, as the authors of this volume do, is to prefigure a "next generation" of critical educational theorizing and methodology that is strongly committed and connected to the transformation of educational struggles taking place in the Asia-Pacific. Today, our educational struggles are personal and global, embracing countries, nations, and individuals. The chapters in this volume provide more complex visions of the past, present, and future; classic and emergent issues; and local dynamics of change, diversity, and conflict within and across countries. Together, they not only map and reframe issues of difference for those of us who work in education in the Asia-Pacific, but also open up and make accessible critical issues of curriculum and policy for teachers, students, teacher educators, and researchers—whether they are in the North, South, West, or East.

REFERENCES

Luke, A. & Luke, C. (2000). A situated perspective on globalization. In N. Burbules & C. Torres (Eds.), *Globalization and education: Critical perspectives* (pp. 275–298) New York: Routledge.

Miyoshi, M. (1994). *Off center: Power and culture relations between Japan and the United States.* Cambridge: Harvard University Press.

Mohanty, C. T. (1991). *Third world women and the politics of feminism.* Bloomington: Indiana University Press.

Smith, L. T. (1999). *Decolonizing methodologies: Research and indigenous peoples.* New York: St. Martin's Press.

Stiglitz, J. E. (2001). *Globalization and its discontents.* New York: W. W. Norton.

Chapter 1

Curriculum, Ethics, Metanarrative

Teaching and Learning Beyond the Nation

Allan Luke

Which grand narratives should count in curriculum making and pedagogy in the national and regional educational systems of Asia and the Pacific? This chapter attempts to reframe this core curriculum question in relationship to ethical and political issues raised by the events following September 11, 2001, the regional political and economic uncertainty following the Bali incident of October 12, 2002, and by reference the ongoing crisis around migration, refugees, and difference in Australia, Southeast Asia, and the South Pacific. Here, I will outline some of the complex ethical and political dilemmas facing curriculum theorists and critical educationists who remain committed to a vision of schooling that engages with issues of social equity and human rights, peace, and the pursuit of new transcultural strategies for addressing diversity. For these remain key curriculum issues in the face of rapid economic and cultural change.

This task and its theoretical terms are, of course, hardly novel. But in many educational jurisdictions of the North/West, we have reached an impasse in theory, policy formation, and classroom work that is leading to passivity and paralysis, as well as an unmarked and unstated acquiescence to a neo-Tylerian curriculum agenda. This model is typified by the new taxonomies of "needs," lists of knowledges, skills, and competences defined as necessary and sufficient for the production and shaping of human subjects for new economic conditions, however defined. The now dominant approach to curriculum making in Australia and New Zealand, as well as in the United States and United Kingdom, involves a positivist listing of attributes, skills, and outcomes of the new *homo economicus*. This model has become a kind of nouveau export commodity through the mandating of International Monetary Fund (IMF) structural adjustment policies, aid programs, and the movement of Western academic experts and transnational

11

educational consultants across borders to countries in the Asia-Pacific, but
also to Africa, Latin America, and elsewhere.

There are, of course, inherent and necessary tensions between grand
narrative and polyvocality; between emergent cosmopolitan identities,
nation and nationalism, and local identity politics; between residual forms
of ethno-nationalism and emergent forms of multiethnic national identity in
curriculum making. These are the very geopolitical, cultural, and "intra"-
national dynamics that are given in curriculum making and secular schooling in current conditions—the inevitable issues that are placed on the table
wherever and whenever decolonization has broken the axiom of empire:
that nation = single race = single language. For it is the disruption of this
formula that unsettles the epistemological and cultural foundations of
colonial curriculum settlements and impositions.

But to offer a normative alternative requires an ethical and political
metanarrative, however self-skeptical this must be. It requires a species of critical educational theory that is hybrid and polyvocal, that articulates visions
of social and cultural utopias and heterotopias, while blending this with a
continued skepticism towards totalization and the kinds of essentialism
that always seem to land grand narratives in deep trouble. It must be, Seyla
Benhabib (1996, 2002) would argue, both encouraging and enabling
of diversity—epistemological, sociopractical, and ideological. But it must
also generate the epistemological and dialogic conditions for an education
that goes beyond relativism to enable the identification and debate over
the normative grounds of social and cultural action, the analysis of common cause and shared identities and differences, and the root sources of
conflict. Such an approach would have to address not only archetypal curriculum questions about which and whose knowledge, and which social
and intellectual fields should be worthy of study, but also the setting and
enabling of face-to-face material and textual conditions in classrooms for
critical, novel, and provocative discourse and intellectual exchange.

At the same time, the issues around difference and fundamental ideological disjuncture that have been placed on the table provide a unique historical opening for curriculum theory and making. Even countries that
work from ostensive or constructed solidarities around national or ethnonational identity (e.g., the "Chinese way," the "Arab way") or have histories of silence around difference in textbooks and pedagogy (e.g., Japan,
Korea), are faced with issues of diversity, solidarity, and identity post
September 11. The opening I speak of is the possibility of disrupting and
questioning the acritical acceptance of a now internationally rampant
vision of schooling, teaching, and learning based solely on systemic efficacy at the measurable technical production of human capital. But if and
how this can be done while building and rebuilding, holding on and holding out, critiquing and maintaining—while negotiating a critical balance

of social cohesiveness and collaborations across differences in the business of everyday life, cultural, and economic exchange—is the key question for secular institutions like schools.

Yet we are slowly being backed into an undernuanced and empirically misleading model that bifurcates us into pro- and anti- "globalization" politics—a model that reifies globalization or whatever we now choose to call it into a singular, universal phenomenon with self-same local effects (C. Luke, 2001; Kellner, 2000). This sits in opposition to equally naïve, one-dimensional notions about both national and nationalistic sovereignty, local homogeneity, integrity and sustainability, and essentialist versions of cultures, whether White or Black, colonial or indigenous. In this regard, one of the most interesting effects of the events of 2001 has been a pan-political revival of the Manichean allegory, whereby political and cultural forces that stand in radical opposition to one another share a fondness for binary argumentation—for the construction of universes of unequivocal "good" and "evil," Black and White, Christian and Muslim, left and right, global and local, and so forth. This constitutes a rhetorical strategy that Wilden (1982) called the "symmetrization" of difference, a "flattening out" of hierarchies and differences within difference—moves aided and abetted by the modes and genres of mass media (Graham & Luke, 2003).

If they do nothing else, September 11 and subsequent events foreground the dilemmas of learning to live together—of identity and relationality in a time when these matters have tended to become altogether subordinated in educational debates. They underline the need for a critical postmodernism that actually begins to envision and "dream" utopias once again; that engages rather than ignores the complexities and diversities that have to be entailed in such utopias, while understanding and retaining a self-skepticism towards the possible effects of such dreaming (Alexander, 2001).

There are signs that neoliberal educational governance and the new globalized political economy of education have colluded with our own well-theorized and fervent, perhaps overstated and overwritten, "skepticism towards grand narratives" (and its attendant foci on theoretical pluralism, cultural relativism, and local "cultural appropriateness"[1]). Taken together, these two ostensibly opposite forces can set the practical and administrative conditions for a fragmentation of the educational work of teaching and learning. This fragmentation is achieved through the narrow instrumental technicism of a test- or package-driven classroom, *and* through an overly developed epistemological sensitivity to the local, the "cultural," the "relevant," *and* the diasporic view that eschews grand constructions of discipline, field, and discourse. However progressivist its intents, the latter orientation can have the effect of a parochial narrowing of the curriculum and its engagement with discipline, field, and institutions (Luke & Carrington, 2002), at a time when a broader, more cosmopolitan analysis of the reciprocal, reflexive, and synergistic effects of economic globalization and, indeed, exploitation, is in order. The challenge is how, and whether, we have the theoretical and practical resources to conceptualize and enact an explicitly normative curriculum reconstruction with/without (self-critical) metanarrative in relation to the current political and national situations.

In recent discussions about new cosmopolitan identities for youths and adults, Cheah and Robbins (1998) ask a simple question that frames the ontological dilemma raised by the unbridled and uneven flows and networks of globalization: What is worth dying (and living) for, beyond and without the nation-state? If we wished to translate this position into key curriculum questions, we might ask: Are there metanarratives other than nationalism or human capital? What is teaching and learning beyond the nation?

At the risk of stepping over the line on what is "speakable" about current events, I would suggest that events since 2001 offer some powerful responses. We have learned that religious belief and political ideology, nationhood and nationalism, human rights, and the physical, psychic, and spiritual search for normative versions of the "good life" remain for some not only worth dying for, but apparently worth risking one's life and family for, and, in some cases, worth killing and inflicting violence for. For some, this entails a restoration or reclaiming of the moral and the communal via transcendental, nonmaterial belief. For others, it entails a will towards the establishment or reconstruction of civil society and civic exchange. As frightening and unsettling, incommensurate and troubling as these signs should be, they sit on a balance beam against the uncontested domination of the human capital rationale.

In response to Cheah and Robbins' question, these events suggest that the reasons we live, teach, learn, and die are not simply or solely for the attraction, expansion, and amelioration of capital, nor exclusively for the building of versions of the self with a will towards capital. For many of us working in education through the postwar (now post-postwar) period, we can be forgiven for believing that since the empire began to bite and write back in the 1960s and 1970s, and since the emergence of a transnational culture of narcissism in the 1980s, that the traverse of educational rationale, policy, and practice has been slowly but inexorably away from any models—pedagogical or philosophical, political or moral, left or right—that do not appear to have at their base the mass inculcation of individuated skills for the production and exchange of economic capital.

The fundamental curriculum question that has been facing Australian education for the last several decades is, ironically, the same question facing many of the postcolonial and emergent nation-states described in this volume. We cannot reconstruct curriculum as long as the unfinished business of nation building remains, with misrecognition of identity and hybridity, ongoing struggles around reconciliation and entitlement, confusion about place and situatedness, and indeed, a very slow coming to grips with our own new, blended, cosmopolitan affinities and networks. Where do we turn on the North/South, East/West axis for geopolitical and military alliance, trade, intellectual and cultural exchange, blended identity, and institutional prototypes and exemplars? The Australian immigration and refugee debate has forcefully restated to us that the stance of neoliberal governance—while all dressed up in the postideological discourses of new economies and new human capital—remains profoundly ideological in the most morally barren way: playing the "race" card at a historical moment when it should be educating or reconstructing the new Australia. This is both in relation to the continuing politics around Indigenous Reconciliation (see Singh's chapter in this volume), the inhumane treatment of refugees and, more generally, the Other (A. Luke, 2003).

It isn't just in response to the moral and political vacuum in curriculum development that we must begin to query the principled response of Australian education to the emergent forms of identity, work, economy, cultures, and institutional life. This is something that is at the foundation of the Queensland New Basics reforms that I, and others, have worked on: a commitment to realign, not uncritically, educational practice, curriculum, and the construction of discourse and identity in schools with emergent, hybrid, and blended forms of life in communities and amongst our students. Whether this or other kinds of futures-oriented curriculum reform in Singapore, Canada, and elsewhere is a plea for a "kinder, gentler" human capital model or, indeed, for a new human subject, is, of course, up for continuing debate and the continuing compromises and appropriations required of state schooling. Yet there is another, equally compelling reason for it: simply, current approaches to curriculum have taken to theorizing and constructing possible worlds by default.

The theoretically eclectic and avowedly practical approaches to curriculum making by Australian state governments are based on a neo-Tylerism, focused on the production of quantifiable, tractable, and "useful" outcomes. There are various ways that we can divine what might count as an outcome: typically, on a continuum that ranges from visible behavioral demonstration or skill acquisition, to knowledge/content bit, to progressive processes or experience deemed essential; or, ranging from psychological capacities, to workplace or field-specific competence, to social outcomes. Each of these approaches to defining "outcomes" indexes a particular view of human agency, covering a full range from behaviorist to progressivist and sociocultural definitions. Yet there are powerful, implicit normative categories, ontological models of the subject, and epistemological models of knowledge at work here. And if the Pinar reconceptualist perspective holds, the framing and specification of the outcomes—taken as a product in and of itself—is always a surrogate for an explicit specification of the human subjects, fields of knowledge, and possible worlds under discourse construction. That is, all curriculum narrates, projects, and "trajects" imagined human subjects into future pathways—a recurrent theme of a decade of work on curriculum futures.

At the same time, there is much to learn from a focus on narrative. This is not just because teaching remains for many as an epic (or rather, mock-epic) journey, but also because of the degree to which indigenous knowledge and epistemology demands that we return to the contingency of existence on narrative—on the dreaming of histories of the present and of the future. If there is something that J. F. Lyotard's original "report on knowledge" to the Canadian government (1992) probably picked up from Aborigines, Torres Strait Islanders, and other Fourth World peoples (though he didn't know it), it is the idea that underlying every discourse of technicality, there is a narrative, an epic poem, whether of peoples, nations, or worlds. Epic poems, however we parse them with story grammars of varying technical sophistication, have protagonists, problems to solve, journeys and attempts, outcomes and consequences, and, most importantly, moral, didactic resolutions.

I make this point, hardly original, not to romanticize the social construction of curriculum. For narratives and epics are not necessarily free-floating forms of textuality or highly personalized representations of identity, as they have become in so much educational research. Such a stance can be justified via literary, phenomenological, and psychoanalytic theory. Grand narratives can be parsed, analyzed, understood, and, indeed, rewritten, as can be their potentially significant material and discourse consequences for peoples, communities, and nations. Racist and sexist curriculum narratives have the material effect of cutting off and curtailing possible life trajectories, forms of gainful employment, civic participation, and familial and intergenerational relations. Triumphalist ethno-nationalist narratives are being used worldwide to both "militarize the body politic" (Graham & Luke, 2003) and to justify social and economic policies that "Other" and marginalize particular populations.

To return to Benhabib's (2002) feminist critique of relativism, all narratives are not equal in their creation or material force. Some grand narratives, their interpretations, and their interpreters, kill people; this is one of Lytoard's simple points that often gets left out of accounts of postmodern "skepticism towards metanarratives." It is this matter of differential material and bodily effects of narratives (and all texts and discourses) that makes the analysis of grand narratives political *and* economic, their psychic and spiritual consequences notwithstanding. And it is this dilemma of how to construct utopias, heterotopias, and dystopias without totalization and essentialism that sits at the heart of the next generation of curriculum making, and will weigh heavily on the development of the blended critical educational theory I have described here.

What's tricky about this is that without narrative, whether grand or small, the task of thinking about, making, critiquing, and transforming curriculum is an empty task. Since I began working for the Queensland state Department of Education in 1999, I have sat in on curriculum policy writing, syllabus writing, and planning sessions in many states in Asia and North America. In many cases, teachers, bureaucrats, and subject experts have set the absurd task of filling in (usually age- or grade- and field-specified) lists of tasks, characteristics, needs, skills, outcomes, and knowledges without any programmatic framework, whether empirical/analytic or narrative/interpretive, beyond a broad commitment to human capital production. As a moment in the local construction of discourse, the phenomenon is fascinating. But in practice it often entails the translation of vague policy statements (e.g., preparation for the new economy) into domain specifications (e.g., mathematics skills), and then into lists of preferred or desired social, discourse, and technical practices (e.g., "knowledge of number facts," "can use number facts to solve problem").

In such contexts, we reconstruct the new human subject piecemeal through a kind of epistemological "pin the tail on the donkey." In practice, this is done on the basis of underexplicated generational wisdom, judged by our capacity to reach "stakeholder" consensus. In this sense, it is necessarily a reproductive, rear view mirror activity, rather than a futures-oriented one. Whether manipulated or genuine, it is likely to need an overall normative vision for education and schooling. And all too often, this occurs in the context of national, state, and regional educational jurisdictions that seem incapable of leading their educational communities anywhere other than to the performance-based production of human capital.

My point here is as salutary for those of us who do educational theory and research as it is for teachers and curriculum bureaucrats. In the case of curriculum making, radical overskepticism towards metanarratives—an oversensitivity to the local and the individual—can lead to fragmentation and paralysis. The irony of the approaches described above is that in practice, they become acts of *bricolage*, a species of professional assembly and regional collage that, by definition, cannot service the aspirations of human capital models with any degree of precision or effect. And if Pinar's position is right, there is not only no place outside of the epic poem, but one writes them by default, and indeed, winds up living them in one way or another. Even one's skepticism towards grand narratives is an epic poem (or at least a sonnet or three-minute radio song), with the deconstructionist as hero.

Let me shift to a narrative of sorts—or actually, an analysis masquerading as a narrative. In the week before September 11, I was in Phnom Penh, Cambodia, for a conference on language and development issues. The conference brought together Cambodian educationists, some Southeast and Northeast Asian bureaucrats and teacher educators, and "Northern" and "Western" language and literacy workers, community workers, curriculum developers, curriculum makers, and implementers working throughout Asia on various aid, development, and corporate programs. These included teachers of English as a Second Language (ESL), textbook developers, basic education workers, educational officials and officers from various nongovernment organizations (NGOs) and national and transnational aid and trade agencies, and some state curriculum bureaucrats from Southeast and Northeast Asian countries. In other words, all of the transnational players in globalized and international education and education in "developing" contexts were represented, not just government and nongovernment sectors, not just aidcrats and educrats, but also the increasingly influential private providers of educational analysis and intervention (many of which were developed as extensions of large-scale engineering and agricultural project management, others of which began as government organizations but have long since been corporatized or privatized), the freelance contractors and subcontractors that these organizations employ, and of course, multinational publishers and the ubiquitous Australian universities hawking for students. This is the new face of education in conditions of global flows. These are the new networks for the exchange of educational capital and goods—hardly the stuff of government-to-government bilateral negotiation, nor that of Freirian negotiated curriculum.

The importance of the conference for Cambodian and regional educators should not be underestimated, both in terms of recognition and analysis of local work, and in terms of refocusing local efforts. But, working from the perspective of Australian education, there were several things that struck me during that visit. First, the disparity of the global distribution of capital is unsustainable, regardless of the complexity of local cultural and environmental effects. Second, the historical effects of genocide and starvation under Khmer Rouge rule meant that Cambodian educational bureaucracy, schools, and higher education institutions were being led by a generation of great youth and energy. They were actively seeking new models, stories, and ways ahead, and with their own healthy skepticism towards a particular totalitarian and totalizing species of grand narratives.

By contrast, the opinions and views exchanged by many of my Australian, British, and American colleagues there were more mixed. As Alaister Pennycook's (1998) groundbreaking work on the English language and colonialism shows, English as a second language has become a contemporary, multinational industry. Where we find the flows of capital, information, and bodies, we find English educators as the new intellectual pieceworkers of economic globalization: Masters in ESL and MBAs seem to be the most heady brew on the educational market. Once the staple of Bible translation, ESL has morphed into ESP (English for Special Purposes) and EAP (English for Academic Purposes). But we would have to search wide and far for the old species of English for Moral Purposes or English for Political Purposes. In this context, English language teachers no longer form an intellectual or nonsecular vanguard, nor do they necessarily act as a deliberate or staged professional instrument of colonialism. For the English language teacher has become a kind of intellectual/semiotic guest worker, usually on contract, shifting from employer to employer, and working increasingly for subcontractors or private providers rather than nations or governments. She/he is moving from site to site of emergent capitalism, often with family in tow—an ostensibly cosmopolitan, but perpetually diasporic subject in her or his own right.

Speaking with many of these teachers, some of whom I worked with when they were trained over two decades ago, what struck me was the degree to which their work had also become fragmented and directionless. Several said as much. Many had started as teachers/backpackers of a particular generation; they were "looking for adventure," but were committed to humanitarian aid, health, and the power of education as well.[2] Some now worked on one of aid projects by NGO aid agencies, others were employed by the growing sector of private "subcontractors" who bid against universities and governments for lucrative contracts to deliver specialized educational services, and some were subcontractees of these organizations. Most remained dedicated and committed educators, but their generational, political commitments had been translated into an abiding concern for the communities in which they worked, expressed as a need to be "culturally sensitive" and "culturally appropriate," to avoid either the aculturalism of technocratic education or the cultural imperialism of colonial education.

They were caught in a shift that has been underway since the 1970s: a shift in who provides educational services, and in what ways; a shift not only in the structural political economy of education, but as well in the kinds of educational subjectivities constructed to act as human *techne* for these new educational markets. This is to say nothing of the comparable, but different historical dilemma of pro-Aboriginal Australian educators who find themselves morally and epistemologically double bound by their own histories and Whiteness.

Peoples of the Asia-Pacific diaspora know well about the stories of education, language, and translation as the disciplinary instruments of colonialism. The resilience of the nexus between Western religion, literacy, and pedagogical discipline across the region is remarkable. The colonialist curriculum was, in many ways, taken to be as nonproblematic as the imperial scientific, and Judeo-Christian discourses that provided its epistemological basis (Pennycook, 1998). While we continue to grapple with the aftermath of colonization, we would have to admit that its agents—whether teachers, missionaries, governors, soldiers, or bureaucrats—clearly had a grand narrative. For our part, we have government commitments to advance the economy and attendant lists of outcomes. This is to say nothing of the particular institutional technologies that are offered: business models of devolved school management, standardized achievement tests, techniques of human resource management, and discourses of "quality assurance."

By contrast, for those who taught in such sites during the postwar period and right through the Colombo Plan era, aid, trade, and development were inextricably linked in a "helping discourse" that was about the expansion of postwar technocratic institutions, modes of information, and production across countries. And so it was with its Other—the discourses of liberation and emancipation embraced by those of us in the next educational generation. We, too, had a powerful normative educational agenda after 1968, drawing on the provocative "point of decolonization" theorizing and activism of Fanon, Freire, Illich, and others.

However fragmentary they may be, these glimpses of local educational work suggest a bigger problem. In the current condition of education for and by globalization, two powerful forces have been brought together. First, having been "burned" by grand narratives before, many of the educators working in such contexts have retreated to a studied subservience and humility towards the local, trying to achieve contextually, "culturally appropriate" local ends within the parameters of their particular institution or task. This is an utterly reasonable move, in spite of its tendency to buy into, and proliferate, a traditional anthropological version of the cultural (Foley, Levinson, & Hurtig, 2001; Kramsch, 2002). Whatever its educational intents, this new culturalism works together with the fragmentation of educational work towards a new transnational political economy of educational reform that speaks the mandates of IMF-style structural adjustment policies. Both generate a concentration on the local, and step away from larger political economy analyses. Much of the educational development and infrastructure work is outsourced, subcontracted, and undertaken by differing governments and NGOs, often with discoordinated means and aims. Hence, many of the now traditional problems of postwar aid and development practices resurface. The work tends to be partial, focused on short- and medium-term goals, fragmented, and temporally and spatially discontinuous.

My point is that three key historical movements have come together in the field: a skepticism towards educational metanarratives; a tendency of Western and Northern educators to assume a post-postwar cultural pluralism that places a great stress on the "local"; and neoliberal governance over the development and provision of new educational services, programs, and interventions. What is missing is a strong, overarching normative vision about the moral and civic purposes of education. In fact, if we are to judge by the quality and depth of state and national education debates in Australia, the United States, Canada, and elsewhere, there is a studied avoidance of such debates. With a few notable exceptions, the great irony of current educational governance is the tendency to engage in large-scale policy "dreaming" about knowledgeable nations, smarter states, intellectual isles, and so forth, while continuing to invest in inward-looking and compilationist approaches to curriculum and pedagogy. Without even the recognition that we need to debate such visions, we are left to work in educational environments that are encouraging piecemeal and partial visions directed at short-term goals.

What has been lost is a powerful, shared normative vision about what education can, and should, be. If there is an epic poem, it is an epic poem by default about how locality might, should, and can engage with global flows of capital, information, and technology. In this regard, whether we're speaking about Queensland's smart state, Tasmania's intelligent isle, India or Hong Kong's recent policies, the emergent agenda in Beijing, or the Cambodian context, the grand narrative of education in new conditions has a striking similarity to each other, as do the trappings of its new administrative forms and systems, and political economy. The dilemma facing government educational systems in Australia and Asia can be divided into two basic functions (A. Luke, 2003):

- **The Attraction Function**: to generate sufficient human capital to attract flows of capital investment, businesses, jobs, and attendant infrastructure development into the region, site, or local community
- **The Amelioration Function**: to mop up the effects of the unequal distribution of capital, including structural unemployment, physical displacement and relocation, population movement, health and environmental problems, political violence, etc.

If we take these two functions and map them against current state educational policy and curriculum development, specific patterns emerge. First, the dissection of key learning areas (hereafter KLAs, or whatever "stand-in" term is used to designate fields of study, core subjects, or disciplines) into lists of outcomes, goal statements, and so on is an attempt, albeit of varying positivist and progressivist degrees, to meet the attraction function. The narrative chain for the attraction principle goes something like this: the student (protagonist) ⇒ acquires skills, knowledges, competences (action) ⇒ dutifully tick boxed in formalized assessment based on quality assurance principles (verification of capital by the system) ⇒ takes these out of the school and is able to both attract and generate economic capital in the social fields of work (consequences).

The amelioration function proves to be a bit more difficult, despite some well-theorized attempts to include particular values and ideologies within curriculum in the areas of studies of society and environment, citizenship, and literacy education. The tendency of most state curriculum documents is to attempt a set of "overlays," or grids, that can verify or guide supra-KLA coverage of various "core skills," "values," or "orientations." Hence, we find teachers and schools grappling to grid issues of "identity," "futures," and "literacy across the curriculum" across their already atomized syllabi and work programs. What this means is that the soft, less-rationalized ameliorative function, by definition harder to quantify than traditional skills or knowledge outcomes, becomes part of a subordinate grid of curriculum specification.

The geopolitical events of the last three years verify matters that have been on the table for nations, governments, and communities for well over a decade now: that learning to live together in difference, the establishment of an ethics of care and empathy, the issues of transcultural and intercultural communication, and the direct education of the Other within what was historically purported to be homogeneous systems are not designer options for curriculum, pedagogy, and education, but must be part of any version of new basics. In the past decade, we have known, written, and spoken about and through, diversity in education again and again; about the possibilities of a complex redistributive justice based not just on economic capital, but on the building of communities' social, cultural, and symbolic capital, and the kinds of networks for exchange that they will need to survive and sustain themselves. We have described how new economies are exacerbating symbolic and physical violence and political division around issues of difference (e.g., Milojevic et al., 2001; Hammer, 2002), and we have pointed out the public pedagogical responsibilities of government, media, and corporation to educate about globalization and diversity, only to be written off as advocates of political correctness.

We have been reminded by commentators as diverse as Francis Fitzgerald (1985) and Manuel Castells (1996) that one of the reactions to globalized economies, technocratic systems, and fast-capitalist economies and cultures is a powerful attraction to simple answers, fundamentalist doctrine, and one-dimensional politics. The same conditions of moral and political uncertainty that have destabilized longstanding institutional systems and canonical knowledge increase the allure of simplified, nostalgic approaches to teaching and curriculum.

To return to our local curriculum settlement: What might a new Australian epic poem look and sound like? Will it be a narrative of nation or a narrative of transnation, a new White diasporic nationalism or a techno-colored cosmopolitanism? It is Benedict Anderson's brilliant and controversial study (1991) of the rise of the nation-state and "print capitalism" that argues that nations and nationalism aren't necessarily the problem; rather, the forms of "statism" are the narratives that do the most harm. Australia's unique postcolonial and neocolonial history has left it not only with unfinished business, but an "underdeveloped" national identity as well. But this truncated national development might now be a powerful advantage to other, more "mature" nation-states with imperial histories and ossified, generationally immobile concepts of identity, such as those of the West and North. This has always provided countries and educational communities like ours with a historical opening—a moment and a possibility that older, more "mature" nation-states do not have: the possibility for the nonviolent formation of a new social and cultural contract.

Taught by the Frankfurt School of the psychically and socially, aesthetically and sexually destructive force of particular regimes of capital; offered a bleaker postwar version of the self by philosophic and literary existentialism; taught by Foucaultians about the impossibility of escape from normative discourses; and taught by postcolonialists and indigenous writers about the genocidal force of those phenomena that purported to know truth, justice, and science, it is no surprise that many of us appear to be allergic to normativity, clinging to the necessary but somewhat safer intellectual haven of critique, and reluctant to get our hands dirty with the sticky matter of what educationally is to be done in these difficult conditions.

Despite the recent events, because of recent events, and in the face of recent events, perhaps we have the space for an epic poem. Such poems, Lyotard suggests, can be fascist and exclusionary, xenophobic and imperialist. As curriculum theorists, developers, and educators, this is our job and our moment to rekindle a robust debate about teaching each other how to live together *in difference* with a more equitable and sustainable distribution of resources and capital. As sociologists and philosophers, intellectuals and theorists, we face a parallel task: to bring together and reframe the "self-limiting, partial and plural utopias" (Alexander, 2001, p. 579) that inform our new politics of the local, with a more truly "global" vision of "repair" of systems of governance and forms of life that have brought us to this unfortunate moment.

Notes

1. For a critique of "cultural appropriateness" in second language pedagogy, see Pennycook, 2000. This is often enlisted as part of an overall progressivist educational agenda that, ironically, may constitute a form of imposition in and of itself (e.g., Lin & Luk, 2002) and elide or ignore local pedagogic histories.

2. Rod Neilsen's doctoral research at the University of Queensland documents these family and career dynamics of nomadic ESL teachers.

REFERENCES

Alexander, J. C. (2001). Robust utopias and civil repairs. *International Sociology, 16* (4), 579–591.

Anderson, B. (1991). *Imagined communities* (2nd ed.). Minneapolis: University of Minnesota Press.

Benhabib, S. (1996). *Critique, norm and utopia: A study of the foundations of critical theory.* New York: Columbia University Press.

Benhabib, S. (2002). *The claims of culture.* Princeton: Princeton University Press.

Castells, M. (1996). *Rise of the network society.* Cambridge: Blackwells.

Cheah, P., & Robbins, B. (Eds.). (1998). *Cosmopolitics: Thinking and feeling beyond the nation.* Minneapolis: University of Minnesota Press.

Fitzgerald, F. (1985). *Cities on a hill.* New York: Harper.

Foley, D., Levinson, B. A., & Hurtig, J. (2001). Anthropology goes inside: The new educational ethnography of ethnicity and gender. *Review of Research in Education, 25,* 37–98.

Graham, P., & Luke, A. (2003). Militarising the body politic. *Body and Society 9,* 149–168.

Hammer, R. (2002). *Antifeminism and family terrorism.* London: Roman & Littlefield.

Kellner, D. (2000). Globalisation and new social movements: Lessons for critical theory and pedagogy. In N. C. Burbules & C. Torres (Eds.), *Globalization and education: Critical perspectives* (pp. 299–322). New York: Routledge.

Kramsch, C. (2002, December 19). Language and culture revisited. Address to the 13th World Congress of Applied Linguistics, Singapore.

Lin, A., & Luk, J. (2002). Beyond progressive liberalism and cultural relativism: Towards critical postmodernist, sociohistorically situated perspectives in ethnographic classroom studies. *Canadian Modern Language Review, 59* (1), 97–124.

Luke, A. (2003). Literacy and the other: A sociological agenda for literacy research and policy in multicultural societies. *Reading Research Quarterly, 34* (1).

Luke, A., & Carrington, V. (2002). Globalisation, literacy, curriculum practice. In R. Fisher, M. Lewis, & G. Brooks, (Eds.), *Language and literacy in action* (pp. 231–250). London: Routledge/Falmer.

Luke, C. (2001). *Globalisation and women in academia: North/West—South/East.* Malwah, NJ: Lawrence Erlbaum.

Lyotard, J. F. (1992). *The postmodern condition: A report on knowledge.* Minneapolis: University of Minnesota Press.

Milojevic, I., Luke, A., Luke, C., Land, R., & Mills, M., Lingard, R., Budby, J., Louie, K., Ip, D., & Alexander, D. (2001). *Moving forward: Students and teachers against racism.* Melbourne: Eleanor Curtain Publishers.

Pennycook, A. (1998). *English and the discourses of colonialism.* New York: Routledge.

Pennycook, A. (2000). *Critical applied linguistics.* Malwah, NJ: Lawrence Erlbaum.

Wilden, A. (1982). *System and structure: Essays in communication and exchange* (2nd ed.). London: Tavistock.

Chapter 2

"... Nothing Objectionable or Controversial"

The Image of Maori Ethnicity and "Difference" in New Zealand Social Studies

Roger Openshaw

In 1840, Britain formally "annexed" New Zealand. The Treaty of Waitangi was signed in the Bay of Islands by representatives of the Crown and Maori chiefs, and was then transported to other areas for more signatures. From the beginning, the treaty was controversial. It ceded the sovereignty of the country to Britain in the English text version, but simply acknowledged *kawanatanga* (literally, governorship) in the Maori version. The English text version promised chiefs and tribes "full and undisturbed possession of their Lands and Estates Forests Fisheries and other properties," whilst the Maori version more vaguely referred to "the entire chieftainship of their lands, their villages, and all their property" (Owens, 1992, p. 51).

It is doubtful that many Maori fully appreciated just what they were signing (Owens, 1992). Others seem to have viewed the treaty as a pragmatic concession to the realities of British power in the mid-nineteenth century (Sorrenson, 1992). The Land Wars which followed, however, resulted in many Maori tribes losing land to government confiscations. During the twentieth century, bitter debate over the implications of the treaty have spanned decades. The result is that New Zealand has retreated from its long-held "one people" stance to officially become a bicultural country, where the two main cultures recognized are Maori (indigenous people) and *pakeha* (descendants of British settlers). Despite this, the exact meaning of Maori culture, particularly the way it should be portrayed to others, remains unclear.

For these reasons, any public debate concerning ethnicity and difference in New Zealand has long been controversial. This was particularly true within the state schools, historically a meeting ground between the two peoples. Within social studies, however, any potential conflict is likely to be intensified for two main reasons. First, there was, and remains, a widespread view in New Zealand that everyone, regardless of ethnic origin, is equal, therefore there can be little racial discrimination. Second, social studies as a school subject was introduced into New Zealand schools during the post–World War II era specifically to replace history and civics as the main vehicle for citizenship training prior to form five[1] (Openshaw & Archer, 1992; McGee, 1998). Thus, perhaps inevitably, it bears the brunt of criticism relating to the difficult question of national identity.

Social Studies and Citizenship Education

Prior to World War II, New Zealand educators and politicians were increasingly regarding schools as miniature social systems. In this environment, citizenship education was envisaged as playing a key role in "repairing" society (McGee, 1998, p. 48). When it was introduced as a post–World War II new curriculum subject, social studies was to provide the focal point of citizenship education for democracy. Moreover, it was to be the vehicle for innovative teaching methods emphasizing active student participation. Thus, the Thomas Report argued that in introducing social studies into the secondary school, the subject's aims were twofold: first, it was to "assist in the development of individuals who [were] able to take their parts as effective citizens of a democracy"; second, it was "to deepen pupils' understanding of human affairs and to open up wide fields for personal exploration" (New Zealand Department of Education [NZDOE], 1943).[2]

Citizenship education, however, posed a significant challenge for social studies educators. Writing in the early 1940s, the prominent New Zealand educator and scholar J. H. Murdoch was among the first to pose some provocative questions. Could schools realistically encourage students to work collaboratively for the benefit of the community? Could they foster respect for other peoples, uphold a high standard of international ethics, and make them aware of spiritual values in their broadest sense? And how was this possible when that same community embraced individualism (narrowly defined as getting ahead), was fearful of external threats, and lauded a crass brand of materialism? The question was whether or not schools could really make much headway:

> A certain fear of thought is ... painfully evident in our community. There is at once a professed desire for intellectual freedom and a dislike of the results of genuine thinking. We are a conventional people, and distrust originality—especially in our preachers and teachers....

All this, with our penchant for political control, reinforces our tendency towards democratic totalitarianism. The heavy handed father finds a little compulsion salutary; and the habit grows. So our educational institutions are consciously virtuous, and conscientiously paternal. (Murdoch, 1944, pp. 435–436)

As a contemporary liberal educator, Murdoch, like many of his liberal counterparts today, saw in the rapidly increasing Maori society a useful counterbalance to what he considered to be undesirable features of his own society:

> ... it is worth while noting that the Maori has a very distinct contribution to make to our common culture. In particular, his essential spirituality is a quality we have tended to lose. The sense of sacredness of certain historical spots, for example, is surely a trait that the pakeha might well develop. For what remains when the sense of sacredness is gone? Again, the strongly developed community life of the Maori is a necessary corrective to the selfish individualism that is so marked a feature of pakeha society. (pp. 429–430)

Taken together, Murdoch's observations underline two factors that were to directly impact early postwar New Zealand social studies. First, Murdoch recognized that there were definite limits to which society, bureaucracy, and politicians would be prepared to countenance controversial issues being discussed in schools. This was particularly true of the early postwar era in New Zealand. New Zealand was a geographically isolated and socially conservative nation. The entire population numbered less than two million people, compared to eighty million sheep. The personal concerns of individuals about the education of their children were frequently expressed directly to the political representatives, who subsequently raised questions in the House. Hence, there were numerous instances of parents, employers, and ministers of religion writing to the director of education and even to the prime minister to complain about objectionable curriculum content. Second, and perhaps even more significantly for this chapter, Murdoch revealed that amongst some liberal educators of the day, a particular conception of Maori culture was being actively promoted as a counterbalance to the evils liberal educators were condemning in modern, industrial, urbanized society. In this aspect, Murdoch was anticipating a trend common in New Zealand today, whereby Maori and pakeha cultures are often counterpoised in educational literature—the former as being peaceful and spiritual; the latter as embodying the evils of materialism, urbanization, and industrialization (Nash, 1990).

Early Textbook Concerns

With the coming of peace in 1945, the New Zealand Department of Education set up a number of syllabus committees to develop syllabi for existing and new subject matters. Syllabus documents at this time functioned as official curricula mandated for all New Zealand schools, though in practice it was always assumed that teachers would exercise professional judgment in their implementation. The Committee on Social Studies duly prepared a new syllabus document for schools entitled "Syllabus of Social Studies in History and Geography," associating the subject matter with history and geography. However, in February 1946, with the polio epidemic forcing the closure of all primary and secondary schools, the senior inspector took the opportunity to call a conference of post-primary principals. As a result, further committees were formed to enable primary and post-primary school representatives to better coordinate the teaching of social studies, English, and arithmetic. A reorientation of method and content in social studies was now deemed highly desirable in light of the new world situation. Moreover, it was understood that social studies now had as its central aim the provision of a philosophy of life for the growing child (Otago Education Board, 1946).[3] The Committee on Social Studies appreciated the dangers of teaching from textbooks, but nevertheless, believed these dangers were outweighed by the need for inexperienced teachers to cover the breadth of the new syllabus.

It was in this postwar revisionist context that the education department sought to place in print a revised version of the widely used social studies text *The Story of New Zealand* (1945), published by the nation's largest publishing house. The preparation of suitable textbooks for social studies and history, traditionally a political process, was about to become even more political. In February 1947, the Cabinet gave its approval for the purchase of some six thousand copies of the revised edition of *The Story of New Zealand* (published by Reed)—one reference copy per school. Despite this fairly limited distribution, the education department, from the very beginning, expressed its intention to exercise considerable discretion in both the choice of writers and the selection of content for the revised text. In practice, this meant that prospective textbook writers had to secure the approval of senior departmental officers, especially the supervisor of teaching aids, who in turn would be expected to consult with the inspectorate. On the bottom of one letter written to the department by a prospective writer, the supervisor of teaching aids, W. B. Harris, wrote: "He has lots of bright ideas and I think he can write. His personal views and general attitude are not always acceptable" (Harris to Reed, 1947).

The education department's preferred author was Ray Chapman-Taylor. A trained teacher and an educational liberal, Chapman-Taylor had worked with army education in occupied Japan, teaching citizenship to

New Zealand soldiers. Subsequently, he had prepared a school journal issue on Japan for use in social studies classrooms (Openshaw, 1991). Arrangements for Chapman-Taylor's transfer to the education department were soon well underway. With many teachers expressing dissatisfaction over delays in publication, however, the department decided to modify its normal procedure of having the book read and approved by a number of senior departmental officers before publication. Instead, a streamlined procedure was adopted whereby the supervisor of teaching aids would be authorized to place an asterisk alongside the titles of those texts of which he approved. Harris's doubts as to his own suitability for such a task were countered in a terse handwritten note from the acting director of education, who pointed out that: "It is essential that the books be read in order to ensure that they contain nothing objectionable or controversial" (Acting Director, 1947).

However, deciding what was objectionable or controversial, and to whom, was, as Harris well appreciated, no easy matter. One particularly thorny question concerned the place and portrayal of Maori in New Zealand history, particularly when the Land Wars were concerned. Within two decades of British annexation, pakeha settlers had outnumbered Maori inhabitants. Maori numbers rapidly declined, and by 1890, pakeha outnumbered Maori by fourteen to one. War was a final arbiter in the pakeha acquisition of land and the establishment of European dominance. In these wars, many Maori tribes suffered from land confiscations; overall, Maori holdings were reduced to less than one-sixth of the country. The impact on Maori, however, was uneven, with some tribes profiting from new technologies and successful pastoral ventures. Moreover, tribe fought tribe, not only for their own survival in a pakeha world, but also to pay off old tribal scores or to eliminate military rivals (Sorrenson, 1992).

Little more than half a century later, memories remained bitter, and at variance. What was written in school texts at this time, therefore, was not just an academic matter. The portrayal of the Rongowhakaata leader, guerilla fighter, and prophet, Te Kooti Arikirangi Te Turiki, in social studies texts provides a classic example of a cautious political compromise arrived at entirely within the bureaucracy, without significant public debate. Te Kooti had once fought against the Maori land resistance movement known as Hauhau, but the Ringatu church, which presented a Maori version of Christianity in opposition to established European denominations, dated its origin from the revelations given to Te Kooti while he was imprisoned in the Chatham Islands in 1867 (Binney, 1990). Whilst Ringatu was not as significant as the Ratana-Labour Pact (which brought the First Labour Government to power in 1935), the government was nevertheless dependent upon continued Maori support as its electoral margin dwindled after the close of World War II.

Te Kooti then, was a controversial figure for both Maori and pakeha for his role in the bitter guerilla struggles during the latter stages of the Land Wars.

The New Zealand's official narrative of its history was situated firmly in the framework of British experience, particularly in pre–World War II school textbooks. Maori who had resisted settlement were not generally well regarded (Gibbons, 1992). Thus, the 1945 edition of *The Story of New Zealand* claimed:

> It might be doing Te Kooti an injustice to call him a Hauhau, but a foolish new 'religion' he had invented, called Ringatu, was so much like it that he and his followers can be looked upon as the successors of the Hauhaus. (p. 341)

A series of letters between the education department and Reed illustrates the determination of the department and the Labour government to avoid undue offense to rival Maori views, while maintaining an essentially British perspective. Thus it was suggested that the passage be altered to read:

> It might be doing Te Kooti an injustice to call him a Hauhau but it is no wonder that the terrible deeds following his escape caused him and his followers to be looked upon as their successors. (Reed to Harris, 1948)

Other passages in *The Story of New Zealand* also appeared suspect in the dawning of the new era in social democracy. For instance, after corresponding with the chief inspector of primary schools, J. L. Ewing, Harris pointed out to Reed that some criticism might be leveled at the original author's justification of Maori land confiscations after the Land Wars. The description of Maori in the text as "a warlike race" was also deemed to be controversial. This was because, especially during the early years of World War II, New Zealand authorities had been more than happy to convey an image of military preparedness and willingness for sacrifice in a righteous cause. When the war ended and the United Nations was firmly established, however, it was feared such sentiments could become a national embarrassment, especially when taken out of context. Accordingly, on page 344 of the text, the description appeared along with a later-inserted reference that seemed to suggest that the country had not done too badly out of the war, financially speaking. Harris pointed out to Reed that: "The Department wishes you to omit the last sentence of the top paragraph and the next paragraph, deleting reference to Maori as 'a warlike race,' and to '... the cost of the war'" (Harris to Reed, 1948).

In response to subsequent allegations that the treatment of Maori in the social studies syllabus was "superficial," Harris could only agree. The supervisor did point out, however, that the breadth of the syllabus was such that something had to be left out of it. Furthermore, he was able to refer to the opinion of the Syllabus Revision Committee. This committee had opined that Maori history had less relevance in the southern areas of New Zealand, where there were fewer Maori (Harris to Hamilton, 1951).

CREATING AN IMAGE OF MODERN MAORI

Potential controversy not withstanding, New Zealand content was sharply increased in social studies during the early postwar years. By the early 1950s, further New Zealand–centered resources for social studies classes were appearing. In April 1952, the school bulletin *Exploring New Zealand* (Taylor, 1953), was awaiting delivery to schools, with *Life in the Pa* (Chapman-Taylor, 1953) expected shortly thereafter. By the late 1950s, an updated draft of the syllabus in social studies, together with a series of handbooks entitled *Suggestions for the Teaching of Social Studies in the Primary School* (hereafter *Suggestions*), with a forward by Chapman-Taylor, were being tested in New Zealand primary schools. Officially released in 1962, *Suggestions* reminded teachers that social studies aimed at: "clear thinking about social problems," "intelligent and responsible behavior in social situations," and "developing an intelligent and sympathetic interest in the various peoples, communities and cultures of the world" (NZDOE, 1962, pp. 7–8).

These new documents attracted critical comment even prior to their official release. An article in the influential fortnightly publication, the *New Zealand Listener*, featured a social studies debate between A. B. Ryan, the headmaster of Wairehau High School and a strong supporter of social studies, and Mrs. Eileen Saunders, a conservative educational commentator and parent. In defense of the subject's approach to knowledge, Ryan restated the progressivist philosophy, whereby learning began with the child's own knowledge, community, and local areas, moving outwards to provide a basis of comparison with those living elsewhere. In response, Saunders asserted:

> I suspect that the whole of the thing is permeated by a vague desire, a vague belief that if you teach children the better things of history, how men have co-operated, how they live together, you will somehow make them better. I think that is nonsense. You are trying to bring the children up in a fool's paradise. The sooner they understand the world as it is, the better, and the world is not like that. (Saunders & Ryan, p. 10)

This was only the beginning. The department was soon to appreciate the fact that good educational intentions have their limitations. Shortly after the release of *Suggestions*, a number of secondary school teachers and university professors claimed that social studies now emphasized liberal social engineering at the expense of academic integrity (Stone, 1963; Gorrie, 1963).

These warnings would prove to be just a taste of what was to come. Attention soon focused on a section of the syllabus devoted to contemporary New Zealand life, incorporated under the theme "How Families Live." To enliven the teaching of this section, the education department and the school publications division planned a series of school bulletins to function as resource material for schools. The first of these, published in early 1964, dealt with a "typical" Maori family. Entitled *Washday at the Pa* (Westra, 1964; hereafter *Washday*), this initial bulletin was profusely illustrated with photographs by Dutch-born, naturalized photographer, Ans Westra. Westra had worked with Maori people on the East Coast, and had subsequently published a number of articles on Maori life in well-respected national journals such as *Te Ao Hou* (Chief Inspector of Primary Schools [CIOPS], 1964).

The controversy that broke out over *Washday at the Pa* was not only the result of this new interest in indigenous case study material and photos for social studies, but also was reflective of rapidly changing demographics within New Zealand society. By the early 1960s, Maori urban drift, with its associated problems of poverty and breakdown of traditional life, had been underway for more than a decade. An important consequence of this for New Zealand society as a whole was that cultural identity became an increasingly contested issue. Maori traditional lifestyles were frequently idealized in glossy tourist brochures, but pakeha identity as "the best of British" was dependent upon Maori exclusion from affluent suburbia (Brookes, 1997, pp. 243–244). While successive New Zealand governments actively promoted a view of harmonious race relations to the world, some Maori commentators increasingly pointed to substandard accommodation and racism (Brookes, 1997).

In this context, graphic portrayals of contemporary Maori urban life, especially for a student readership, were almost bound to result in controversy. Somewhat surprisingly, the *Washday* manuscript does not appear to have been read by education departmental officers prior to publication, as was often the case with school publications. The photos and text outline, however, were apparently shown to the secretary of Maori affairs, who expressed "some qualms because of the living conditions shown." Despite the secretary's concern, some thirty-seven thousand copies of *Washday* were subsequently printed and dispatched to public primary schools during May and June of 1964 (CIOPS, 1964).

Image, Controversy, and the State

The Maori Women's Welfare League was to play a pivotal role in the subsequent development of the *Washday* controversy. Officially founded in 1951, the league had actively lobbied to improve housing and to combat negative stereotyping of Maori. This entailed portraying, and indeed, embracing, an image of successful adaptation by Maori to modern suburban New Zealand life, with its new houses and material comforts. In this context, reminders of a lifestyle many league members had discarded, however artistically portrayed, were patently unwelcome. In July 1964, the league held its annual conference, during which many members expressed their concern over the new school bulletin. Mrs. J. Heta, speaking on behalf of Ngtai Porou, claimed that "the living conditions shown [were] not typical of Maori life, even in remote areas," and that if the aim of the publication was to depict a happy Maori family, "a more average, typical family background" could have been selected for the photographs ("Maori Women," 1964). Mrs. J. Baxter, delegate to the Board of Trustees of the Maori Educational Foundation, asserted that such threats to Maori confidence and self-respect were, "a bigger problem than land tenure, living conditions, health or education." As a result, conference delegates passed a resolution calling for the bulletin to "be completely and immediately withdrawn from publication and from issue to all schools, and that similar future publications be referred for approval to the Maori Education Foundation Board of Trustees" ("Maori Women," 1964).

With the minister of education temporarily out of Wellington on official business, the press approached the director of education, A. E. Campbell, for his comments on the league's concerns. In response, Campbell pointed out that *Washday* was the first in a series of bulletins aiming to show how both Maori and pakeha families lived in New Zealand:

> None of the bulletins is intended to be completely typical or representative of families in general; nor is it intended to be a comment on Maori housing. Rather, it is intended to bring out the affectionate and co-operative relationship between parents and children, and among the children themselves. I am sorry that some Maori people have found cause to object to the Bulletin. When its purpose is understood, and it is considered as whole, there seems to me to be little ground for criticism. (Campbell, 1964)

As the senior department officer, however, Campbell was soon to discover just how insistent a minister could be, especially when prompted by cabinet colleagues who were mindful of an emerging political power, in this case, the Maori middle class. On July 29, 1964, the league's dominion secretary, Jane F. Bell, sent a letter to the minister of education, the Honorable A. E. Kinsella, citing the resolution and protesting against *Washday*. Bell emphasized that the "feeling was high and delegates much disturbed." Bell pointed out that the photographs had been taken in a private home, not a *pa*; that the primitive living conditions shown were not typical of contemporary Maori life; that the family depicted could be identified and suffer shame; and the bulletin would have a detrimental effect on racial attitudes given the drift of the Maori population to the cities (Bell, 1964).

On the same day, in a letter to Campbell (appropriately stamped "VERY URGENT"), Kinsella outlined the press coverage of the league's objections and requested Campbell's comments, as he was expecting an approach from the minister of Maori affairs over the matter. The minister's private secretary had already advised the minister that Campbell had been similarly involved with another school publication during the last Labour government (1957 to 1960), when Sir Eruera Tirikatene had taken exception to a statement in one of the publications dealing with the failure of Tiri's potato crop. Thus, the minister insisted, that:

> I would like to have your comments on this particular publication so that I am already armed should I receive an approach from the Minister of Maori Affairs. No doubt it is desirable that we should let our pupils know something of the Maori way of life but I feel that while we are promoting the advances of Maori education, it might be as well for any proposed school publication dealing with any aspect of Maori life to be seen by yourself or the Assistant Director before it finally goes to print. (Kinsella, 1964a)

Campbell responded a day later, on July 30, reiterating his previous comments to the press. He pointed out that the bulletin was "a positive attempt to depict healthy family life to young children." While he realized that "… sensitive Maoris might take exception to the photographs," he nevertheless felt that "if instructions were to be given to have the bulletin withdrawn, it would serve to increase the attention it is receiving" (Campbell, 1964).

The government, however, had no desire to be subjected to parliamentary criticism on racial issues. On August 3, a brief press statement from Kinsella was released to the evening radio news. The statement acknowledged the strength of the league's concerns. While no one had denied that the family relationships portrayed were "affectionate, good-humored and cooperative," Kinsella conceded that it was now "clear that the publication has given offense and I have, therefore, decided that it be withdrawn from the schools" (Kinsella, 1964b). A *Gazette* notice on August 15 advised schools to return all copies of *Washday* directly to the government printer in Wellington where they were to be pulped (Internal memo, 1964). Neither adverse reaction in the national press to evident censorship, nor protest from many other Maori groups on the grounds that the bulletin was both enjoyable to read and accurate, was to make the slightest difference. By late August 1964, Campbell had penned a brief but revealing postscript on his original memo:

> On future consideration, and after being made aware of the strength of the objections from the Maori Women's Welfare League, I came

to the conclusion that, on balance, it would be better to withdraw the bulletin. I particularly feared the damage that could result if the matter became one of Party political controversy. (Campbell, 1964)

Over the next few months, thousands of copies of *Washday* were returned. Press reaction was largely adverse, with the government accused of censorship, and the department, of tame compliance. It was all to no avail. Political interference and government sensibilities had effectively eliminated the first attempt in New Zealand social studies to portray contemporary Maori life in a realistic manner. It was not to be the last time that such a phenomenon would occur.

CONCLUSION

History has a habit of repeating itself. In the 1990s, the education department's successor, the New Zealand Ministry of Education, was obliged to confront difficult political issues surrounding the portrayal of Maori and pakeha following the 1994 appearance of *Social Studies in the New Zealand Curriculum: Draft* (Openshaw, 2000). Defenders portrayed the document as an attempt to redress past colonialist injustices and to assert Maori claims to sovereignty under the Treaty of Waitangi. In addition, they commended it for upholding Maori values and culture in the interests of creating a new bicultural understanding (Harrison, 1998). Opponents, however, criticized the document as an example of political bias, special pleading, and double standards in the interests of a new form of political correctness known as "Waitangism" (Partington, 1998). A revised draft, which appeared in 1996, failed to satisfy any of the parties, and the document was again withdrawn. According to material subsequently released under the Official Information Act, the ministry then consulted a private Maori consultancy agency while revising the bicultural component for the third, definitive document: *Social Studies in the New Zealand Curriculum*. This document became, in effect, the official curriculum, and was officially launched by the minister of education, the Honorable Wyatt Creech, in October 1997.

This recent incident of official tampering, together with the various historical examples provided, underline a stark reality that many New Zealanders, for their own reasons, tend to ignore: Where the controversial issue of ethnic difference arises, social studies texts, materials, and curricula, no matter how realistic or innovative they may claim to be, are ultimately shaped by political rather than educational factors. In New Zealand, social studies textbooks were rapidly revised in the early post–World War II period to accommodate new political and international realities. In light of this process, it was, perhaps, predictable that when the *Washday* controversy broke, all departmental attempts at educational justification for the innovation were rapidly overwhelmed by political priorities—which were deemed to outweigh any adverse press reaction and criticism from those within education.

A number of related points can be made. First, it can be argued that, especially where Maori culture and history are concerned, social studies in New Zealand has historically degraded into little more than a political correctness dressed in constructivist clothing; it serves in the interests of conveying an image of economic and social success to the world. Thus, the particular version of Maori culture taught by schools has always been a carefully selected one, both in terms of those deemed to be "qualified" to make the selection, and of the actual selection of qualities held to best serve the desired political ends. Hence, during the early postwar years the portrayal of Maori culture and history in social studies was subject to the prior approval of the minister of education and the minister of Maori affairs, together with the selected few who were deemed to be the appropriate authorities for expert consultation. By the early 1960s, this limited policy-making community was being increasingly challenged by new suburban-based groups, such as the Maori Women's Welfare League, with immediate consequences for the future portrayal of Maori in social studies.

The results can be seen today in a "new" middle-class Maori grouping, which has been largely successful in forging a working partnership with Wellington-based pakeha educational policymakers. Both groups, for their own particular purposes, desire a more "upmarket" image for Maori culture, one that emphasizes a particular brand of ethnicity and difference. Consequently, the dominant interpretation of Maori culture that filters down into schools is more likely to emanate from Maori in management positions, or from Maori consultancy agencies expressly set up to function within today's neoliberal economic environment, where global image is everything. In this glossy brochure culture, warriors are usually "out." Also strongly discouraged are positions that might muddy the official line on biculturalism, such as research that points to social-class divisions among Maori, or accounts of colonial history that reveal the multidimensional nature of culture contact. Again, this selective amnesia suits the current neoliberal ethos that emphasizes individualism and commercial success through enterprise. However, on a deeper plane, it also graphically attests to the ways in which indigenous peoples too, can appropriate, consume, and reproduce knowledge and images as part of the postcolonialist drive for national identity (Keesing, 1989; Moeran, 1990; Nozaki & Inokuchi, 1996).

Second, it is likely that the social studies program will always face insurmountable political problems when innovatory materials and programs are perceived to directly challenge the prevailing myths and values of those who have political influence, especially where these values are actively promoted by successive governments. Elsewhere in the world, educational bureau-cracies have proven to be highly vulnerable to political pressure as well, especially in regard to controversial social studies programs. Goodson and Marsh have observed that, in Queensland, the state government has shown willingness on occasions to override the educational bureaucracy and cen-sor the use of controversial curriculum materials. In the case of MACOS,[4] the strength of the opposition ultimately proved irresistible. "The Premier and his Cabinet clearly held the trump card and had a dominant influence over the events leading up to the banning of MACOS in Queensland state schools" (Goodson & Marsh, 1996, pp. 142–143).

Finally, this chapter reveals a common thread of educational experience. As we have seen, the past battles between educational bureaucrats, teachers, parents, and others were to be repeated in the most recent social studies controversy over ethnicity and difference. Today, just as in the 1940s and the 1960s, the portrayal of ethnicity and difference in contemporary New Zealand social studies, and what is currently acceptable, continues to be driven by political judgments. The introduction to this book makes it abun-dantly clear that textbooks and official curriculum documents are mod-ernist educational technologies of a pervasive type. Acting as major modes of information, they are continuously being negotiated and contested in a postcolonial environment that has seen power relationships change markedly. Accordingly, the New Zealand situation, and the compromises it demands, has parallels elsewhere in the Asia and Pacific regions.

NOTES

The author would like to acknowledge the kind assistance of Archives New Zealand in preparing this research.

1. At this time, New Zealand adhered to the British system of standards and forms in describing school classes, rather than the American system of grades. Thus, form five stu-dents were usually fifteen to sixteen years of age.

2. The Thomas Report advocated a common core curriculum for secondary schools. It also supported the idea of secondary schools catering to the nonacademic majority of their pupils in addition to the more academic interests of the minority. The report was sub-sequently to become the key document in shaping the postwar New Zealand secondary school curriculum, and is still often mentioned in educational policy documents today.

3. All archival materials cited in this chapter is from Archives New Zealand's ABEP. W 4262 accession. In order to clearly distinguish them from nonarchival material, these citations end with a file reference. The bibliography is accordingly divided into archival and nonarchival materials.

4. Man A Course of Study (MACOS) was a controversial social studies program developed in the United States during the 1960s. It was subsequently used in schools in both Australia and New Zealand during the following decade.

REFERENCES

Archival Materials

Acting Director. (1947, October 21). ABEP. W4262. Box 1850. 30/2/15. Social Studies. Part 1 1947–1959.

Bell, J. F. (1964, July 29). Letter to Minister of Education. ABEP. W4262. Box 556. 5/1/14. Washday at the Pa. National Archives: Wellington.

Campbell, A. E. (1964, July 30). Memo to Minister of Education. ABEP. W4262. Box 556.5/1/14. Washday at the Pa. National Archives: Wellington.

Chief Inspector of Primary Schools (CIOPS). (1964, July). Memo to Director. ABEP. W4262. Box 556. 5/1/14. Washday at the Pa. National Archives: Wellington.

Harris, W. B. to Reed, A. W. (1947, September 4). ABEP. W4262. Box 1850. 30/2/15. Social Studies. Part 1 1947–1959.

Harris, W. B. to Reed, A. W. (1948, April 9). ABEP. W4262. Box 556. 5/1/14. Washday at the Pa. National Archives: Wellington.

Harris, W. B. to Hamilton, S. (1951, September 13). ABEP. W4262. Box 1850. 30/2/15. Social Studies. Part 1 1947–1959.

Internal memo. (1964). No author given. ABEP. W. 4262. Box 556. 5/1/14. Washday at the Pa. National Archives: Wellington.

Kinsella, A. E. (1964a, July 30). Memo to Director of Education. ABEP. W4262. Box 556. 5/1/14. Washday at the Pa. National Archives: Wellington.

Kinsella, A. E. (1964b). Press statement. ABEP. W 4262. Box 556. 5/1/14. Washday at the Pa. National Archives: Wellington.

Otago Education Board. (1946, August). Report of the Committee on Social Studies. ABEP. W4262. Box 1850. 30/2/15. Social Studies. Part 1 1947–1959.

Reed, A. W. to Harris W. B. (1948, February 22). ABEP. W4262. Box 1850. 30/2/15. Social Studies. Part 1 1947–1959.

Nonarchival Materials

Binney, J. (1990). Te GFKooti Arikangi Te Turiki. In *The dictionary of national biography* (Vol. 1, pp. 462–466). New Zealand Department of Internal Affairs, Wellington: Bridget Williams Books.

Brookes, B. (1997). Nostalgia for 'innocent homely pleasures': The 1964 New Zealand controversy over Washday at the Pa. *Gender & History, 9* (2), 242–261.

Chapman-Taylor, R. (1953). *Life in the Pa.* Pauls: Auckland.

Gibbons, P. J. (1992). The climate of opinion. In G. W. Rice (Ed.), *The Oxford history of New Zealand* (2nd ed., pp. 308–336). Auckland: Oxford University Press.

Goodson, I. F., & Marsh, C. J. (1996). *Studying school subjects.* London: Falmer Press.

Gorrie, A. M. (1963). Jam for breakfast, dinner and tea. *Education, 10* (12), 17–23.

Harrison, K. (1998). Social studies in the New Zealand curriculum: Dosing for amnesia or enemy of ethnocentricism? In P. Benson and R. Openshaw (Eds.), *New horizons for*

New Zealand social studies (pp. 63–82). Palmerston North: Educational Research and Development Center Press.

Keesing, R. M. (1989). Creating the past: Custom and identity in the contemporary Pacific. *The Contemporary Pacific, 1* (1 & 2), 19–42.

Maori women incensed by bulletin issued by department. (1964, July 23). *Otago Daily Times.*

McGee, J. (1998). Curriculum in conflict: Historical development of citizenship in social studies. In P. Benson and R. Openshaw (Eds.), *New horizons for New Zealand social studies* (pp. 43–62). Palmerston North: Educational Research and Development Center Press.

Moeran, B. (1990). Rapt discourses: Anthropology, Japanism and Japan. In E. Ben-Ari, B. Moeran, B. & J. Valentine (Eds.), *Unwrapping Japan* (pp. 1–17). Manchester: Manchester University Press.

Murdoch, J. H. (1944). *The high schools of New Zealand: A critical survey* (Educational Research Series No. 19). Christchurch: New Zealand Center for Educational Research.

Nash, R. (1990). Society and culture in New Zealand: An outburst for 1990. *New Zealand Sociology, 5* (2), 99–124.

New Zealand Department of Education (NZDOE). (1943). *The post-primary school curriculum.* Wellington: Government Printer. (Report of the Committee appointed by the Minister of Education in November 1942, [The Thomas Report]).

New Zealand Department of Education (NZDOE). (1962). *Suggestions for the teaching of social studies in the primary school* (Vol. 1). Wellington: Government Printer.

Nozaki, Y., & Inokuchi, H. (1996) On critical Asia literacy. *Curriculum Perspectives, 16* (3), 72–76.

Openshaw, R. (1991). Schooling in the 40's and 50's: An oral history. *Research resources,* No. 1. New Zealand: Massey University Educational Research and Development Center Press.

Openshaw, R. (1995). *Unresolved struggle. Consensus and conflict in state post-primary education.* Palmerston North: Dunmore Press.

Openshaw, R. (1998). Citizen who? The debate over economic and political correctness in the social studies curriculum. In P. Benson and R. Openshaw (Eds.), *New Horizons for New Zealand social studies* (pp. 19–42). Palmerston North: Dunmore Press.

Openshaw, R. (2000). Culture wars in the Antipodes: The social studies curriculum controversy in New Zealand. *Theory & research in social education, 28* (1), 65–84.

Openshaw, R., & Archer, E. (1992). The battle for social studies in the New Zealand secondary school 1942–1964. In R. Openshaw (Ed.), *New Zealand social studies: Past, present and future* (pp. 19–33). Palmerston North: Dunmore Press.

Owens, J. M. R. (1992). New Zealand before annexation. In G. W. Rice (Ed.), *The Oxford History of New Zealand* (2nd ed. pp. 28–56). Auckland: Oxford University Press.

Partington, G. (1998). Social studies in the New Zealand curriculum. In P. Benson and R. Openshaw (Eds.), *New horizons for New Zealand social studies* (pp. 83–102). Palmerston North: Dunmore Press.

Saunders, E., & Ryan, A. B. (1961, December 8). Social studies—for and against. *New Zealand Listener, 45* (1161), 10.

Scott, D. J. (1996). *The Currie commission and report on education in New Zealand 1960–62.* Unpublished doctoral dissertation, University of Auckland.

Sorrenson, M. P. K. (1992). Maori and pakeha. In G. W. Rice (Ed.), *The Oxford History of New Zealand* (2nd ed. pp. 141–167). Auckland: Oxford University Press.

Stone, R. C. J. (1963, July). Humane studies are not enough. *New Zealand Post Primary Teachers' Association Journal, 10* (6), 27–29.

Story of New Zealand, The. (1945). Wellington: A. H. Reed.

Taylor, N. (1953). *Exploring New Zealand.* Wellington: New Zealand Department of Education.

Westra, A. (1964). *Washday at the pa.* Wellington: New Zealand Department of Education.

Chapter 3

State Formation, Hegemony, and Chinese School Curricula in Singapore and Hong Kong, 1945–1965

Ting-Hong Wong

Using a Gramscian notion of hegemony, this chapter compares the strategies adopted by post–World War II Singapore and Hong Kong to serve their state formation projects by reforming the curricula of Chinese schools. Hegemony, according to Antonio Gramsci, is a form of domination built upon the culture of the subordinated. When hegemony is formed, the ruling group, instead of sweeping away the culture of the ruled, seeks to incorporate it and then reorganize its elements into a form that advances the dominant group's own advantageous position (Gramsci, 1971). State formation is the historical process through which the ruling group struggles to construct a local or national identity, integrate society, win the consent of the subordinated group, and outmaneuver political antagonists (Green, 1990; T. H. Wong, 2002). The relationship between hegemony building and state formation is by no means direct and mechanical, especially when the culture in question is that of a subordinated ethnic group. In monoracial milieus, the ruling regimes can construct state power through incorporating and then remaking the culture of the dominated race. However, in multiracial societies, the project of state formation can limit the state's capacity for cultural incorporation, because the ruling regime's attempt to accommodate the culture of a dominated ethnic community might perpetuate racial segregation and elicit opposition from other ethnic communities.

This chapter demonstrates the conjunctural connection between cultural hegemony and state formation in the historical cases of Chinese school curricula in Singapore and Hong Kong. I will advance that the ruling authorities of Hong Kong had a much higher capacity to incorporate Chinese culture into the hegemonic curriculum than its counterpart in Singapore.

This was because Hong Kong was by and large a monoracial Chinese society, and the state's action was not constrained by other racial groups in the civil society. Also, I would argue that because the state in Singapore had a low capacity for turning Chinese culture into official knowledge, it opted to remove the culture of the Chinese people from the official curriculum. To explicate this argument, I will first briefly outline the background of Chinese school curricula and state formation in the two cities.

BACKGROUND

After the World War II, Chinese schools in both Singapore and Hong Kong continued the prewar practice of adopting curricula and textbooks from mainland China. As these instructional materials were produced under the aegis of the Ministry of Education of the Kuomintang (KMT) government in Nanjing, they inculcated a Chinese nationalistic and anti-imperial consciousness in students within the two British dependencies (e.g., Gopinathan, 1974). This undesirable situation soon became intolerable: In the early 1950s, the decolonization process triggered by the Rendel Report—a document prepared by an advisory body commissioned by the British to suggest future constitutional change of the colony—demanded that the state of Singapore create a local consciousness shared by all four of its ethnic communities (e.g., Yeo, 1973). The Chinese school curriculum, which had been promoting a centrifugal outlook and preventing integration between the Chinese and other racial groups, became an obstacle hindering the construction of the new state (Loh, 1975).

Regarding Hong Kong, the colonial regime entered a new stage of state formation when the Chinese Communist Party (CCP) became the new ruling power in China in 1949. The Communist and Chinese patriotic ideology fostered by Beijing could produce antagonism and endanger the position of the colonial state. The British authorities needed to contain these threats by drawing a clearer line of demarcation between Hong Kong and mainland China. Also, the new scenario propelled the British authorities to monitor the influences of Taiwan upon the colony; otherwise, Hong Kong Chinese might develop a strong anti-Beijing identity and turn Hong Kong into an explosive battleground between the two Chinese nations (Tsang, 1997).

Though the ruling regimes in both Singapore and Hong Kong needed to control Chinese school curricula, by virtue of their diverse agendas of state formation, they had different objectives and capacities in carrying out these pedagogic reforms. In Singapore, since one of the major objectives of state building was to blend the Chinese with other racial groups into a national whole, the state was under strong pressure to undermine the elements of Chinese culture present in the educational sphere. This imperative for *de-Sinicization* was especially important because after Japan's occupation (from 1942 to 1945), the relationship between the Malays and the Chinese had deteriorated. The Malays, the dominant group in Malaya according to the constitution, launched a strong nationalistic movement to protect their interests against possible infringement from the Chinese (e.g., Cheah, 1983). To avoid alienating the Malays and inciting further racial animosity, the ruling authorities needed to prevent the "overformation" of the Chinese people's ethnic identity. In addition, after 1949, the Singapore government, with more than 70 percent of its citizenry being racially Chinese, had to allay the fears of neighboring countries (such as the Federation of Malaya and Indonesia) who believed that Singapore was a "Little Beijing" used by the CCP to expand its influences in Southeast Asia. This external dimension of racial politics added impetus for the Singapore government to de-Sinicize its school system.

In sharp contrast, the racial politics of Hong Kong were relatively simple. With a 98 percent racially Chinese population, the British were spared the challenge of harmonizing diverse indigenous ethnic communities, and the ruling regime's behavior was not restricted by any powerful non-Chinese racial groups within the local society. In addition, Hong Kong's colonial state was not threatened by any anti-Chinese nation in the surrounding region. In the two decades following World War II, the forces most likely to produce social cleavage and elicit antistate movements in the colony were Beijing and Taipei, two Chinese nations. Given this background, the British authorities in Hong Kong could protect their ruling power by *denationalizing*, which meant preventing the school system from inculcating in pupils a strong identification with either of the Chinese states, but not de-Sinicizing Chinese school curriculum; the colonial state had more room to absorb Chinese culture and then transform it into a "selective tradition" that consolidated British domination.

SINGAPORE: DE-SINICIZING THE CHINESE SCHOOL CURRICULUM

Singapore implemented many reforms to regulate Chinese school curriculum in the two decades after the war. However, due to space limitations, I will discuss in this section only the reforms of the early 1950s, when the island was still a British dependency, and the early 1960s, when Singapore had already become a completely self-governing state under the leadership of the People's Action Party (PAP). The reforms of these two periods reveal the impasse of the state in Singapore, which had a low capability for hegemonizing Chinese culture. In the early 1950s, the British de-Sinicization policy elicited tough opposition from the Chinese. By the late 1950s, although the state authorities successfully removed Chinese elements at the level of syllabi, it failed to de-Sinicize school knowledge beyond the level of official curriculum documents because of hindrances from pedagogic agents with strong embodiments of Chinese culture.

The Early 1950s: De-Sinicization and Resistance from the Chinese

In 1951, the Fenn-Wu Committee, an advisory body appointed by Kuala Lumpur to make suggestions for Chinese school policy, released its report. *Inter alia*, the report suggested that the governments eliminate the separateness and foreign politics of Chinese schools and make them contribute to the formation of a common Malayan culture (Department of Education, Federation of Malaya, 1951). To achieve this objective, the report proposed localizing the Chinese school curriculum and bringing it into line with the curricula of other schools. After accepting this recommendation, the governments in the Federation of Malaya and in Singapore assigned E. C. S. Adkins, the secretary of Chinese affairs in Singapore, to translate suggestions from Fenn-Wu into workable policy. The curriculum reform preferred by the British authorities had a strong tendency toward de-Sinicization, because many British colonial bureaucrats, including Adkins, in Malaya, was strongly distrustful of the Chinese.[1] After Adkins submitted his report in early 1952, the government of the federation followed his advice and installed a General Textbook Committee (GTC) and a Teachers Advisory Committee (TAC) to implement the textbook reform. According to *Sin Chew Jit Poh*, a vernacular newspaper, the TAC was made up of teachers and principals from Chinese schools (*SCJP*, 18 March and 16 April 1952). To ensure successful imposition of their own will, the British authorities signed a pact with the United Publishing House Limited (UPHL), an amalgam of four major Chinese publishing firms. This agreement bound the UPHL to follow the government's instruction when compiling textbooks. In return, the British promised to grant an imprimatur solely to the UPHL. The colonial authorities hoped that this pact would make the books produced under their tutelage the only available texts and give all Chinese schools no choice but to use these state-preferred materials.[2] To minimize influences from the Chinese educators, the British authorities also made the TAC a purely advisory body (*SCJP*, 11 and 17 April 1952).

The actions of the British, perceived by the Chinese as designed to eliminate their culture, provoked determined resistance. The United Chinese School Teachers' Association (UCSTA), the most prominent teacher organization in the federation, avowed that because Chinese people bore a distinct cultural heritage, this new curriculum should not be identical with curricula of other institutions (*SCJP*, 24 April 1952). In late May 1952, a leading vernacular newspaper in Singapore tried to protect the elements of Chinese culture in the curriculum by countering the claim of E. M. Payne, the chairman of the GTC, that the new syllabi should follow the principle of "starting from proximity" and include more topics about Malaya (*SCJP*, 23 and 24 May 1952). It delineated the concept of "proximity" into two aspects—geographical and psychological—and maintained that as psychological distance meant more for students, the new curriculum should give equal attention to both China and Malaya (*SCJP*, 27 April 1952). Furthermore, Chinese educators also struggled against de-Sinicization at the level of individual subjects. For instance, before the Singapore Chinese School Conference (SCSC) representatives in the TAC scrutinized the compiling guidelines for civics, the document addressed Singapore and the Federation of Malaya as "nations," advised that the new textbooks cover the Commonwealth, and tended to undermine the importance of China. But after it was examined by the TAC, the same document was changed to classify the Federation of Malaya and Singapore as "places" and suggest that new textbooks assign more curriculum space to topics about China and less to topics about Malaya (*SCJP*, 20 and 21 June 1952).

To strengthen their position in the anti–de-Sinicization campaign, the Chinese educators in both Singapore and the peninsula challenged both the accord between the colonial state and the UPHL and the procedure for textbook examination. In April 1952, the UCSTA asserted that the TAC should have the final say on all textbook manuscripts (*SCJP*, 24 April 1952). At almost the same time the SCSC challenged the British for giving special privilege to the UPHL, it also insisted that the government should encourage free competition for textbook production (*SCJP*, 27 April 1952). Later, the SCSC asked Payne to either withdraw the privilege bestowed upon the UPHL or to confer the same right to all publishers (*SCJP*, 25 June 1952). In October, the SCSC escalated their protest by assembling a large meeting, which was attended by representatives from some forty-six Chinese schools (*SCJP*, 13 October 1952).

Under firm opposition, the colonial regime was forced to yield from time to time. In late May 1952, Payne accepted that the new syllabi should preserve the essence of Chinese culture. More importantly, he ceded control over text production, agreeing that all publishers were free to publish textbooks written according to the official syllabi (*SCJP*, 23 and 24 May 1952). In October 1952, the colonial authorities granted the Chinese community more power to influence the final form of textbook manuscripts when they promised that all textbook manuscripts would be finalized by a joint meeting of the GTC and the TAC (*SCJP*, 31 October 1952). Finally, in late 1953, after some Chinese schools decided to use the old textbooks despite the fact that the UPHL had already published the new series (*SCJP*, 12 December 1953), the Department of Education in Singapore yielded by reaffirming the discretion of Chinese schools to make textbook selections (*SCJP*, 23 December 1953). These compromises, though averting further agitation of the Chinese community, perpetuated the Chinese people's non–local-oriented consciousness and slowed state formation in Singapore.

The Early 1960s: A De-Sinicized Official Curriculum Without a De-Sinicized Recontextualizing Field

After a landslide victory in the general election of May 1959, the People's Action Party (PAP), led by Lee Kuan Yew, became the new ruling power in the now self-governing Singapore. Steering Singapore towards complete independence, the PAP was under more intense pressure than all its predecessors to blend the Chinese with all other racial groups into a unified whole. After assuming office, the PAP took swift actions to implement curriculum reform. In October 1959, a Committee on Syllabi and Textbooks (CST) was formed to revise school syllabi and encourage the Malayanization of teaching materials. Shortly afterward, the CST installed fourteen subject committees, which were made up of teacher representatives from four types of schools, to carry out this reform. From October to December 1959, the Ministry of Education approved thirty-three new syllabi (*SCJP*, 13 October and 11 December 1960). In late 1960, the PAP announced that starting in early 1961, all schools in Singapore would adopt the new common curriculum (*SCJP*, 20 December 1960).

From the new syllabi of history and geography—two vital subjects for the production of citizenship—one can see that the state had successfully de-Sinicized the official syllabi. The official curriculum of these two subjects included a very small amount of Chinese content. For instance, the geography curriculum was packed with topics on geographical skills and physical geography; its section of regional geography covered Australia, Africa, the Americas, Europe, and Asia, as well as the local settings of Singapore and the Malay Peninsula. Within this framework, China was treated as only one country among many in Asia and assigned an extremely limited amount of curriculum space (Ministry of Education, Singapore, 1961a). Regarding the subject of history, the official syllabus, following a world history approach, contained the histories of many countries and covered a very long timespan. Thus, the history syllabus allowed a very limited amount of curriculum space for Chinese history and placed it within the context of Western history (Ministry of Education, Singapore, 1961b). Besides minimizing the proportion of Chinese topics, this arrangement also de-Sinicized Chinese history and geography by placing them under the temporal and spatial matrix of the West.

Although the PAP regime had removed a large number of Chinese cultural elements at the level of official syllabi, this de-Sinicization of curriculum was not executed without any mediation. In fact, a very wide gap existed between the state-promulgated syllabi and the textbooks used for classroom teaching. To take an example, the history textbooks produced by World Bookstore, a Chinese publisher, devoted four whole volumes, out of a total of six, to Chinese history. This amount of emphasis given to China was much larger than that recommended by the PAP. In addition, the whole series started with a chapter entitled "The Periodization and Special Characteristics of Chinese History." These treatments brought Chinese history back to the center of human history and violated the world history, or de-Sinicization approach, promoted by the state.

The de-Sinicization plan was impeded when it went beyond the level of official syllabi because the publishers for Chinese schools had embodied a Sinicized culture. The strategy of de-Sinicization presupposed a process of deculturation. However, it was quite difficult for the local Chinese publishers to eliminate the cultural habits built up throughout many years of immersion in Chinese culture. This was because many of these publishers were founded by well-established publishing firms from mainland China before World War II as overseas branches; and in the postwar decades, many of them still maintained a close tie with their headquarters in other Chinese societies, such as Hong Kong (Carstens, 1988). In addition, the state's capacity for de-Sinicizing the Chinese school curriculum beyond the level of official syllabi was limited by the fact that an ideal substitute—a locally centered pedagogic model shared by all racial groups—simply did not exist. This is because Singapore had been a colonial society and the intellectual discourse, and the educational spheres, of different racial groups coexisted in a segregated manner (e.g., Loh, 1975; T. H. Wong, 2002).

HONG KONG: DENATIONALIZING CHINESE SCHOOL CURRICULUM

Though the government of Hong Kong started to regulate local Chinese schools in the early twentieth century with the purpose of containing the influences of Chinese politics (e.g., Ng Lun, 1977; Sweeting, 1990), it did not intend to make the curriculum in Hong Kong too different from that of China during the prewar era. Hong Kong was a steppingstone by which the British could enter China, and it served to facilitate communication between East and West. Drawing a categorical distinction between the curricula in the two territories would undermine Hong Kong's value. Also, the prewar Hong Kong government needed to ensure a certain level of coherence between the curricula in the two places, because many pupils completing secondary education in the colony went back to China for higher education (e.g., C. L. Wong, 1983). The policy, nevertheless, changed after 1949. The victory of the Chinese Communist Party (CCP) in the Chinese civil war suddenly left the colonial regime facing a unified and potentially hostile Chinese state, which had also been an adversary of Whitehall during the Cold War (Catron, 1971). To prevent the leftists from spreading Communism and expanding their following in Hong Kong, the colonial state now became very adamant about drawing a definite boundary with mainland China. In addition, the British had to monitor Taiwan's activities in the colony, because Chiang Kai-shek's attempt to enlist the support of the Hong Kong Chinese for its anti-CCP cause could endanger the relations between the colony and Beijing. Within this context, the colonial regime toiled to bar the Hong Kong Chinese from strongly identifying themselves with either of the two Chinese nations.

Articulating the Denationalization Principle

In September 1952, the colonial government appointed a committee to consider the position and aims of Chinese studies in the local school system (Hong Kong Government, 1953). In their report, the members of this committee (which included education officers from the government and some leading figures in local education) admitted that they had borne in mind "the intimate ties that bind Hong Kong to the Great Britain" when making their recommendation (p. 1). In comparison to a similar committee appointed three years earlier, which had been asked to bear in mind "Hong Kong's position to China" when suggesting the policy[3], the position of the 1952 committee represented the colonial state's desire to make a curriculum distinctive from that of mainland China. After pointing out that the subjects of Chinese language, Chinese literature, and Chinese history in local schools had been closely following the trends in China, the committee recommended severing this bond on the grounds that the curriculum of the old Nanjing government produced "arrogant and bigoted Chinese nationalists" (p. 19). To correct this nationalistic bias, the committee declared that Chinese studies in Hong Kong should develop pupils' abilities of expression in their mother tongue and help them to understand and appreciate Chinese thought, literature, and traditions. To buttress this goal of denationalization, the committee connected it discursively to the notions of communication and democracy:

> In a free and democratic society, the art of communication has a special importance. A totalitarian state can obtain consent by forces, but a democracy must persuade, and persuasion is through speech ... The function of Chinese Language lesson in local schools is, therefore, to develop Chinese pupils' power of expression and communication in their mother tongue, so as to fit them to make their way in Hong Kong. (p. 17)

In addition, the committee removed the nationalistic theme inscribed by the Kuomintang (KMT) by positioning the "West" as a subject for academic investigation, rather than an enemy to be fought, and a comparative yardstick to help the Chinese people deepen their self-understanding. It also rearticulated Chinese studies as a means to cultivate harmonious East-West relations:

> [H]aving attained proficiency in their own language, literature and history, Chinese pupils should guide another steps [*sic*] further to utilize this as a basis for making comparative studies of Eastern and Western thought and language. It is only through such studies that Hong Kong children can become more Chinese, conscious of their own culture and at the same time having a liberal, balanced and international outlook. (p. 19)

This direction of denationalization can also be found in many other state education policies during the 1950s and 1960s. For example, in 1952, the government created a Chinese School Certificate Examination (CSCE) for students completing their education in Chinese middle schools in Hong Kong. The CSCE, designed by the British to de-link the Chinese school curriculum in Hong Kong from that in mainland China (Cheng, 1954), enabled students of Chinese schools to learn a great deal about Chinese language and culture. For instance, the regulations of the CSCE made passing Chinese language a requirement for obtaining a CSCE certificate (*Special issue on Hong Kong*, 1954); and the history and geography syllabi of the CSCE allowed students taking these two subjects to focus predominantly upon Chinese history and Chinese geography.[4] However, the Chinese cultural elements included were a "selective tradition" that hindered the creation of a strong pro-Beijing, pro-Taiwan, or Chinese national identity. For example, the history syllabus covered only the period from the early Ching Dynasty to the end of the anti-Japanese war in 1945 and skipped entirely the Chinese civil war and the post-1949 era. Its treatment of the period between 1912 and 1945 took the Nationalist government in Nanjing as the center of Chinese history and ignored the CCP. It reconstituted the history of confrontation between China and imperialism by accentuating the offenses of oriental imperial powers (such as Japan and Russia), omitting many confrontations occasioned by Western invasions, and by suggesting that the May Fourth Movement was only a literature reform.[5] In addition, the geography syllabus for the CSCE only requested that students who chose the section on China for their regional geography paper have some general understanding about the landscapes, climates, products, and cities in various parts of China. By desentimentalizing the pedagogic topics, "China" was transformed from a motherland to be loved and devoted to, into only an external object to be studied.

The colonial state took several steps to execute the denationalization strategy at the level of textbooks. In 1952 and 1953, as newspapers such as *Wen Wei Pao* and *Wah Kiu Yat Poh* reported, the Hong Kong government furnished a list of approved textbooks, which included many titles produced in Taiwan or under the old Nanjing Nationalist regime (*WWP*, 19 August 1952; *WKYP*, 5 and 6 July 1953). This was an expedient step taken by the colonial state before something better became available. The British then localized school textbooks by inducing the publishers in Taiwan to adjust their texts to the situation of Hong Kong and encouraging local publishers to produce instructional materials. Throughout this process, the colonial regime created a number of subject syllabi as guidelines for compiling textbooks (T. H. Wong, 2002). If the desired text still did not appear, the colonial authorities would invite writers to draft suitable materials. For instance, Professor S. G. Davis, head of the Department of Geography and Geology at the University of Hong Kong, was asked by the government to write a geography series for Chinese middle schools. When extending the invitation to Professor Davis, the government requested he avoid offending either Beijing or Taipei in the new text.[6] Perhaps because denationalizing a text-producing field was easier than deculturalizing it, the publishers compiling textbooks for Chinese schools in Hong Kong appeared to adjust better to the demands of the state than their counterparts in Singapore. Consequently, school textbooks in Hong Kong became very different from those in mainland China and Taiwan. This helped to create an identity that was very distinctive from those promoted by the two Chinas (Chen, Wang, and Chen, 1995).

DeNationalization of the Pedagogic Discourse and Counter-Hegemony

Unlike the de-Sinicization strategy in Singapore, the denationalization approach, which did not generate a widespread sense of cultural crisis, helped the Hong Kong colonial state avoid provoking tough resistance from a substantial section of the Chinese community. The denationalization tactics positioned the pro-Beijing and pro-Taipei camps—the two major nationalist powers in the colony—as counter-hegemonic. However, due to the weaknesses of their mobilizations, their antistate challenges were far less powerful than those launched by the Chinese community in Singapore.

Hong Kong had a number of pro-Beijing schools in the educational arena. Before 1949, educators from these schools had criticized the official curriculum sponsored by the Nanjing Kuomintang government for making young people docile and conservative (Heung Tao Middle School, 1949). Right after the victory of the CCP, these leftists advocated that all schools in the colony adopt new teaching materials complied by the new

China (*WWP*, 26 January 1950). In late 1951 and early 1952, when the Hong Kong government was about to inaugurate the CSCE, a number of leftist middle schools, such as Hon Hwa, Sun Kiu, Chung Hwa, and Pui Kiu, publicly declared their unwillingness to participate in the exam (*WWP*, 24 December 1951, and 10 and 14 March 1952). Through its mouthpiece newspaper, the leftist educators also denounced the CSCE curriculum as "enslaving the minds of pupils" (*WWP*, 26 February 1952), "creating a colonial mentality," "hiding the fact that the young people were the future masters of new China," "hindering students from understanding the glorified tradition of Chinese people's struggle against oppression," "deleting topics on western invasions" (*WWP*, 11 March 1952), and "wittingly leaving out achievements of the Chinese people under the leadership of the CCP" (*WWP*, 17 March 1952).

Though this counter-hegemonic discourse posed some threat to the denationalization cause of the colonial state, the weaknesses of the leftists' mobilization prevented them from winning a wider support base among the Hong Kong Chinese and expanding this "oppositional moment." The pro-Beijing educators by and large followed a defensive withdrawal strategy—they had never organized other schools to campaign against the curriculum reforms launched by the British. Also, with insufficient funding, leftist schools were unable to enlarge their enrollment.[7] The small enrollment of leftist schools was due, in part, to the fact that Beijing did not support a large expansion of patriotic schools in Hong Kong (Catron, 1971). This relatively nonaggressive tactic was in line with the policy of Beijing, which treasured the political and economic values of the colony and opted to tolerate, rather than challenge, the colonial situation of Hong Kong (Heaton, 1970; Tang, 1994).

Hong Kong had two major types of schools under the pro-Taiwan umbrella. On the one hand, there were some ultra-nationalistic and outright pro-KMT schools in Rennie's Mill, the stronghold of the KMT in the colony. These schools were mostly inaugurated in the early 1950s with the assistance of the Hong Kong government, Taiwan, and other international agencies.[8] These schools were registered at Taipei, followed the curriculum promulgated by the KMT, and used textbooks compiled or approved by the Ministry of Education of the Republic of China. The pedagogic activities of these schools were minimally regulated by the colonial state, because they neither registered with the Hong Kong government nor participated in local public examinations, and because many of their students pursued higher education in Taiwan (Ming Yuen Middle School, p. 1; Rennie's Mill Middle School, 1985). Given this minimum regulation, these schools endeavored to teach *San Min Chi I* (the Three Principles of the People) and projected a nationalist and pro-Taiwan identity. Though the schools in Rennie's Mill confronted the hegemonic curriculum of the colonial state, their influence in Hong Kong was very limited—in the late 1950s, while the enrollment in Hong Kong's registered primary and secondary schools totaled about 370,000 (Hong Kong Government, 1963), the nine schools at Rennie's Mill enrolled only 4,560 students (Society for Social Problem Study, 1959–1960).

There was a larger number of pro-KMT schools outside of Rennie's Mill, the secluded "little Taiwan." These institutions, however, were more ready to compromise themselves to the colonial society. For example, Tak Ming, the largest pro-Taiwan schools in the colony, had 7,697 pupils enrolled in their kindergarten, primary, and middle divisions during the 1959–1960 school year. This number exceeded the total enrollments of the nine schools in Rennie's Mill. Tak Ming proclaimed that its objectives were to support national development of the free motherland, produce national pillars of the future, and further develop the good tradition of Chinese culture. Every year, a substantial number of Tak Ming students completing middle school education went to Taiwan for higher education. However, the pedagogic practices of Tak Ming were more susceptible to regulations from the colonial authorities, because the textbooks it adopted were approved by both the Hong Kong and Taiwanese governments, and because it entered students for public examination held by the colonial state. Owing to these practices, the opinions expressed in the school magazine of Tak Ming in the 1950s and 1960s on the local official curriculum were, unsurprisingly, very mild.

Conclusion

In this chapter, the historical cases of Singapore and Hong Kong are used to demonstrate that the state's capacity to incorporate and then transform an ethnic culture into a hegemonic curriculum depends upon the relationship between the state authorities and other racial groups in the civil society. After World War II, the ruling regime of Singapore was under pressure to reform school knowledge in Chinese schools. This was the case because the government, in a context of decolonization, needed to construct a local identity and integrate its several ethnic communities, namely, the Chinese, the Malays, and the Indians, into a national whole. Chinese schools, traditionally following the official curriculum in mainland China, spread a sectional, China-centered outlook, and so undermined the state formation project of the ruling authorities. Nevertheless, as Singapore was a multiethnic society, the state authorities, under intense pressure from the Malays, had very little latitude to compromise with the Chinese residents and accommodate Chinese culture in educational policy. Hence, it sought to eliminate Chinese culture from the local curriculum. This strategy of de-Sinicization, however, entrapped the ruling regime in deeper contradictions, because it provoked tough resistance from the Chinese and damaged the regime's position as the governing power.

In Hong Kong, the colonial authorities were also under intense compulsion to reform the curriculum of Chinese schools during the postwar era. This was because after 1949, the Chinese Communist Party became the new ruler of mainland China. To shield young people in the colony from political influences from Beijing, which spread anticapitalist and anti-imperial ideologies, the Hong Kong government had to discontinue local schools' reliance upon the curriculum used on mainland China. In addition, the Hong Kong government had to reduce influence from Taiwan on the school system in the territory and prevent young people from harboring strong anti-Beijing sentiments. Since Hong Kong was basically a monoracial Chinese society, the British, not being besieged by other racial communities, could focus on developing an effective concessionary approach. To do so, the colonial authorities exercised the strategy of denationalization. This tactic accommodated Chinese culture as part of the official knowledge in the colony, but remade it into a form that did not impart a dangerous pro-Beijing, pro-Taipei, or anti-British identity. By not attempting to oust Chinese culture, a move that would have met with strong resistance from the Chinese masses, the policy of denationalization was implemented quite smoothly. This development, as a result, helped consolidate the position of the colonial government.

The comparative history of my two cases allows for a clear look at a number of theoretical implications involving hegemony building and state formation. In the states of Singapore and Hong Kong, the handling of the Chinese curriculum shows that some specific hegemonic approaches could be used to consolidate ruling power under some particular forms of state–civil society relations, but that in other contexts, the same hegemonic tactics could slow state formation. These conjunctural relations hint strongly that the thesis of state formation as the process of constructing a ruling hegemony is too crude. Such a statement, provided by some scholars following a Gramscian approach (Curtis, 1988, 1992; Green, 1990) proves inadequate for analyzing the formation of ruling power in concrete historical milieus, for it makes no distinctions regarding the different approaches in forming hegemony. Worse still, the general statement associating state formation and hegemony disguises the fact that not all approaches to forming hegemony or cultural incorporation will buttress state power. To overcome this theoretical inadequacy, more historical and conceptual work needs to be done to help distinguish various hegemonic strategies and diverse forms of relationships between the state and various racial groups in civil societies. Then, based upon the foundation of these conceptual works, we should formulate theoretical statements about the compatibility of, and contradictions among, various kinds of hegemonic strategies, state–civil society relations, and state formation projects.

Working from the historical cases of Singapore and Hong Kong, I would like to theorize the consequences of different hegemonic strategies. When the state has a low capacity for incorporating the culture of a particular ethnic group, it might switch to substitute that cultural tradition. Such an approach, however, might hurt state formation by creating a wider front of resistance, and such opposition is likely to arise for two reasons: first, the substitution strategy might create a sense of cultural crisis and provoke opposition from the groups whose cultures are being replaced; second, since the substitution approach is also a tactic for deculturalization, it would position all of the pedagogic agents embodying that culture as counter-hegemonic. To overcome the obstacles, the state would have to accomplish the difficult task of changing the cultural predispositions of these pedagogic agents. If the approach proved unsuccessful, the state could modify its tactic and build its power through other means, perhaps by articulating other elements within the cultural totality of the ruled, by minimizing its involvement in matters of racial identity, and by allowing concession in other spheres (but not ethnic culture). This secondary tactic, however, if successfully implemented, might only result in a temporary stability of state power, because the issues of ethnic culture and identity would remain latent, and so could be rearticulated by an antagonistic force.

NOTES

The Chinese version of this article appeared in Wong, T. H. (2002). *Guojia quanli xinggou yu Huawen xuexiao kecheng gaige: Zhanhou xingjiapo ji xianggang de gean bijiao* [State formation and Chinese school curriculum reform: A comparative study of Singapore and Hong Kong], *Jiaoyu yu shehui yanjiu 4*, 111–133. I deeply appreciate the editorial board of the journal for allowing me to publish the English version in this volume.

1. For instance, Adkins had judged that the only way to resolve the problem of Chinese schools was to replace it by English institutions. The British civil services in Singapore and the Malay Peninsula had this anti-Chinese predisposition partly because they considered the Malays the only indigenous ethnic group and had put very little effort into learning the language and culture of the Chinese.

2. The Draft Agreement attached to Memorandum from Member for Education on Chinese Textbooks, Executive Council Paper No 10/10/52; and Extract from Federation of Malaya, Sav. 2064, 9 October 1952. Both in a declassified confidential file Colonial Office 1022/285.

3. Report of the Committee on Chinese Studies in Anglo-Chinese Schools, 27 August 1949, in a declassified confidential file Hong Kong Record Service: 147, D&S: 2/2 (I).

4. The history exam consisted of two papers, namely Chinese and World History. This arrangement ensured that half of the history curriculum was about Chinese history. The geography exam also had two subject matter areas—Physical Geography and Regional Geography—and candidates were required to select only one among (1) Asian Geography, (2) Chinese Geography, and (3) British Imperial and Commonwealth Geography, for Regional Geography.

5. The May Fourth Movement happened in 1919 when students and workers in China staged demonstrations to protest the terms of the Treaty of Versailles, which allowed Japan to retain control over the Shangdong Peninsula, formerly a territory leased by China to Germany. This movement eventually evolved into an intellectual revolution championing science, democracy, and fundamental change in traditional Chinese society.

6. K. T. Attwell, Report on the Two Series of School Textbooks by Professor S. G. Davis, 10 September 1962, in Hong Kong Record Service: 457, D&S: 2/10 (2).

7. Gary Catron estimated that in the mid 1950s, when the total enrollment in the colony was about 250,000, only about 10,000 to 12,000 attended pro-Beijing schools (Catron, 1971).

8. In 1950, the Hong Kong government resettled destitute KMT soldiers in a new refugee camp at Rennie's Mill after some pro-Beijing unionists violently clashed with those ex-KMTs in the refugee camp at Mount Davis in Hong Kong island. The Hong Kong government, however, minimized their involvement soon after setting up the new refugee camp.

REFERENCES

Published Official Documents

Department of Education, Federation of Malaya. (1951). *Chinese schools and the education of Chinese Malayans: The report of a mission invited by the federation government to study the problem of education of Chinese in Malaya.* Kuala Lumpur: Government Printer.

Hong Kong Government. (1953). *Report of the Chinese studies committee.* Hong Kong: Education Department.

Hong Kong Government. (1963). *Report of education commission.* Hong Kong: Government Printer.

Ministry of Education, Singapore. (1960). *Annual report, Singapore, 1959.* Singapore: Government Printer.

Ministry of Education, Singapore. (1961a). *Syllabus for geography in primary and secondary schools.* Singapore: Government Printer.

Ministry of Education, Singapore. (1961b). *Syllabus for History in Primary and Secondary Schools.* Singapore: Government Printer.

Newspaper Sources

Sin Chew Jit Poh (SCJP).
Wah Kiu Yat Poh (WKYP).
Wen Wei Pao (WWP).

Books and Articles

Carstens, S. A. (1988). Chinese publications and the transformation of Chinese culture in Singapore and Malaysia. In J. Cushman & G. Wang (Eds.), *Changing identities of the southeast Asian Chinese since World War II* (pp. 75–95). Hong Kong: Hong Kong University Press.

Catron, G. (1971). *China and Hong Kong, 1945–67*. Ph.D. dissertation, Harvard University, Cambridge, Massachusetts.

Cheah, B. K. (1983). *Red star over Malaya: Resistance and social conflict during and after the Japanese occupation, 1941–1946* (2nd ed.). Singapore: Singapore University Press.

Chen, J., Wang, A., & Chen, E. (1995). Opening a "window" on ideology: A comparison of school textbooks in Taiwan, Hong Kong and Mainland China. *Sinorama 20* (6), 6–27.

Cheng, T. C. (1954). The Hong Kong Chinese school certificate examination. *Journal of Education* (12).

Curtis, B. (1988). *Building the educational state: Canada West, 1836–1871*. Philadelphia: Falmer Press.

Curtis, B. (1992). *True government by choice men? Inspection, education, and state formation in Canada West*. Toronto, Ontario: University of Toronto.

Gopinathan, S. (1974). *Towards a national system of education in Singapore, 1945–1973*. Singapore: Oxford University Press.

Gramsci, A. (1971). *Selections from the prison notebooks*. London: Lawrence and Wishart.

Green, A. (1990). *Education and state formation: The rise of education systems in England, France, and the USA*. London: Macmillan Press.

Heaton, W. (1970). Maoist revolutionary strategy and modern colonialism: The Cultural Revolution in Hong Kong. *Asian Survey, 10* (9), 840–857.

Loh, P. F. S. (1975). *Seeds of separatism: Educational policy in Malaya, 1874–1940*. Kuala Lumpur: Oxford University Press.

Ng Lun, N. H. (1977). Consolidation of the government administration and supervision of schools in Hong Kong. *Journal of the Chinese University of Hong Kong, 6* (1), 159–181.

Sweeting, A. (1990). *Education in Hong Kong: Pre-1841 to 1941, fact and opinion*. Hong Kong: Hong Kong University Press.

Tang, J. T. H. (1994). World War to Cold War: Hong Kong's future and Anglo-Chinese interactions, 1941–55. In M. K. Chan (Ed.), *Precarious Balance: Hong Kong between China and Britain, 1842–1992* (pp. 107–129). Hong Kong: Hong Kong University Press.

Tsang, S. Y. S. (1997). Strategy for survival: The Cold War and Hong Kong's policy towards Kuomintang and Chinese communist activities in the 1950s. *Journal of Imperial and Commonwealth History, 25* (2), 294–317.

Wong, C. L. (1983). *A history of the development of Chinese education in Hong Kong*. Hong Kong: Po Wen Book Company.

Wong, T. H. (2002). *Hegemonies compared: State formation and Chinese school politics in postwar Singapore and Hong Kong*. New York: Routledge/Falmer.

Yeo, K. W. (1973). *Political development in Singapore, 1945–55*. Singapore: Singapore University Press.

Others

Special issue on Hong Kong school certificate examination (1954). Hong Kong: Cairo Printer Limited.

Heung Tao Middle School. (1949). *Experiment on democratic education: Three years of experience from Heung Tao Middle School.* Hong Kong: Author.

Ming Yuen Middle School. (1990). *Ming Yuen Youth: Special issue for the 40th anniversary of school inauguration.* Hong Kong: Author.

Rennie's Mill Middle School. (1985). *Thirty-five years of Rennie's Mill Middle School.* Hong Kong: Author.

Society for Social Problem Study. (1959–1960). *Research report on refugee camp at Rennie's Mill.* Hong Kong: Author.

Chapter 4

Official Knowledge and Hegemony

The Politics of the Textbook Deregulation Policy in Taiwan

Jyh-Jia Chen

Introduction

The process of building a liberal-democratic, capitalist, native-dominated state in Taiwan has involved mass struggles over the control of cultural institutions such as schools, the appropriation of language, curricular development, and textbook production.[1] In postwar Taiwan, the combined power of these elements generated the dynamics of textbook deregulation: the opening up of textbook publication at all levels of education. People in Taiwan tend to believe that the opening up of textbook production contributes to more democratic educational policymaking and to more diverse curricula through a less-controlled textbook market. Most scholarly research on textbooks in Taiwan has focused strictly on the imposition of the state's political ideology (e.g., Xie, 1988), patterns of omission and misrepresentation of gender and ethnic minorities (e.g., Ou, 1989), or the impact of deregulation on the content of textbooks (e.g., Ke, 1998).[2] Other research has examined how local governments have practiced textbook selection (e.g., Huang, 1997), or the fluctuation of market shares of private publishers and the gradual concentration of the textbook industry (e.g., Zhang, 1996). Very little attention has been directed towards understanding the political complexity and ideological subtlety of the textbook deregulation policy as it was formulated during a period of dynamic transformation of the state.

This chapter examines the sociopolitical process of deregulating national standardized textbooks within the context of state transformation in Taiwan over the last two decades. It analyzes how the state, as well as opposition forces, constructed discourses and adopted methods of textbook reform, and how these reform practices were gradually incorporated into the official textbook deregulation project. This chapter argues that the historical formation of textbook deregulation policy involved a series of hegemonic struggles over school knowledge and textbook production. Through these struggles, state and opposition forces forged strategic alliances to nativize education, decentralize curricular decision making, and marketize textbook production. Despite contesting interpretations of nativization, decentralization, and marketization, the state and opposition forces gradually converged to adopt a "Taiwan first" stance, as well as curricular deregulation. Thus enabled, the state strategically determined the scope and timetable of textbook deregulation.

A HEGEMONIC APPROACH

Hegemony, according to Gramsci (1971), refers to a historically specific moment of leadership when the leading group is able to form historic projects with which to articulate and rearticulate the interests of subordinate groups, thereby winning the active consent of the masses and maintaining leadership. To win popular consent, the leading group must take into account the moral and intellectual elements of the subordinated in order to pursue a new historic agenda that represents the collective will. It is this process of coordinating the interests of a dominant group with the general interests of other groups, as well as with the life of the state as a whole, that constitutes the hegemony of a particular historical bloc (Hall, 1996; Mouffe, 1979).

Jessop (1990, p. 209) has argued that the realization of a hegemonic project is partially dependent upon the state's "strategic selectivity," which involves the structural privileges inscribed in a given state form, including its forms of representation, intervention, and internal articulation. The selectivity of the state emerges from different representation systems (e.g., clientelism, parliamentarianism, or pluralism) and allots varied degrees of institutional access and opportunities to different political forces pursuing their specific interests. Moreover, the internal articulation of the state refers to the distribution of power among different parts of the state. Finally, government intervention involves regulating civil society and the economy. Jessop argues that a national-popular oriented, hegemonic project will favor the structurally privileged class in the long run, given the selectivity of the specific state form.

Considering the significance of school knowledge in the production, reproduction, and transformation of power relations, the dominant groups in economic, political, and cultural spheres pursue their own interests when attempting to control what counts as legitimate knowledge in schools. However, the control over "official knowledge" is never a top-down imposition, but rather depends on a balance of forces (Apple, 1993). Specifically, textbooks signify particular constructions of reality and particular ways of selecting and organizing the vast universe of possible knowledge. Textbooks function not only as economic commodities in the publishers' pursuit of market profit, but also as regulated products controlled by the state and as cultural artifacts in the struggle over legitimate knowledge (e.g., Apple, 1989). Textbooks, then, are the result of political, economic, and cultural activities, conflicts, and compromises, through which the hegemonic bloc and its alliances consistently attempt to control the content and form of official knowledge (Apple, 1995).

The following sections will demonstrate how centralized, China-centered education in Taiwan helped to create common interests among opposition forces, which, together, strove for textbook reform. With no popular participation and little consensus connected to the existing state-authored textbook policy, the first wave of textbook deregulation in the late 1980s was initiated by the Ministry of Education. By contrast, textbook deregulation in the 1990s—which could be called the second wave of textbook deregulation—embodied hegemonic struggles over the nativization of curricula, decentralization of educational decision making, and marketization of textbook production. To maintain hegemonic control, the state was forced to compromise by adopting a strategy of steering the production of official knowledge at a distance.

THE CRISIS OF THE KUOMINTANG'S LEGITIMACY AND THE FIRST WAVE OF TEXTBOOK DEREGULATION

Due to an unresolved dispute over sovereignty, education in postwar Taiwan was shaped by the perceived necessity of national survival, ideological consolidation, and the legitimization of state power. After World War II, Taiwan fell to the Chinese Nationalist Party (the Kuomintang, or KMT) as a result of a complete transfer of power from the Japanese colonial government to the party. In 1949, the KMT fled to Taiwan and declared martial law after being defeated by the Chinese Communist Party (CCP). As émigré rulers, the KMT felt compelled to reinvent and invoke "Chinese tradition" in order to legitimize its version of the sovereignty of the Republic of China (ROC), which, in fact, only ruled Taiwan, but supposedly represented all of China. This state-led nation building articulated and merged conflicting ethnic identities into a homogeneous sense of Chineseness.[3]

The nationalizing experiences in curricula led to the introduction of a Sinicization education policy that focused on the legacy of Chinese culture. For example, standard Mandarin was taught as the sole official language in schools; native languages were downgraded to "Taiwanese dialects" and

prohibited on official occasions. A strongly centralized educational administration system was established. The Ministry of Education controlled the
overall direction of national policy as it related to educational revenue, teacher
education, curricula, textbooks, instruction, and evaluation. A national
curriculum was implemented and administered by the National Curricular
Standards (hereafter, the Curricular Standards), which regulated the goals of
schooling and curricula, prescribed the subjects that should be taught and
their specific content, and determined acceptable teaching and evaluation
methods. Starting in 1968, all schools in Taiwan began to use the national
standardized textbooks, which were written, published, and distributed by
the National Institute for Compilation and Translation (NICT), a branch
of the Ministry of Education.[4]

Mounting external threats in the 1970s (including diplomatic setbacks
and a global economic downturn) prompted opposition forces to question
the legitimacy of the KMT's rule. In turn, the KMT modified itself by instituting a Taiwanization policy,[5] economic upgrading, and cultural reconstruction, all while maintaining Chinese nationalism in its curricula. The
emergence of "democratization" discourse and practice characterized the
transformation of the KMT state in the 1980s. A simultaneous opening of
institutional access and opportunity enabled previously repressed voices to
stake their cultural claim in the contested political arena. The proliferation of
political and social opposition movements challenged not only the KMT's
authoritarian regime, but also its corporatist structure, thereby redrawing
social-political boundaries and politicizing the civil society. As a result, the
KMT attempted to transform itself by proposing liberalization projects,
which included lifting martial law in 1987, removing bans on news media in
1988, and legalizing the founding of new political parties in 1989.

The redefinition of culture and identity by political and social opposition
movements helped to legitimize emerging educational reform movements in
the late 1980s. Counter-hegemonic discourse further altered the ways power
relations in schools were perceived. Along with raising textbook contro-
versies, in this climate of liberalization national curricula and the national
standardized textbook policy were also called into question. The Ministry
of Education soon initiated textbook liberalization, which could be called the
first wave of textbook deregulation. From 1989 to 1991, the national standardized textbook policy was gradually replaced with a dual system consisting
of state-authored textbooks and privately produced textbooks approved
by an authorization system. The NICT would continue to control the writing
of core subjects in elementary schools (Mandarin, math, social studies, the
natural sciences, life and ethics, and health education), as well as testing-
related areas in high schools (Chinese literature, history, geography, citizenship, and the Three Principles of the People[6]). Private publishers were
allowed, after screening and approval by the NICT, to produce textbooks in

certain subject areas, including the arts, physical education, and non required vocational courses. The first wave of textbook deregulation represented the state's attempt to partially decontrol the textbook market without modifying dominant ideologies in curricula.

The KMT reconstructed itself under the leadership of Lee Teng-hui, who succeeded to the presidency in 1988 after the death of President Chiang Ching-kuo. Economically, greater privatization and globalization aimed to accommodate capitalist interest in the accumulation of capital. Politically, the nativization of state power sought to incorporate local factions and conciliate political and social opposition movements.[7] Of equal significance was the undertaking of "nation building from above," in which elements of both Chinese and Taiwanese identity were incorporated into an ideological invention of "ROC on Taiwan." At the core of Lee Teng-hui's Taiwanese nationalism was a community of life of the "New Taiwanese" with an independent sovereign state called "ROC on Taiwan" (Wu, 2002).

THE SECOND WAVE OF TEXTBOOK DEREGULATION

Deregulating Elementary School Textbooks, Late 1980s–1994

The year of 1989 saw the advance of the opposition discourse over localized curricular making. Driven by a politics of autonomy, the opposition aimed at fostering opportunities for teachers and parents to select teaching materials autonomously. The state's direct control over the revision of the Curricular Standards excluded educational reform groups from the decision-making process, triggering a request for popular participation in the making and selection of curricula. From February to September, educational reform groups held a series of conferences called the National Education Conferences by Civic Organizations, which concerned curricular decentralization, textbook liberalization, and school autonomy (National Education Conferences by Civic Organizations, 1989). The teacher-parent alliance requested, in particular, that teaching materials be written by teachers and professionals and chosen by individual schools.

Along with the process of redistributing the hierarchical and horizontal powers in the state apparatus, the conflict between the Sinicization of education and the indigenization of curricula represented the struggle for symbolic power, where the construction and reconstruction of native identity was at stake. First, the opposition demanded that native languages be recognized as languages of instruction.[8] Ethnic minorities demonstrated on the streets, appealing for equal access to the use of mass media, as well as for a bilingual education. Bilingualism arose at the local level when the opposition Democratic Progressive Party (DPP) won six seats out of a possible twenty-one in the 1989 mayoral elections. More and more local governments invested in the development of the *xiangtu*, or the nativist curriculum supplementary (additive) to the existing curriculum, so as to encourage students to identify with their hometowns, native cultures, and languages (Legislative Yuan, 14 April 1993).

Second, the dispute over the indigenization of education intensified in the reconstructed Congress, which provided the conditions for modifying the Curricular Standards (which were still based on the old KMT's version of Chinese nationalism). In particular, the DPP's ability to secure 50 of the 160 seats in the 1992 elected legislature made it a determinant minority; as such, it enjoyed veto power and could influence the legalization of national policymaking, profoundly transforming the power relations between the executive and legislative bodies. Considering language to be the medium of cultural production and circulation, in 1993, DPP legislators proposed an amendment called the Mother Tongue Article, which delegated children's native language education and the publication of teaching materials to the Ministry of Education (Legislative Yuan, March 17, 1993). The legalization of native language education called into question the taken-for-granted ranking of language education in schools. These legislators further demanded a multilingual education.

Along with the intensification of oppositional nativization discourse and the formation of "ROC on Taiwan" ideology were efforts by the Taiwanese KMT—a nativized KMT under Lee Teng-hui's leadership—to modify its pedagogic discourse as represented in the slogan "Rooted in Taiwan, Mindful of the Mainland, Looking out to the World." Based on this principle, the Ministry of Education decided to revise the Curricular Standards so as to invent the first-ever mandatory indigenization of curricula (Ministry of Education [MOE], 31 July 1993). The new curricula included three separate subjects: Xiangtu Instructional Activity for the third grade to the sixth grade, and Xiangtu Art Activity and Getting to Know Taiwan for the seventh grade. The implementation of Xiangtu Instructional Activity, according to the ministry, was based on the guideline of "from near to far" (township-county/city), which aimed to "provide students the opportunity of learning dialects, and enhance their understanding of *xiangtu* culture" (Legislative Yuan, 31 December 1994; MOE, 28 February 1995). City and county governments, schools, and teachers would be in charge of the composition of decentralized teaching material. Furthermore, teaching of the subject Getting to Know Taiwan involved a three-part junior high school textbook series that dealt with Taiwan's historical, social, and geographical studies, "to get students to better know and love the place where they are living, and to develop an awareness and confidence that all people in Taiwan have a shared identity, regardless of what ethnic group they belong to or where they come from" (MOE, 31 August 1993, 28 February 1995).

The revised Curricular Standards and textbooks became effective in 1996. It suffices to say that the official xiangtu curricula could practice depoliticized ethnic politics, applying them to learning psychology and teaching methods (for example, the notion of "from near to far") without confronting "dangerous" issues such as the complexity of interrelationships between political dominance, cultural oppression, language inequality, and ethnic assimilation (Mao, 1997). On the other hand, the invention of Getting to Know Taiwan could serve as a politicization of the identity formation of students for the construction of a "new Taiwanese consciousness."

The implementation of the indigenized curricula articulated counter-hegemonic discourses, but it did not jeopardize the Ministry of Education's control over textbook production. After the first wave of textbook deregulation, the mandatory nature of textbooks guaranteed a national market of twenty-four million books. Since textbooks provided a mass market, steady turnover, and stable profit, private publishers aligned themselves with legislators to pressure the Ministry of Education to decontrol the text market. During a public hearing in October 1993, debates over the termination of national standardized textbooks may have crystallized a variety of discourses espoused by private publishers, legislators, and government officials. In that public hearing, legislators of the New Party (NP)[9] noted the trend towards the globalization and privatization of state-owned enterprises to justify a less-regulated text market. Moreover, representatives of newly emerged private publishers targeted the inertia of the government, which had monopolized the textbook industry for decades and thus had no incentive to improve the quality of textbooks. Private publishers asserted that they were more capable of "updating textbooks to satisfy students' needs." They also argued that diversified textbooks—a result of textbook deregulation—would significantly improve the quality of all textbooks (Zhou Quan's Congressional Office, 1993a, 1993b).

The Ministry of Education, which gradually manufactured the rhetoric of "liberalizing textbooks increases students' burden," identified the national entrance exams as the major obstacle to a free text market. Ministry officials explained that, given the competition of the national entrance exams, students would have to master all editions of authorized textbooks in order to succeed. Inevitably, it would increase the pressure on students preparing for the exams. Further, under these circumstances, economically disadvantaged students would be less able to purchase different editions of textbooks or attend private tutoring classes; this would result in reduced access to advanced levels of education. However, government officials agreed that the ministry needed to consider a timetable for thorough textbook deregulation (Jiao ke shuquan, 1993). Given the close linkage between the school system, educational qualifications, and the labor market, the stress to "reform the entrance exam first, liberalize textbooks later" may have captured support for the Ministry of Education from social groups that tended to benefit from an elitist educational evaluation system.

The need for decentralized educational policymaking and nativized curricula may have contributed to the forging of strategic alliances between educational reform groups and opposition forces within the legislature. They collectively endeavored to amend the Compulsory Education Law, which gave the Ministry of Education the power to produce and authorize use of textbooks. Democratic Progressive Party legislators proposed two amendments: One, in December 1993, took a pro-evaluation stand, and the other, in April 1994, took a pro-authorization stand (Legislative Yuan, 25 December 1993, 23 April 1994). Both amendments claimed that only by opening up textbook publication could diverse ethnic groups preserve their native cultures, schools enhance the autonomy to develop curricula, and teachers and parents become empowered to select textbooks. However, DPP legislators and educational reform activists also saw that the need to open up textbook production as a means of nativization/decentralization could conflict with popular beliefs in "upward mobility through education" and the fears of educational failure. Yet as concern mounted over the constraints that national entrance exams imposed on modes of textbook production, the textbook authorization proposal gradually acquired favor and efficacy in terms of mobilizing support from groups of people (for a more comprehensive discussion of the historical and contemporary examination system in Taiwan, see Chen, 2003, pp. 175–176, 247, 267).

The opposition's demands to nativize curricula, decentralize decision making, and marketize textbook production posed severe threats to the legitimacy of the state's dominance over education. Facing massive pressure from opposition movements and educational reform groups, the ministry decided to make selective accommodations to the opposition's demands for nativization, decentralization, and marketization, so as not to lose its overall hegemonic control. Minister Guo Wei-fan initially managed to weave an official textbook reform discourse into the Seventh National Education Conference in order to muster favorable public opinion (Legislative Yuan, 2 April 1994). However, the ministry's tactics failed when legislators allied across party lines to target the illegitimacy of nationally standardized textbooks. In April 1994, legislators of the Chinese new party, a pro-unification party, the DPP, and surprisingly even the KMT, all of whom were serving in the Education and Culture Committee of the Legislative Yuan (ECCLY), passed a resolution to reform textbooks. This resolution required that the Ministry of Education thoroughly open up textbook publication within two years, and appointed the ministry to be in charge of formulating textbook screening criteria. The ECCLY passed the same resolution again in June after the KMT-controlled Congress voted down the ECCLY's initial resolution (Legislative Yuan, 25 June 1994).

The ministry eventually compromised and included the opposition's demands for textbook reform in its deregulation project. This official textbook reform was intended to create a partial opening up of the textbook market while still maintaining the principle of "Rooted in Taiwan, Mindful of the Mainland, Looking out to the World" in curricular development. The ministry announced the deregulation of elementary school textbooks in June 1994, and finalized this policy in 1995. The policy indicated that national standardized textbooks in core subjects (Mandarin, math, social studies, the natural sciences, and moral and health education) at elementary school levels would no longer be used. After 1996, a national textbook authorization system would be in charge of screening and approving textbooks. Considering the intensified controversy over the NICT's role in textbook censorship, Minister Guo delegated the task of screening both public sector and private sector textbooks to the Taiwan Provincial Institute for Elementary School Teacher In-Service Education (TPIE). Following a rigid screening procedure formulated by the Ministry of Education, the TPIE would recommend several textbooks in each subject area for approval by the ministry. Finally, individual schools would have to set up textbook committees, comprised of administrators and subject-area teachers, to choose approved textbooks. However, the principal of each school would exercise the authority of final approval (MOE, 31 July 1994).

Deregulating Senior High School Textbooks, 1994–1997

Compared to the discourse of xiangtu instruction, the notion of nativization education was more counter-hegemonic and oppositional, undergoing a subtle transition in line with the prevalent nationalist politics of the 1990s. Several features characterized the nationalist nativization discourse that was taking place within the educational domain. First, elements of indigenization tended to be articulated from the perspective of Taiwan-centered education rather than from that of hometown-based curricula. Opposition legislators targeted the extreme underrepresentation of Taiwanese history, geography, and literature in national curricula. A thorough indigenization of education, DPP legislators argued, would reconstruct the China-centered educational system into a Taiwan-centered one. Second, the road that was paved for the indigenization of education was not intended to produce xiangtu teaching materials supplementary to the existing materials. Nativizing education involved a fundamental reform of educational guidelines and policies, educational institutions, teacher education, curriculum development agents, and national curricula. Lastly and ultimately, the indigenization of education was intended to familiarize children with Taiwan to enculturate a sense of a "Taiwanese community of fate" (Legislative Yuan, 28 April 1993).

From 1994 to 1995, the expressions "Getting to Know Taiwan" and "indigenization curricula" sparked debates over the remaining Chinese nationalist ideology in textbooks. Democratic Progressive Party legislators and independent legislators argued that the title "Getting to Know Taiwan" explicitly marginalized Taiwan studies as a local curriculum instead of as a fundamental principle in organizing school knowledge. Particularly, Taiwan's history, culture, and languages were still treated as mirror images of China in the rest of the national curricula. Conservative pro-unification forces still occupied the official agencies in charge of creating curricular guidelines. Two such agencies were the Directing Commission on Humanities and Social Sciences Education (hereafter, Directing Commission) and the Curricular Standards Revision Committees (CSRCs). Aiming to establish Taiwanese subjectivity in education, the DPP and independent legislators proposed abandoning the Directing Commission and CSRCs, revising the Curricular Standards and national curricula, and abolishing national standardized textbooks. Specifically, the curricula would comprise up to 60 percent of Taiwan's history, literature, and geography (Legislative Yuan, 18 January 1994, 25 January 1994, 26 October 1994, 25 December 1994, 28 December 1994 & 31 December 1994).

This pro-independence force in education—consisting primarily of legislators, scholars, teachers, and cultural workers—soon consolidated and attempted to transform Chinese cultural hegemony into Taiwan-centered curricula. In 1995, pro-independence forces established the Textbook Reform Coalition (TRC) right after the ECCLY passed a resolution that required the Ministry of Education to open up high school textbooks from 1996 on. The TRC identified curricula in Taiwan as "anti-Taiwan" and "antireality," alienating students from the motherland where they had grown up. The TRC thus proclaimed, "the real goals of the textbook reform movement are the reconstruction of Taiwan's spirit and the re-creation of Taiwan's culture" (Jiao ke shugai, 1995). Broadcasting its ideas in public hearings, press conferences, and newspapers, the TRC called for:

- the abolition of the Directing Commission, the NICT, and the Curricular Standards in order to localize curricula
- the development of textbooks to establish Taiwan-centered education
- and the implementation of multilingual education for diverse ethnic groups (Legislative Yuan, 22 March 1995; Da dao, 1996)

In April 1996, an intensified sentiment for Taiwanese independence prompted the TRC to reorganize itself into the Taiwanization Education Coalition (TEC) (Jiao yu, 1996). The TEC targeted the Curricular Standards in order to speed up the decentralization of curriculum development.

The semi-official Commission on Educational Reform (CER) under the Executive Yuan represented another emerging force in the struggle over curricula reform. This two-year-term commission, established in September 1994, could be viewed as an institutional mechanism for dealing with educational reform demands from below. Comprised mainly of liberal economists, law scholars, and educational reform advocates, the CER identified the idea of education deregulation—the discontinuation of inappropriate intervention by the state in education—as the major goal of educational reform (Legislative Yuan, 23 October 1996). The CER further set the agenda of educational liberalization and decentralization, which, to a large degree, challenged conservative/reactionary forces within the Ministry of Education and other state apparatuses. One site of conflict was curricula reform and textbook deregulation. In 1996, the CER recommended the dismissal of the NICT, the replacement of the Curricular Standards with minimum guidelines, the complete deregulation of textbook production, the establishment of a U.S.-style textbook council to screen textbooks at the city and county levels, the selection of textbooks by individual schools, and the integration of subject-centered curricula (Commission on Educational Reform of the Executive Yuan, 1996). Viewed by the opposition forces as the "super–Ministry of Education," the CER found itself in conflict with the ministry, which preferred to maintain continued control over high school textbook production. The more popular the CER became, the more the ministry-led educational reform lost legitimacy.

As the primary target of opposition attacks, the ministry responded by affirming the constraints of the national entrance exam and the need for government-controlled decentralization (Legislative Yuan, 26 October 1994). Minister Guo reiterated that only a complete transformation of the national entrance exam could open up high school textbook publication. The ministry implemented the Diverse High School Entrance Program in 1995, which offered diverse channels for applying to senior high schools, expanded six-year integrated high schools and comprehensive high schools (MOE, June 30, 1995, July 7, 1995). The ministry's strategy involved loosening or modifying its control over evaluation mechanisms, represented by the national entrance exam, in exchange for continued intervention in textbook production.

Taiwan's first presidential election and the competition between the two main parties for the electorate's votes made it vitally important for the presidential candidates to invoke the support of a majority indigenous population by deliberately constructing Taiwanese identity. The emergence of the notion of "Taiwan First" represented a political tendency towards a convergence of hegemonic and counter-hegemonic ideologies at a time when both the KMT and the DPP, in competing for the votes of the electorate, focused on China's military threat more than ever (Shu, 1997/1998).[10]

Lee Teng-hui won a landslide victory in the presidential election of March 1996. Enjoying the symbolic legitimacy of being "the first native president," he eagerly sought to enjoy the hegemony of state power over Taiwanese society—not only politically, but ideologically as well. One of the state's hegemonic projects was to reform education, the administration, and the justice system. The goal of educational reform, Lee Teng-hui claimed, was to emphasize nativization and community education, as well as to build up a "community of life." The former referred to shifting the center of education from a "Great China" perspective to a Taiwan-centered orientation. The latter sought to firmly established a Taiwan-based community of life regardless of ethnicity and partisanship (Li zong tong, 1996). By appealing to a seemingly more inclusive notion of the "New Taiwanese," which sought to bind "four major ethnic groups" together, the official educational reform discourse articulated the opposition's need to create the subjectivity of Taiwan through education, and may have contributed to legitimizing Lee Teng-hui's power bloc.

Official educational reform discourse affected the principle of textbook production, curricular development, and educational policymaking at different speeds. That is, initially the official textbook reform furthered textbook marketization, but not the latter two aspects. When Wu Jing was appointed as the new minister of education, the ministry discussed two reform proposals: (1) revision of the 1995 version of the National Curricular Standards for Senior High Schools; and (2) decontrol of high school textbook production (D.-X. Su, personal communication, 5 July 2000). For the ministry, deregulating high school textbooks and maintaining the Curricular Standards better served its interests in controlling the production of official knowledge. The expected withdrawal of the NICT from the writing of humanities subjects also contributed to a dismissal of the opposition's critique of the NICT's role in the reproduction of the KMT's ideologies. In September 1996, the ministry announced the opening up of high school textbook production for 1998 (MOE, 14 September 1996, 24 September 1996). However, it was not until the Diverse College Entrance Program was in place that the conditions were right for deregulating high school textbooks. The ministry had been formulating the Diverse College Entrance Program, which included school recommendations and a two-stage entrance exam, so as to expand the opportunities for senior high school graduates to attend universities (Legislative Yuan, 29 March 1997). The ministry eventually finalized the deregulation policy for senior high textbooks in March 1997. After screening by the NICT, private publishers were allowed to produce senior high school textbooks in subjects including Chinese literature, citizenship, history, geography, the Three Principles of the People, and military education. This policy was slated to start in 1999, the first year in which the 1995 version of the National Curricular Standards for Senior High Schools was implemented (Gao zhong, 1997).

Deregulating Junior High School Textbooks, 1997–2001

Starting in 1996, demands for curricular deregulation became one of the determinants for deregulating junior high school textbooks. Textbook reform advocates claimed that textbook content remained highly regulated by the Curricular Standards despite the opening up of the textbook market. First, decentralization forces called for the replacement of the Curricular Standards with curricular guidelines for diversified textbooks and "life- and experience-centered" curricula. Second, nativization/Taiwanization forces sought to alter the national curricula so as to expand Taiwan's representation in textbooks, and to organize Taiwan-centered curricula. Last, but no less important, marketization forces requested a loosening of state control over curriculum production in order to create a "free" textbook market (Legislative Yuan, 18 December 1996). Opposition to state intervention intensified with the idea of curricular deregulation—a notion that incorporated various demands from the opposition for curricula reform, so as to challenge the legitimacy of the Curricular Standards and national curricula.

Along with intensified demands for curricular deregulation came the dismissal of the CER in December 1996 and the establishment of the Educational Reform Committee of the Executive Yuan in February 1997. Opposition forces within the CER were recruited into the Educational Reform Committee, and the CER's general report was incorporated into the official educational reform agenda. This, in effect, revealed an ongoing tendency towards a convergence of oppositional and official educational reform (Jiao gai, 1996; MOE, 30 April 1997). To contest the popular demands for curricular deregulation, and to shape the hegemonic interpretation of textbook reform to its own ends, the Ministry of Education appointed a curricular development committee in April 1997 to formulate the National Curricular Guidelines (hereafter, the Curricular Guidelines) and the "New 1-9 Curriculum" (Legislative Yuan, 17 October 1998). This curricular development committee, which included education officials, industrialists, legislators, scholars, former members of the CER, educational reform activists, principals, teachers, and parents, represented a deregulation-oriented alliance aimed at replacing the Curricular Standards with the Curricular Guidelines (MOE, 31 May 1997). Moreover, the stress of the New 1-9 Curriculum on school-based curricular development made the national standardized textbooks problematic, leading to the opening up of junior high school textbook production.

However, the demand for a Taiwan-centered education may not have been satisfied because the Curricular Guidelines only referred to individuals' capacities and ten basic competencies for compulsory education. The official discourse regarding the measure of basic competency positioned students as unique individuals without mentioning their ethnicity, gender, and class background, thereby lessening the transformative potential of education for constructing collective identities for subordinated groups. Furthermore, the integrated New 1-9 Curriculum required teachers to transform both their subject-centered instruction into a student-centered one and their role as textbook transmitters into one of curricular developers. These transformations shifted the boundaries around school knowledge and profoundly impacted institutions in charge of teacher education. Three major teachers' universities strongly argued against the integration and "simplification" of curricula and asked for a reformulation of the Curricular Guidelines (MOE, 31 May 1999). Finally, given their large class sizes and overwhelming teaching loads, teachers resisted the implementation of the New 1-9 Curriculum, challenging the legitimacy of top-down curricular decision making.

The momentum of amending the Compulsory Education Law gained steam within educational reform groups when textbook reform became part of the official agenda. Teachers' and parents' organizations, in particular, advocated for participation in the national curricular committee, textbook development committee, and school councils so as to develop and select textbooks. However, the ministry suggested choosing teachers' representatives by recommendation because "whether or not teachers' organizations could reflect opinions in the school was questionable" (Legislative Yuan, 2 October 1996). The request for parental participation in these committees was disregarded during the bargaining process due to the lack of strong alliances among teachers' groups, parents' groups, and opposition legislators, and the ministry, privileged by the majority rule of parliamentarianism, maintained control over formulation of the Curricular Guidelines in the amended Compulsory Education Law (Legislative Yuan, 20 January 1999).

Although the ministry intended to deregulate junior high school textbooks as soon as the New 1-9 Curriculum was implemented, the uncertainty of this policy dissatisfied legislators, who adopted the strategy of cutting or freezing the government budget in order to effect the complete opening up of textbook production. When scrutinizing the government budget, members of the Coalition for Educational and Cultural Reform—an alliance of eleven legislators from different parties—repeatedly urged that junior high school textbooks be deregulated in 1999 and that the NICT withdraw from textbook writing. In order to get its budget approved, the ministry was forced to compromise by declaring the Curricular Guidelines in 1998, deregulating junior high school textbooks in 1999, and withdrawing from textbook writing in 2001 (Legislative Yuan, 30 April 1997, 17 October 1998 & 22 May 1999). The opening up of junior high school textbook production put a conclusive end to the national standardized textbook policy, which itself dated back thirty-odd years.

CONCLUSION

Curricular policy in postwar Taiwan involved an ongoing process of nation-alizing Chinese culture. As Taiwan underwent a transition to a liberal-democratic, native-dominated nation-state, the demand for textbook deregulation crystallized the struggle over discourse surrounding nativization, decentralization, and marketization, all of which shaped the contours of market-driven textbook production under the state's authorization. While the first wave of textbook deregulation was initiated by the Ministry of Education, the second wave of textbook deregulation involved struggles over nativizing curricula, decentralizing educational decision making, and commodifying textbook production. To maintain hegemonic control, the state was forced to compromise by adopting the strategy of steering the production of official knowledge from a distance.

The centralized, China-centered education system created common interests among opposition forces to transform the very nature of both school knowledge and textbook production. For nativization forces (mainly represented by the DPP and pro-independence organizations), textbooks were vitally important in forming a Taiwanese identity, and were essential for overthrowing the ROC symbolic system. Furthermore, decentraliza-tion forces (mainly represented by educational reform groups) preferred to restrict the role of the state in curricular decision making. It was the decen-tralization of curricular decision making that provided parents and teach-ers with the space in which to engage in textbook development and selection. Lastly, for marketization forces (mainly represented by private publishers), it was a "free market" that would allow them to compete with each other for the profit of commodified textbooks. Given their height-ened political liberties, opposition forces acquired institutional access to curricular policymaking. They collaborated strategically and advocated textbook deregulation by articulating different interpretations of the "opening up of textbook publication," along with a chain of associated demands such as nativization education, Taiwanization, school autonomy, diversification, curricular deregulation, and textbook liberalization.

Considering the external threat of the Chinese Communist Party and the internal dissent of mainlanders, the Taiwanese KMT adopted a pragmatic strategy of nativizing state power and manufacturing the discourse of "ROC on Taiwan" to consolidate its power. Through this strategy, the KMT trans-formed the nature of its selective tradition that had shaped the form and con-tent of its textbooks. A dominant Taiwan-first discourse and the emergent notion of "Rooted in Taiwan, Mindful of the Mainland, Looking out to the World" gradually replaced the orthodox framework of Chinese nationalism. The two new principles operated as a hierarchical filter for recontextualizing school knowledge. The orientation towards nativization in official curricula reform defused the radicalism of Taiwan-centered education by introducing xiangtu subjects as additive curricular enclaves. Moreover, the request for school autonomy proposed by educational reform groups was incorporated into the official creation of textbook committees and school councils, where parents and teachers were positioned as competent individuals rather than as collective agents in terms of participating in textbook selection and curriculum making. Last and equally important, the demand for opening up textbook publication was articulated via a free-market ethic. Only the state and private publishers had the capacity to produce textbooks, excluding subordinate groups from collective textbook development.

The present study suggests that, while the discourse of deregulation often identifies itself with democracy, this discourse can, and indeed does, come to satisfy part of the state's need for the legitimization and maintenance of hegemonic power. This study marks something of a new departure for research on theoretically informed education policy analyses, not only in its application of the Gramscian approach to education systems in Third World countries, but also in its attempt to incorporate the perspectives of opposition movements into the analyses of state formation and pedagogic principles. As discussed in this chapter, the effects of textbook deregulation have been contradictory. To a certain degree, the New 1-9 Curriculum offers room for school-based curriculum development. At the same time, however, tendencies arise for a privatization of textbook production that diminishes the common-good purpose of educational knowledge. It is important to think about what Connell (2001/2002) has identified as a strong model of public education, a model that both delegitimates the marketization of schooling and reinvents the public-good nature of education. In this regard, any critique of the market agenda in education must incorporate a reconsideration of the proper role of the state, if that state as deregulator or decentralizer is inadequate, which is to say, ineffective. Of equal significance to the successful existence of a democratic curriculum at the classroom level is the role of secondary associations (teachers' councils, parents organizations, neighborhood associations, and grassroots groups) in the realm of democratic governance.

NOTES

An earlier version of this material appeared in Chen, J.-J. (2002). Reforming textbooks, reshaping school knowledge: Taiwan's textbook deregulation in the 1990s. *Pedagogy, Culture and Society*, 10(1): 39–72. The earlier version has been substantially revised. I am indebted to Michael Apple for his comments and Peter Seelig for his editorial assistance.

1. In this chapter, "textbooks" refers to the whole set of state-mandated materials, including textbooks, teachers' manuals, and students' workbooks at elementary and high school levels.

2. This chapter adopts the pinyin system to transliterate Chinese characters and names (with family names preceding given names) into the Roman alphabet. However, if a name has a publicly known romanized form, the original form will be used to avoid confusion (e.g., Lee Teng-hui, Chiang Ching-kuo).

3. The retreat of the KMT to Taiwan and the large number of Chinese immigrants who fled to the island changed Taiwan's demographic composition. In the following decades, it became a place of constant constructions and interpretations of ethnic-related self-identification. Up to the 1990s, Taiwan's population was conventionally classed into four ethnic groups according to origin, time of arrival in Taiwan, and language. The non-Han residents—the aborigines (*yuanzhumin*)—are of Malay-Polynesian origin and comprise slightly more than 1 percent of the population. The Han Chinese can be divided into "Taiwanese" (*bensheng ren*), who moved to Taiwan in line with the waves of Chinese migration over three hundred years, and "mainlanders" (*waisheng ren*), who were born on the mainland and fled to Taiwan with the KMT government around 1949. Because of their languages, Taiwanese are usually referred to as "Hoklo" and "Hakka," which together comprise about slightly less than 85 percent of the population. See Shu, 1997/1998, pp. 84–185.

4. For empirical research on the origins, dynamics, and consequences of struggles over textbook production in postwar Taiwan, see Chen, 2003.

5. The Taiwanization policy was intended to enhance the role of Taiwanese in policy making by selectively coopting them into the upper echelons of the power hierarchy in the party and government.

6. The Three Principles of the People, canonized as the founding principles of the ROC, address the issues of nationalism, democracy, and people's livelihood.

7. "Nativization" in the 1990s involved a fundamental shift in the distribution of political power from mainlander elitists to the Taiwanese situated within the state.

8. Linguistic activists used the term *native language* to refer to Hoklo, Hakka, and aboriginal languages.

9. Splitting from the KMT, some pro-reunification mainlander politicians established the New Party in August 1993.

10. The main difference between how the KMT and the DPP interpreted "Taiwan First" discourse had to do with their expectations about Taiwan's relations with China: rhetorical reunification for the KMT and possible independence for the DPP.

REFERENCES

Primary Sources

Commission on Educational Reform of the Executive Yuan. (1996). *Jiao yu gai ge zong zi yi bao gao shu* [General report on educational reform]. Taipei: Author.

Legislative Yuan. (1986–2000). *Li fa yuan gong bao* [Communiqué of the Legislative Yuan]. Taipei: Author.

Ministry of Education (MOE). (1986–2000). *Jiao yu bu gong bao* [Communiqué of the Ministry of Education]. Taipei: Author.

National Education Conferences by Civic Organizations. (1989). *Di er jie quan guo min jian tuan ti jiao yu hui yi ji lu* [Minutes of the first meeting, the second meeting, and the third meeting]. Taipei: Author.

Zhou Quan's Congressional Office. (1993a). *Biao zhun ben jiao ke shu he shi liao* [When will the national standardized textbook be abolished? Public hearing minutes]. Taipei: Author.

Zhou Quan's Congressional Office. (1993b). *Guo min zhong xiao xue jiao ke shu ying quan mian kai fang wei shen ding ben shuo tie* [Textbooks for compulsory education should all be authorized by the government]. Taipei: Author.

Daily Newspaper Articles with No Author

Da dao kuo fu gai zao jiao ke shu [Reforming textbooks from the ground up]. (1996, January 7–10). *Min zhong ri bao.*

Gao zhong jiao ke shi ba shi ba xue nian quan mian kai fang [Senior high school textbooks to be deregulated in the 1999 school year]. (1997, March 12). *Lian he bao.*

Jiao gai xiao zu kua bu hui cheng li, kuan lie liang bai qi shi ba yi yi zhu [Inter-ministry educational reform committee established, 278,000,000 NT dollars allocated]. (1996, December 3). *Zhong yang ri bao,* p. 1.

Jiao ke shu gai zao lian meng xuan yan [A statement by the Textbook Reform Coalition]. (1995, January 28). *Min zhong ri bao.*

Jiao ke shu quan mian min ying hua, guan xue shang she zhan [Contention among governmental officials, scholars, and publishers over the thorough privatization of textbooks]. (1993, October 31). *Lian he bao.*

Jiao yu ben tu hua lian meng ti chu shi wu xiang zhu zhang [The Nativization Education Coalition announces fifteen demands]. (1996, April 30). *Min zhong ri bao,* p. 1.

Li zong tong: jiao gai xu zhong shi xiang tu she qu jiao yu [President Lee: Educational reform should emphasize *xiangtu* and community education]. (1996, May 27). *Lian he bao,* p. 1.

Secondary Sources

Apple, M. W. (1989). Regulating the textbook: The socio-historical roots of state control. *Educational Policy, 3* (2), 107–123.

Apple, M. W. (1993). *Official knowledge.* New York: Routledge.

Apple, M. W. (1995). *Education and power* (2nd ed.). New York: Routledge.

Chen, J.-J. (2003). *State formation, pedagogic reform and textbook (de)regulation in Taiwan, 1945–2000.* Unpublished doctoral dissertation, University of Wisconsin, Madison.

Connell, B. (2001/2002). Renovating the "public": The future of public education. *Education Links, 63,* 7–12.

Gramsci, A. (1971). *Selections from the prison notebooks* (Q. Hoare & G. N. Smith, Trans.). New York: International Publishers. (Original work published 1948–51)

Hall, S. (1996). Gramsci's relevance for the study of race and ethnicity. In D. Morley & K. H. Chen (Eds.), *Critical dialogues in cultural studies* (pp. 411–440). New York: Routledge.

Huang, Z.-C. (1997). *Guo min xiao xue jiao ke shu xuan yong fang an zhi yan jiu* [A study of the selection of elementary textbooks]. Unpublished master's thesis, National Hua-Lian Teachers College, Hua-Lian, Taiwan.

Jessop, B. (1990). *State theory*. Pennsylvania: Pennsylvania State University.

Ke, Z.-Z. (1998). Guoyu jiao ke shu di san ce bu tong ban ben zhi bi jiao fen xi [A comparison of different editions of volume three of the Mandarin language textbooks]. *Jiao shi zhi you, 39* (5), 48–58.

Mao, C.-J. (1997). *Constructing Taiwanese identity: The making and practice of indigenization curriculum*. Unpublished doctoral dissertation, University of Wisconsin, Madison.

Mouffe, C. (1979). Hegemony and ideology in Gramsci. In C. Mouffe (Ed.), *Gramsci and Marxist theory* (pp. 168–204). London: Routledge & Kegan Paul.

Ou, Y.-S. (1989). *Zhi de yan jiu* [Qualitative research]. Taipei: Shi da shu yuan.

Shu, W.-D. (1997/1998). The emergence of Taiwanese nationalism: A preliminary work on an approach to interactive episode discourse. *Berkeley Journal of Sociology, 42,* 73–121.

Wu, R.-R. (2002). Toward a pragmatic nationalism: Democratization and Taiwan's passive revolution. In S. Corcuff (Ed.), *Memories of the future* (pp. 196–218). New York: M. E. Sharpe.

Xie, Q.-D. (1988). *Wo guo er tong zheng zhi she hui hua zhi yan jiu: you guan guo xie jiao ke shu de nei rong fen xi* [Research on the political socialization of children in Taiwan: A content analysis of elementary textbooks]. Unpublished master's thesis, Wen-Hua University, Taipei, Taiwan.

Zhang, Q.-L. (1996). Zhong xiao xue jiao ke shu kai fang hou min jian shu ju bian ji chu banqing xing zhi tong ji fen xi [An analysis of post-deregulation textbook publishing by private firms]. *Ren wen ji she hui xue hui ke jiao xue tong xun, 6* (3), pp. 50–58.

Chapter 5

Thai English Language Textbooks, 1960–2000

Postwar Industrial and Global Changes

Noparat Suaysuwan and Cushla Kapitzke

INTRODUCTION

As in many modern educational systems, in Thai schools, the main print-based pedagogical technology is the textbook. Inadequate teacher education preparation and the pressures of large classes predispose Thai teachers to depend heavily on textbooks as both instructional resources and student learning materials. This is especially the case for English language curriculum in Thai primary schools. Textbooks, in the form of primers and basal readers, play an important role in teaching and learning by providing written language text, graded language content, and leveled class activities. While curriculum development comprises the most challenging and time-consuming work for Thai teachers—many of whom lack appropriate training—English language textbooks are used as sources of ideas for lesson planning, instructional strategies, and assessment tasks.

Yet, as curricular commodities, textbooks transmit more than information and content knowledge. They are sites par excellence of ideological and cultural hegemony in the lives of small children who have little input in the selection of curricular materials (Apple & Christian-Smith, 1991; Luke, Carrington, & Kapitzke, 2003). From this perspective, students not only learn subject matter from textbooks, but they also acquire values, interests, and knowledge that form desires, habits, and identities. Practitioners and parents alike impute the status of educational and social authority to the content of textbooks, and so the child reader, too, views information in textbooks as neutral, natural, and "the way things are and should be" (Luke, 1994, p. 16).

This chapter interrogates such an assumption by examining the representation, production, and uptake of knowledge in English language textbooks of Thai primary schools. We examine the knowledge that is presented as "official" and to be learned by students, and argue that much more than English as a foreign language—by way of vocabulary, sentence structure, and conversation—is learned, or not learned, by Thai school children. While it is true that English is the current international lingua franca, here we will look beyond language learning to investigate the Western ideas and attitudes that are inscribed in textbooks and reflected in students' lives. This entails the application of critical discourse analysis to unmask the ideologies and politics of simple, and seemingly innocuous, narratives in three textbooks used by Thai children to learn the English language.

RESEARCH ON SCHOOL TEXTBOOKS IN ASIAN CONTEXTS

A few studies have been conducted by North American, European, and Australian scholars on school textbooks used in Asian contexts. For example, Altbach and his colleagues (Altbach, 1992; Altbach, Arboleda, & Gopinathan, 1985) investigated the neocolonial pedagogies of textbooks in the Third World. Other Western researchers have examined the commercial issues around book production such as style, layout, cost, and distribution (Farrell & Heyneman, 1988). In more recent work, Bray and Kwok-Chun (1994) explored the not-so-subtle ideological messages within Chinese mathematics textbooks, such as students being asked to calculate the number of Mao's textual works, or the number of years since the formation of the Communist Party.

Gupta and Lee Su Yin conducted a study on two English basal reader programs used in Singaporean primary schools; the programs were published in 1985—one in Britain and the other in Singapore. The study showed how both texts portrayed the sexes unequally (cited in Gupta, 1991). In a similar study, Lee (2000) used critical discourse analysis to analyze dominant ideological influences in Korean language textbooks, and found that during the colonial and neocolonial eras, textbooks were infused with Japanese and American values. National Korean cultures and local histories were either omitted or misrepresented.

Written and spoken texts represent particular selective views of the world (i.e., subject positions), and establish certain social relations between texts and readers (i.e., reading positions) (Kress, 1989). By establishing reading positions, texts interpellate readers by situating and positioning them in identifiable relations of power and agency in relation to the text. The study of subject and reading positions constructed by textbooks focuses on selective traditions of values, voices, ideologies, and representations. Discursive analyses aim to describe social and cultural assumptions of text, and interrogate the work of lexical choice and grammatical representation in framing agency and action.

This study, by using use lexical and grammatical analyses, and semiotic and visual cues to disclose ideological and cultural pedagogies, examines the content of three English language textbooks used in Thai primary schools from 1960 to 2000: *The Oxford English Course for Thailand* (Burrow, 1960a, 1960b), *English Is Fun* (Department of Curriculum and Instruction Development [hereafter, DCID], 1982a, 1982b, 1983a, 1983b), and *On the Springboard* (DCID, 1993, 1996a, 1996b, 1997). These texts are produced and distributed nationally for the purpose of serving Thai educational goals with respect to the nation's English language needs.

The language and illustrations used in each series textually represent social conditions, economic formations, and cultural values in Thailand during the period 1960–2000. Until the 1960s, for example, the Thai economy was largely agricultural, with over 80 percent of the population engaged in activities such as growing and exporting rice (Krongkaew, 1995, p. 33). Capitalist industrialization accelerated during the 1970s when the economy shifted towards the manufacturing, mining, electricity, and construction industries. Thailand joined the global economy—characterized by extra-national interdependence and a transnational flow of information, finance, people, goods, and services—in the 1990s.

THE OXFORD ENGLISH COURSE FOR THAILAND: THAI ENGLISH TEXTBOOKS IN THE POSTWAR PERIOD

A two-textbook series entitled *The Oxford English Course for Thailand* (Burrow, 1960a, 1960b) was written by H. Coulthard Burrow and illustrated by Douglas Hall, both of whom were British language educators. The texts were printed by the Thai-based Kurusapa Press, but their distribution and sale in both Thailand and Laos required authorization from Oxford University Press. Therefore, curricular legitimacy and financial gain resided with this British-based multinational firm. The books were used over a span of two decades until 1982: book one for fifth grade students and book two for sixth grade students.

Although portraying the "everyday life" activities of Thai children aged ten to twelve years old in rural and urban settings, the books were textual artifacts of postwar British colonialism, the aim of which was to spread British culture to developing countries like Thailand by means of English language textbooks. This occurred through language patterns which were typical of formal written text, but not of the spoken language of everyday life. A majority of the three hundred words displayed in the texts comprised concise, declarative, interrogative, and imperative sentences of short narrative. The assumption underlying this rhetorical style was that students learn vocabulary and sentence patterns best by reading and rote learning. In later editions, audio-lingual methods using language in more natural social settings were included.

Agricultural Economy of the Postwar Period

In books one and two of *The Oxford English Course for Thailand*, traditional forms of Thai life are portrayed through depiction of the agrarian economy. In table 5.1, the semantic classification of keywords reflects and reconstitutes this representation of Thai life.

In the text, the words used to construct language learning draw from the lexical categories of plants, animals, and nature. The variety of fruits, vegetables, and flowers implies that the land is fertile, and that villagers are able to consume or sell their natural produce. These kinds of plants are familiar to the child reader since fruits such as mangoes, bananas, and coconuts were planted in home gardens. Their inclusion represents the agricultural economy of the postwar period, and acknowledges the rural life of most Thai people and their dependence on nature. Villagers are portrayed as growing fruits and vegetables, and fishing in canals or rivers. They raise pigs, hens, and ducks, and occasionally share their produce with neighbors. The people are portrayed as horticulturally productive, consuming agricultural products but not engaged in buying or selling them. Hence, in rural areas, capitalist market relations are not dominant within

TABLE 5.1   Categories of plants, animals and nature
presented in *The Oxford English Course* books one and two
(Burrow, 1960a, 1960b)

Plants	Animals	Nature
Trees	Ants	Sun
Mangoes	Elephants	Star
Bananas	Hen	Moon
Oranges	Pig	Season
Coconuts	Dog	Summer
Corn	Cat	Cold
Bamboo	Bird	Winter
Flowers	Monkey	Rain
Grass	Snake	
Rice	Duck	
	Buffalo	
	Horse	

traditional social life. The following description of Porn's father, who is an ideal farmer, illustrates this:

> Porn lives in a small village. His father has a cart, a buffalo, twenty-five hens and forty ducks. Next year he will have four pigs. Porn's father is working in the fields today. He is cutting the rice and putting it in a boat. He will finish tonight and will pull the boat to his house. (Burrow, 1960b, p. 31)

Here, subject-verb-complement sentence structures convey a process of attribution: Porn's father is an agent, and the verb "has"/"have" shows possession. A "cart" is a farmer's necessary tool, and his helper is an animal, a "buffalo." The modal "will" suggests possibility and expectation, thereby portraying the ideal farmer as reliable and productive. The verbs "cut," "put," and "pull" convey material processes, which portray the farmer as physically strong and energetic. The word "finish" implies completion of the task and connotes success and reward from hard work. Readers can infer that farmers must work all day, from early morning until late at night. Note, however, that the farmer owns, or "has," animals and the capacity to work, but is not portrayed as owning the land. The reason for this is that, at the time, most Thai farmers were poor tenants who had to pay landowners half of their produce for using the land.

The Middle Class in the Postwar Period

A second category of character in *The Oxford English Course for Thailand* is that of a middle-class male who works in a city office. The text describes him as follows:

> Their father can not go to the beach because he is working in the city.
> He has a fan on his desk because it is hot in the city.
> He is writing on a piece of paper.
> He will go to Hua-Hin next week.
> The sun will shine but it will not be hot.
> The wind will blow.
> He will teach his boys to swim. (Burrow, 1960b, pp. 44–45)

This narrative presents a different job and a different social context. Because this man is literate, he is privileged to work at a desk and have a fan because it is hot. Note that the topic of unpleasant weather was not mentioned in the previous text about the farmers. The words "writing on a piece of paper" implies that the work is not as hard as "put[ting] the rice and cut[ting] the rice in the field" (Burrow, 1960b, p. 35). The description of the weather at the beach as sunny, but with a cooling breeze, implies an attractive location. Repetition of the word "will" suggests a high level of intention and expectancy. This implies that middle-class people are privileged enough to have holidays, whereas the farmer's land is their place of both work and recreation. The fact that the texts do not depict farmers as having time off reflects the distinctions between social classes, according to levels of education, money, and career in Thailand during the postwar period.

The Ideal Thai Child in the Postwar Period

School textbooks tend to construct the notion of an "ideal" child: one who is "perfect" in every aspect and lives in a stable, happy family. Thai English language textbooks are no different. Traditionally, the Thai child is expected to be obedient, docile, and submissive towards his/her parents, and to show loyalty at an early age. They are expected to behave well, pay respect to their elders, and speak politely.

In *The Oxford English Course for Thailand*, children are portrayed as well behaved and intelligent, but there is no emotional involvement in anything the children say or do. In one of the stories, a boy is illustrated and described as follows:

> In this picture there is a boy sitting on a chair. His name is Chab. He has three pencils in a jar on the table. He is drawing a boat in his book. On the boat there is a man. This man is not sitting in a boat, he is standing on it. Chab has a black cat. His cat is sleeping under the table. There are ten marbles on the floor. Chab has a brown dog. It is not in the picture. (Burrow, 1960a, p. 59)

The verb "has" denotes attribution. The fact that Chab has "three pencils in a jar on the table" suggests he is a responsible student. Moreover, he has a "black cat" and a "brown dog," which implies that, because he has a connection to two pets, he has well-developed emotional sensibilities. The word "draw" implies aesthetic perception and skill, which depicts him as intelligent and creative. This middle-class boy is constructed as a diligent student who is expected to further his education, which reflects Western attitudes towards education. "Ordinary" boys of a playful or mischevous nature are conspicuously absent. Furthermore, Chab is sitting on a chair working at a table with a lamp. In 1960 when the book was first published, most Thai children did not have furniture like tables and chairs in their homes—they usually sat or lay on the floor. Tables and chairs represent

TABLE 5.2 Comparison of boys' and girls' activities in the home as portrayed in *The Oxford English Course,* book one (Burrow, 1960b)

Boys' activities in the home	Girls' activities in the home
Work in the garden (p. 35)	Wash her blouse (p. 23)
Grow flowers and trees (pp. 35, 37)	Dry her blouse (p. 23)
Put water on his flowers (p. 35)	Go to market to buy things for mother (p. 49)
Fish in the canal (p. 33)	Go to the temple (with her brother) (p. 29)
Give fish to mother for cooking (p. 33)	
Cut the grass every week (p. 36)	
Go to the temple with father (p. 29)	

Western values in the child's possible world. This portrayal of a male child represents an adult theory of childhood (Baker & Freebody, 1989), which constructs the child's possible identity as studious and well-mannered.

Roles and Identities of Female and Male Children

In the texts, different identities for boys and girls are constructed through gendered activities and roles. As table 5.2 shows, boys are perceived as being active in a greater range of pursuits than are girls.

As the table shows, in the textbook seven activities are attributed to boys, and only four activities are attributed to girls. Verbs associated with boys signify physical activity and imply that boys are strong and energetic. The words "work," "grow," "put," "fish," and "cut" designate the manual labor of boys, who are depicted as adopting their fathers' roles and responsibilities in the family as they grow up. Boys must learn and practice their fathers' duties. On three occasions, book two states that boys attend temple with their fathers. This implies that boys must learn the teachings and practices of Buddhism so that they see themselves as Buddhists when they grow to adulthood.

The activities of girls are similar to those of their mothers, namely, domestic work. Girls do chores such as washing clothes and running errands for their mother at the market. This is unpaid work, and in this way, girls are constructed as being less capable and having less responsibility than boys. By reading this text, girls are socialized into women's identities and domestic roles.

ENGLISH IS FUN: THAI ENGLISH TEXTBOOKS IN THE INDUSTRIALIZATION PERIOD

English Is Fun is a series of English course textbooks used by fifth- and sixth-grade students (DCID, 1982a, 1982b, 1983a, 1983b). The Ministry of Education assigned a committee of American and Thai scholars to develop the textbooks, which were based on the 1978 English language curriculum and published by Kurusapa Latphrao Press. The four-book series—books one and two for fifth grade and books three and four for sixth grade—began to be used in schools in 1982 and are still in use currently.

This series was the first attempt to produce an authentic Thai educational language learning product through the input of Thai educators and practitioners. Yet, at the same time, the texts employed an approach to English language learning that was derived from "Western" education, namely, the communicative approach. Altogether, there are about eight hundred and fifty words represented in the four books, the content of which focuses on the functional uses of language.

Thai Children in a Cash Economy

The textbook series *English Is Fun* presents a social world different from that of the immediate postwar period of the 1960s. The children who are portrayed in the textbooks clearly belong to the middle class in the representation of their home environments, the way they dress, and the food they eat. Vocabulary that is used in these texts signifies a shift from a rural lifestyle to an urban, middle-class lifestyle based upon the consumption of material goods.

To provide practice in asking and answering questions, book three in the *English Is Fun* series provides illustrations of items that people use in their daily lives, and asks students to answer questions regarding these items:

A: What can you do with this/these?
     I can wear it/them.
B: Can you drive this/these?
     No. I can't drive it/them, but I can ride it/them. (DCID, 1983a, p. 49)

The lexical items supplied as answers to the questions are: a glass of iced tea, a cup of coffee, a shirt, skirts, a bus, a van, a cartoon (Mickey Mouse), a television set, oranges, a plate of rice, two watches, two mops, a car, two pairs of shorts, a radio, and a bicycle. The verbs supplied for the exercise are: "eat," "drink," "watch," "ride in," "look at," "use," "wear," "read," "sell," "buy," and "listen to" (see figure 5.1).

A plate of rice is the only lexical item remaining from the postwar era. Iced tea and coffee are not traditional Thai drinks, and blouses and skirts signify modern, urban fashion for women. A bus, a van, a car, and a bicycle were not common in remote areas, and such transportation signifies the improved mobility of Thai people, especially in rural communities. The television set, radio, and Mickey Mouse cartoon are forms of mass media,

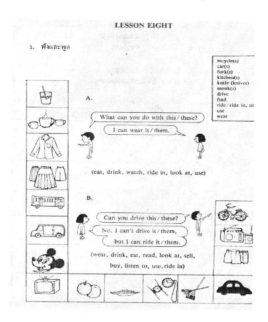

FIGURE 5.1   Illustration from *English Is Fun,* book three (DCID, 1983a, p. 49)

linked to new cultural formations and social identities and mediated by television programs and advertisements. In figure 5.1, a small boy and girl are shown pointing to consumer goods; this constitutes a representation of the reader, who is invited to value these goods.

The Ideal Thai Child in the Period of Industrialization

Table 5.3 shows how verbs are classified in association with boys and girls, in *English Is Fun.*

Verbs associated with boys—kick, hit, ride, and jump—represent them as biologically strong and energetic. The verb "sleep" refers to leisure and relief from such activity; it is a reward to them for their active roles. The text represents boys as both asleep and awake, but not the girls. Verbs associated with girls include iron, wash, sew, cook, and feed. These verbs refer to domestic tasks.

The characteristics of boys are described in the following story:

(1) Wasan is Wasana's little brother.
(2) He isn't very quiet and he isn't very good, either.
(3) He likes to play and to make noise.
(4) He doesn't like to listen to his parents or his teacher or his big sister.
(5) Wasan is a naughty boy. (DCID, 1983b, p. 5)

TABLE 5.3   Verbs used to distinguish boys
and girls in *English Is Fun*

Verbs used with boys	Verbs used with girls
Kick	Sing
Hit	Iron
Ride	Wash
Jump	Sew
Sleep	Cook
Make noise	Feed

This story describes one boy's character traits in relation to his sister. The term "little" is used to indicate that he is younger; the term "big" is used to describe his older sister. The verb "is" in lines one, two, and five denotes relational processes that identify the subject, "Wasan." The verb "like" in lines three and four denotes mental processes of feeling or affection. The story portrays the boy as a naughty child who likes to play, make noise, and disturb other people. The double negatives "He isn't very quiet and he isn't very good, either," and "He doesn't like to listen to his parents or his teacher or his big sister," emphasize Wasan's unacceptable behavior. The text informs the child reader of what is, and what is not, appropriate behavior. Traditional Thai values regarding social hierarchies and relations are stated in the sentence, "He doesn't like to listen to his parents or his teacher or his big sister."

Girls are not portrayed in the same way as boys. Rather, their characteristics are described in the following story:

(1) Yesterday was Sunday and Kanda was at home.
(2) She helped her mother and father in their food shop.
(3) First she cleaned the floor with a broom.
(4) She put tissue paper, fish sauce and sugar on each table.
(5) At twelve o'clock she helped her father cook noodles, fried rice and curry.
(6) Her brother Manop did not help his mother and father.
(7) He played football at school with his friends from eight to ten o'clock and watched TV from ten to twelve.
(8) At two o'clock Kanda's mother said, "Thank you, Kanda. You help Father." (DCID, 1983b, p. 10)

This story introduces a nuclear family: Kanda, Manop, and their parents, who own a food shop in a market. Kanda helps her parents in the shop. The verbs "helped," "cleaned," and "put" in lines two, three, and four are material processes, describing Kanda's role as a domestic helper. The text constructs a female character who works to support her parents one day a week, on Sundays. This implies that she does not go to school on Sunday, and she is portrayed as helpful and responsible. The verbs associated with her brother, Manop, in lines six, seven, and eight describe physical activities of play and entertainment. Unlike Kanda, who works by herself without parental direction or control and is depicted as responsible and mature, Manop does not help his parents.

ON THE SPRINGBOARD: THAI ENGLISH TEXTBOOKS IN THE PERIOD OF GLOBALIZATION

On the Springboard is a series of four English language textbooks for Thai students at the beginner level (DCID 1993, 1996a, 1996b, 1997). These textbooks were developed by a subcommittee of the Ministry of Education, comprised of English language instructors and Thai scholars; book one in the series was published in 1993, by Kurusapa Latphrao Press. Their content focuses on oral communication, grammar, vocabulary development, and phonic awareness.

The textbook series *On the Springboard* differs from the two previously discussed series in that their content shows the influence of new technology and visual literacy. These textbooks aim to capture the attention of young readers through the use of textualities and techniques derived from mass media and popular cultural forms. Today, graphic designers communicate meaning in textbooks through a range of verbal and visual modes, such as images, pictures, layout techniques, and words. The format of the book constitutes multimodal communication, as it not only contains words and flat illustrations, but borrows techniques from a wide range of nonprint media (Goodman & Graddol, 1996). Multicolored cartoons, illustrations, varied typefaces, and icons enhance the book's comprehensibility to students, but also make it more ideologically persuasive.

Textbooks are constructed for pedagogical purposes, but they are also purposely built for the selection, construction, and transmission of certain attitudes and knowledges (Luke, 1999). Objects and processes presented in *On the Springboard* reflect the writers' selective tradition with reference to the impact of globalization on Thai society. The text's vocabulary privileges Western values and middle-class versions of identity (see table 5.4).

The *On the Springboard* textbook series presents Western-style housing, including sitting rooms, bedrooms, dining rooms, and kitchens. These rooms are not found in most Thai homes. For working-class Thai people, the sitting room, the dining room, and the bedroom are one and the same room. The words such as "building" and "mansion" refer to the homes of affluent city people. Furniture such as sofas, beds, desks, chairs, and tables are included; the word "sofa" is used seven times in book one.

TABLE 5.4   Household goods cited in *On the Springboard*

Housing	Furniture	Electrical appliances
Sitting room	Sofa	Fan
Bedroom	Bed	Radio
Dining room	Chair	Television
Kitchen	Table	Lamp
Mansion	Desk	Light
Building		

TABLE 5.5   Food presented in *On the Springboard*

Postwar period	Industrial period	Globalization
Fish	Beef	Hot dog
Chicken	Pork	Hamburger
Duck	Cake	Sandwich
Egg	Coffee	Salad
Tea	Ice cream	Sausage
	Bread	Bun
	Milk	Lettuce
		Onion
		Tomato

This connotes rest, comfort, and leisure. Consumer appliances such as electric fans, radios, televisions, lights, and lamps are presented as necessary household items.

Food can be used to convey messages about eating and lifestyle. Many different kinds of food are presented in the *On the Springboard* series textbooks (see table 5.5). Fish, eggs, chicken, and duck are staple foods for Thai people, but cake, ice cream, bread, and milk are Western foods that were introduced in the texts of the industrial period (see figure 5.2).

In figure 5.2, images of food types are presented like those of fastfood restaurant advertisements. However, they are represented as being an integral part of the Thai diet, which is not the case. This promotes a culture of consumption, and encourages children to desire a Western lifestyle. But Thai people know that foods such as hamburgers, sandwiches, hot dogs, and sausages have only recently become part of the Thai lifestyle. The consumption of fast foods and the "McDonald-ization" of eating habits (Burbules & Torres, 2000) represent new patterns of consumerism. Because fast foods are standardized and value convenience over quality, they are popular among middle-class youth in Thai cities. Increased consumption of these foods is changing the tastes and nutritional practices of Thai people. It is noteworthy that traditional Thai foods such as rice and curry are not mentioned in the texts.

FIGURE 5.2   Western food in book two of *On the Springboard* (DCID, 1996a, p. 43)

The Ideal Thai Child in the Period of Globalization

Whereas the traditional ideal child is shown in earlier textbooks as being submissive and obedient towards parents and adults, children in *On the Springboard* are portrayed as active, independent, and assertive individuals. Boys and girls play together and are not sex-segregated. The text's cover shows how children and the parameters of their identity are semiotically constructed (see figure 5.3).

The illustration depicts children enjoying themselves in and around a swimming pool. The pool's diving board is located at the central point of the picture, which signifies its relation to the title of the book. The cartoon-like illustration constructs children as happy, energetic, and highly mobile. A fair-haired girl is about to jump off the springboard into the pool, which symbolically represents a take off, or launch, into a new world that can be accessed through the English language.

The possible world presented on the text's cover reflects the selective tradition of the book. The children are constituted within an imaginary world of fantasy. In considering the identities, attitudes, and values that are constructed by the textbook, the cover reflects a middle-class activity and lifestyle. These privileged children have time for leisure and exercise in an affluent setting, which is not the norm for most Thai children. To swim in a pool requires an amount of funding that most parents do not have.

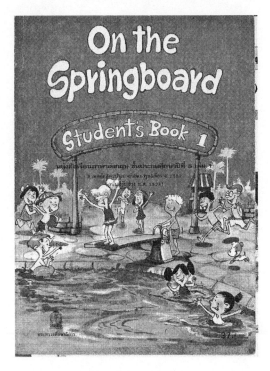

FIGURE 5.3 Cover of *On the Springboard,* book one (DCID, 1993)

The picture, therefore, signifies particular economic and social values, which exclude most Thai people—especially those who live in villages.

  Furthermore, the absence of adults and their usual participation and supervision signifies a high degree of autonomy and freedom for the children. The effect of having similarly aged children engaged in the same activity, dressed in the same way, and playing together suggests common interests, values, and a sense of belonging. This constructs the power of the peer group, especially with regard to the adoption of Western consumer practices and lifestyles. Furthermore, it opens up the possibility for children to imitate these social and cultural practices and become autonomous and independent, even while they are financially and emotionally dependent upon their parents.

  The illustration does not portray gender role segregation, as both boys and girls are socialized into the same activity. In the picture, six boys and five girls play together. The girls are portrayed as more salient and/or dominant than the boys, since it is a girl who is on the springboard. Also, note the boy in the pool; the positioning of his face and body directs the reader to the girl, and signals that he is encouraging her to jump. Different hair colors—black, blond, and brown—signal a multiracial group, but both the girl on the springboard and the boy climbing onto it have blond hair. In reality, there are no blond Thai children, and so this places Anglo-American children at the center of the narrative. The ideal child is, therefore, portrayed as a Western child, which could encourage Thai children to aspire to look like, or be like, this Western ideal. The text has a global focus, which means that the Thai reader must learn to negotiate cultural and economic relationships within regional and international communities.

Identity and Language

Language enables and constrains the possibilities of identity construction. The textbook series *On the Springboard* uses the verbs "like" and "hate" to express children's emotions about, and in relation to, material objects. Because of the blunt phraseology used in this lexical and syntactic exercise, robots, rather than human children, are used as actors. Robotic children are depicted as "liking" domestic pets such as dogs, cats, and birds, and "hating" nondomesticated animals such as bears, elephants, and snakes. Proclivities for particular animals are gendered, as boy robots like different animals than girl robots. Boys are represented as liking dogs, while girls purportedly like cats and birds. One female character claims to "hate" dogs (DCID, 1993, pp. 103–104).

These expressions are also used by children in relation to foods, such as "salad," "sausage," "hot dog," and "milk" (DCID, 1996a, p. 47). In reality, Thai children do not express emotion with the word "hate." Rather, they use the phrase, "I don't like it." Further, heavy use of the pronoun "I" emphasizes self-expression and individuality, which runs contrary to the communitarian values of Thai society. Another notable feature of the text is the absence of interpersonal feeling expressed through the term "love."

Children's Interests and Attitudes

Children's interests and attitudes are constructed through words and illustrations in the text. In lessons like "Making an Invitation," book four of *On the Springboard* (p. 105) depicts children's lives as filled with pleasure and fun (see table 5.6).

The terms "party" and "disco" signify singing and dancing, which, along with going to "dinner" and "the movie," are activities popular with middle-class youth. Girls are portrayed as liking "shopping," while boys prefer going to the "football match." These outings enable youth to mix with peers away from adults, which makes them feel free and independent.

TABLE 5.6   "Making an Invitation" from book four of
On the Springboard (DCID, 1996b, p. 105)

Activities	Occasions and places
Come to my party	Birthday
Go to the disco	Restaurant
Go to dinner	Concert
Go to the movie	Video
Go to the football match	Disco
Go shopping	Weekend

These new forms of sociality reflect Western values. The social practices and relations constructed in the textbooks represent a selective and hegemonic tradition of fast capitalist consumption and production.

CONCLUSION

Textbooks are important tools of English language teaching in Thai elementary schools because they provide convenient pedagogical materials and curricular resources for Thai teachers. Their content—vocabulary lists, simple sentences in short narratives, conversational exchanges, and instructional illustrations—purportedly depicts routine activities from the lives of ordinary children. More than this, however, they play an important role in the portrayal of possible social worlds to the child reader. The textbooks comprise much more than neutral exemplars of common English words and sentence structures: They are the loci of ideology, values, knowledge, and power (Baker & Freebody, 1989; Luke, 1988).

Our analysis has shown how three different series of English language textbooks, produced in different periods, present different linguistic and visual images, thereby signifying profound social change in Thailand during those years. In the first, postwar period, Thai people lived close to, and depended upon, the natural world. But this changed when Thailand became industrialized. Social changes included an emphasis on productivity, improvements in the standard of living, widespread educational and employment opportunities, improved health care, modern communication, and transportation. On the other hand, these developments were accompanied by a weakening of kinship and family ties and a decline in religious and spiritual belief. This visible shift to modernity, a cash economy, and a new industrial order is embodied in these textbooks. The language and illustrations in the texts show Thai society in a state of transition. Social life and cultural customs were henceforth linked to science, technology, and the market and, as a result, values of consumption and materialism were imposed upon Thai students through English language lessons. The authors' choices concerning vocabulary, visual images, and formatting constructed particular ideologies and versions of childhood and knowledge for children.

This analysis has also demonstrated changes in textbook design and composition over a three-decade period. Texts today are comprised of blends of multimodal media—borrowing and blending visual and verbal modes from other media such as comics, cartoons, newspapers, and television. Thai teachers, therefore, need to think about visual literacies and multiliteracies, which are central to meaning making, even in the sterile and formalized discourses of English language textbooks.

As sociocultural and poststructural studies show, childhood is a social construction where children's identities are made, not born (C. Luke, 1991). Textbooks are social and cultural artifacts of literacy education and are constructed for pedagogical purposes. Purposely built for the selection, construction, and transmission of valued knowledge and practices to readers (A. Luke, 1999), textbooks both represent and construct "subjects" of the social and natural worlds. In so doing, they position and construct a model reader. Certain ways of reading, writing, speaking, thinking, and being are therefore inscribed in these texts and on the bodies and minds of readers.

In Thai English language lessons, hegemonic cogency in textbooks encourages child readers to adopt Western ideas, values, and practices such as those of consumer cultures. While oblique reference is made to traditional ways of Thai life in *The Oxford English Course for Thailand*, indigenous knowledges are excluded altogether from *English Is Fun* and *On the Springboard*. Most Thai students do not belong to the middle class, yet these texts privilege middle-class lifestyles and values. What are the reasons for this? Is it because the affluent middle classes are both the semiskilled workforce for the global information economy and significant consumer groups for the products and services of global capitalism (Hewison, 1996)? Given Thailand's increasing engagement with global orders and economies, institutions and ideologies, Thai people need knowledge and skills that will enable them to confront and transform those forces on their terms. Critical studies of language will help Thai educators to recognize the ideological and political role of language in social life, including the social life of English language classrooms.

Notes

The authors would like to thank the Department of Curriculum and Instruction Development, Ministry of Education, Thailand, for granting permission to use the textbook illustrations.

References

Altbach, P. G. (Ed.). (1992). *Publishing and development in the Third World.* Portsmouth, NH: Heinemann.

Altbach, P. G., Arboleda, A., & Gopinathan, S. (Eds.). (1985). *Publishing in the Third World: Knowledge and development.* Portsmouth, NH: Heinemann.

Apple, M. W., & Christian-Smith, L. K. (1991). *The politics of the textbook.* New York: Routledge.

Baker, C. D., & Freebody, P. (1989). *Children's first school books:* Introductions to the culture of literacy. Oxford: Blackwell.

Bray, M., & Kwok-Chun, T. (1994). Imported textbooks, non-interventionist policies and school curricula in Macau. *Curriculum and Teaching, 9* (2), 29–43.

Burbules, N. C., & Torres, C. A. (Eds.). (2000). *Globalization and education: Critical perspectives.* New York: Routledge.

Burrow, H. C. (1960a). *The Oxford English course for Thailand. Book one.* Bangkok: Kurusapa Press.

Burrow, H. C. (1960b). *The Oxford English course for Thailand. Book two.* Bangkok: Kurusapa Press.

Department of Curriculum and Instruction Development (DCID), Ministry of Education, Thailand. (1982a). *English is fun. Book I: A beginning course for Thai students.* Bangkok: Kurusapa Latprao.

Department of Curriculum and Instruction Development (DCID), Ministry of Education, Thailand. (1982b). *English is fun. Book II: A beginning course for Thai students.* Bangkok: Kurusapa Latphrao.

Department of Curriculum and Instruction Development (DCID), Ministry of Education, Thailand. (1983a). *English is fun. Book III: A beginning course for Thai students.* Bangkok: Kurusapa Latphrao.

Department of Curriculum and Instruction Development (DCID), Ministry of Education, Thailand. (1983b). *English is fun. Book IV: A beginning course for Thai students.* Bangkok: Kurusapa Latphrao.

Department of Curriculum and Instruction Development (DCID), Ministry of Education, Thailand. (1993). *On the springboard. Student's book 1.* Bangkok: Kurusapa Latphrao.

Department of Curriculum and Instruction Development (DCID), Ministry of Education, Thailand. (1996a). *On the springboard. Student's book 2* (2nd ed.). Bangkok: Kurusapa Latphrao.

Department of Curriculum and Instruction Development (DCID), Ministry of Education, Thailand. (1996b). *On the springboard. Student's book 4.* Bangkok: Kurusapa Latphrao.

Department of Curriculum and Instruction Development (DCID), Ministry of Education, Thailand. (1997). *On the springboard. Student's book 3.* Bangkok: Kurusapa Latphrao.

Farrell, J., & Heyneman, S. (1988). Textbooks in developing countries: Economic and pedagogical choices. In P. G. Altbach & G. P. Kelly (Eds.), *Textbooks in the Third World: Policy, content and context* (pp. 119–144). New York: Garland.

Goodman, S., & Graddol, D. (1996). *Redesigning English: New texts, new identities.* London: Routledge.

Gupta, A. F. (1991). The unequal sexes in primary school readers. *Singapore Book World*, Festival of Book, 22.

Hewison, K. (1996). Emerging social forces in Thailand: New political and economic roles. In R. Robinson & D. S. G. Goodman, *The new rich in Asia*. London: Routledge.

Kress, G. (1989). *Linguistic processes in sociocultural practice*. Oxford: Oxford University Press.

Krongkaew, M. (1995). Contributions of agriculture to industrialization. In M. Krongkaew, (Ed.), *Thailand's industrialization and its consequences* (pp. 33–65). London: Macmillan.

Lee, D. B. (2000). *The ideological construction of culture in Korean language textbooks: A historical discourse analysis*. Unpublished doctoral dissertation, University of Queensland, Brisbane.

Luke, A. (1988). *Literacy, textbooks and ideology: Postwar literacy instruction and the mythology of Dick and Jane*. London: Falmer Press.

Luke, A. (1994). *The social construction of literacy in the primary school*. South Melbourne: Macmillan Education Australia.

Luke, A. (1999). Social perspectives on primers and textbooks. In D. A. Wagner, R. L. Venezky, & B. V. Street (Eds.), *Literacy: An international handbook* (pp. 186–191). Boulder, CO: Westview Press.

Luke, A., Carrington, V., & Kapitzke, C. (2003). Textbooks and early childhood literacy. In N. Hall, J. Larson, & J. Marsh (Eds.), *Handbook of early childhood literacy* (pp. 249–257). London: Sage.

Luke, C. (1991). On reading the child: A feminist poststructuralist perspective. *Australian Journal of Reading, 14* (2), 109–116.

Chapter 6

The Construction of Culture Knowledge in Chinese Language Textbooks

A Critical Discourse Analysis

Yongbing Liu

INTRODUCTION

Chinese language education has always been used by the government and cultural elites as an important means of transmitting dominant ideology (e.g., Price, 1992). However, few studies on language textbooks in China have been conducted from the perspective of critical curriculum theory. What dominant government/elitist ideology is legitimated through language textbooks? How do language textbooks construct official cultural knowledge, and how do they shape the moral and political identities of the child reader in China?

This chapter examines the discursive construction of cultural knowledge in Chinese language textbooks currently used by primary school students in China. Using critical discourse analysis techniques (e.g., Fairclough, 2002; Lemke, 1995; Luke, 1995), I will discuss how language textbooks introduce the child reader to cultural knowledge constructed by the government and cultural elites. In particular, I will describe how language textbooks construct official cultural knowledge and shape the child reader. Furthermore, I aim to show how these constructions are articulated in relation to sociocultural ideologies, how the passages in the textbooks build up particular relationships with the child reader, and how the relationships of power and knowledge are established by means of the choices of lexicogrammatical and macropropositional structures.

CHINA, 1970S–PRESENT: THE ECONOMIC AND SOCIOCULTURAL CONTEXT

In the late 1970s, China began to reform its economic system and opened its doors to the outside world. After roughly two decades of reform, China has seen an unmistakable emergence of activities that mark a "capitalist society": the privatization of means of production, the commodification of labor, the rise of a new rich class, and so on (e.g., Naughton, 2000; Wang, 2002). The changes have brought about economic prosperity for the Chinese people. Between 1979 and 1997, the annual growth rate of China's gross domestic product (GDP) was 9.8 percent—about three times greater than the world average (Wang, 1999; Yan, 2000).

Due to the rapid growth of the economy and the increase in personal income, a large consumer market has formed. The 1990s were even described by some scholars (e.g., Yan, 2000) as the "consumption revolution" in China. According to Yan, the hot areas of mass consumption shifted to apartments and interior decoration, personal computers, communication devices, air conditioners, body-building machines, and tourism. For example, during the 1990s, the number of mobile phones jumped from fifty thousand to more than thirteen million. Accounts for the Internet, which were almost non-existent in the early 1990s, increased from one million in 1998 to more than twenty million in 2000 (Yan, 2000).

The growing consumer market has, in turn, attracted investment from multinationals who view China's 1.3 billion people as the largest potential market in the world. In many big cities, the neon lights that brighten the evening skies are not only displayed in the Chinese language, but in English, German, Japanese, and a number of other languages as well, reflecting the presence of multinationals like General Motors, Sony, Coca-Cola, McDonald's, Hewlett-Packard, and Arco, to name just a few. In a word, China quickly became part of the world market and entered the World Trade Organization (WTO) in 2001.

However, income gaps have widened enormously. The disparities take various forms—between the east and west, between the coast and inland, between the industrial and agricultural sectors, between the managers and workers, between the private and public sectors, and so on. Coupled with the widening gap between the rich and poor is a soaring rate of unemployment. Within the free market, many state-owned enterprises have lost their battle with the competition, and as a response, in 1998 the government began the practice of eliminating or selling insolvent state industries to private entrepreneurs or foreign companies (Naughton, 2000). In other instances, the government has promoted "share holdings"—a new form of ownership in which the state sells "shares" to investors, domestic or foreign.

In either case, the end result is that the workforce has been substantially downsized and millions of workers have been laid off.

The disparities between the rich and the poor, along with the soaring rate of unemployment, have caused a psychological and ideological crisis for many Chinese people and generated untold resentment against reform, globalization, and the government. Within China, it is publicly argued that the high unemployment rate and the gap between the rich and poor could cause social instability (e.g., Q. L. He, 1998; Hu, 1999). The market economy has caused the state to lose control over society, and has placed the Chinese working class at the mercy of new capitalist exploitation.

The growth of the free market has had implications beyond economic structure: It has opened up a Pandora's box of social evils, such as corruption, drug abuse, prostitution, and counterfeit products, which have appeared and developed at a terrifying speed (He, 1998; Wang, 2002). Human compassion towards the poor and underprivileged has reached a historical low level. Some scholars (e.g., He, 1998; Wang, 2002) believe that all of these problems are caused by the "get-rich mentality" driven by the free market. In other words, people seem to live in an utterly valueless condition where the goal of life is simply to make money. Scholars go on to predict that the most severe crisis in China's future is not just economic, but the collapse of Chinese cultural or moral structure as well.

Defenders of the reform, especially those in the government (e.g., Xiao, 1994; X. He, 1996), argue that a growing income gap and increased unemployment rate are inevitable as China transforms into a free-market economy; the problems should be seen as "growing pains" necessary to the process. They also argue that the reform has led to a renewed sense of citizenship and cultural renaissance, not a cultural crisis. Some even argue that the Chinese cultural system has displayed an internal resilience and a capacity for adjustment (see Oakes, 2000). Social problems, as "pains of the process," can gradually be eased within the system by renewed social order, legality, and education.

In an effort to address the social problems and the cultural crisis, some advocate political changes, which would mean an introduction of Western institutional structures and their value systems (see Wasserstrom & Petty, 1992). For example, one-party totalitarianism should be replaced with democracy in the form of free elections, a parliamentary system, and separation of powers. It is hoped that through these changes, China's free market will be matched by its social and political order, which, in turn, will create a balance between economic and social order. Some even believe that a new type of person, "the bourgeois subject" who is conducive to the capitalist system, will be produced (see Wang, 2002). This person will possess values and motivations that are, in essence, ascetic rather than hedonistic.

However, many cultural elites (e.g., X. He, 1996; Hu, 1999; Xiao, 1994) agree with the government's argument that China cannot be guided by any Western models. If a Western institutional structure is introduced to solve Chinese problems, China will not be able to avoid "the Russian disaster." According to cultural elites, Russia's sudden abandonment of socialist tradition and rapid introduction of Western political principles to guide economic reform did not produce social and economic progress, but rather caused a disaster. In order to prevent Westernization, they agree with the government that a new discourse based on China's own development experiences needs to be developed. Mao's socialist legacies and Confucian traditional Chinese cultural values will have to be the major sources for such a new discourse.

In the new discourse, rule by the present government is justified on three pragmatic grounds: first, this government has protected the sovereignty and territorial integrity of the country; second, it has maintained China's unity and domestic stability; and third, it has achieved a steadier, more rapid economic growth and a higher standard of living for the majority of the people (Oksenberg, 2001). Based on these grounds, the present government form and its political principles are not viewed as the sources of social problems, but instead as a rallying force for coping with the problems. For the government and many cultural elites, the resolution to problems regarding morals and beliefs lies in the hands of education.

In the recent education reform called "quality education," one of the most important tasks of basic education cited is to transmit the desired moral code to students and build up the correct beliefs (Liu, 1995). It is axiomatic in studies of contemporary Chinese education that curriculum form and content has been driven by textbook selection. This is due, in part, to the absence of a formal syllabus or outcome statements other than what is specified in textbooks. It is also due to the difficulty of achieving consistent teacher quality and systems communication across geographic and regional diversity. How are the views I have described here sanctioned, and how are these ideological tensions represented in Chinese language textbooks? Having provided a broad sketch of the context, I now turn to textbook analysis.

The textbooks I will examine here are contained in *Yuwen: Jiunian yiwu jiaoyu liunian xiaoxue jiaokeshu* (Yuwen bianjishi, 1999), a twelve-volume set of textbooks that are still in use nationwide. The series covers six grades of primary school, with two volumes for each year or grade. Due to the space constraints of this chapter, my analysis is limited to the first six volumes and is only partial in nature.

THE DISCURSIVE CONSTRUCTION OF CULTURAL KNOWLEDGE

Through examination of the corpus texts and their intertextual relations, in terms of their themes and orientations, I have identified three major discourses that are constructed in the textbooks used by primary school students: the discourse of patriotism, that of cultural values and beliefs, and that of pro-science and technology. In addition, I have further identified several subcategories that I call "perspectives," from which each discourse is defined and verified.

Table 6.1 shows the number of passages that occur in each category of discourse and their related subcategories of perspective. A series of passages is designated as having an intertextual relation, in terms of theme and orientation, in accordance to the primary concern of the texts, and is assigned to one of the perspectives from which a specific discourse is constructed. In the analysis that follows, the discourses will be discussed separately, first through simple statistics of frequency, and then through concrete textual analysis of passages from the corpus. Since space is limited within this chapter, I cannot provide a detailed analysis of the texts from all perspectives identified in the study; instead, I will analyze one or two texts as examples from each discourse.

TABLE 6.1   Dominant discourses and perspectives in textbook series

Discourses	Perspectives	Number of passages (148 in total)
Patriotism		41 (27.7%)
	• the love of the country	15
	• a happy life people enjoy in the country	10
	• work or sacrifice for the country	16
Cultural values and beliefs		43 (29.1%)
	• concentration on, and hard work in, study	13
	• collective spirit	11
	• respect for authority	7
	• modesty	7
	• honesty	5
Pro-science and technology		38 (25.7%)
	• scientific attitude and rational mind	16
	• scientific knowledge and modern technologies	22
Others	Riddles, word plays, descriptions of rocks, animals, and so on	26 (17.6%)

DISCOURSE OF PATRIOTISM

As shown in table 6.1, 41 out of 148 passages are classified as constructing a discourse of patriotism, accounting for 27.7 percent of the texts. The discourse of patriotism is found to be constructed from three major perspectives, namely, the love of the country, a happy life people enjoy in the country, and work or sacrifice for the country. The perspective of the love of the country is represented in 15 passages that describe the natural beauties and cultural sites of China. The descriptions are oriented towards generating pride in, and a sense of love for, the country. The second perspective involves 10 passages that portray the happy life people enjoy in the country. Finally, the perspective of work or sacrifice for the country is realized through a series of 16 passages. These texts tell stories about workers, national leaders, heroes, and scientists as models of patriotic people. For example, one of the texts describes Beijing, China's capital, as follows:

Beijing
   Beijing is the capital of our country. It is a beautiful city.
   Tiananmen is located at the centre of Beijing with its red walls and yellow tiles. It is solemn and beautiful. In front of Tiananmen is a broad square. In the middle of the square is erected the Monument to the People's Heroes.
   There are many broad and long streets in Beijing. Along both sides of the streets, green trees are shady and flowers are in full bloom. Beijing has recently built many three dimensional freeway bridges. Surrounding the bridges, there are green carpet-like lawns and picture-like flowerbeds. Various kinds of vehicles are running constantly on and under the bridges from different directions....
   How beautiful Beijing is! We love Beijing. We love our motherland. (Yuwen bianjishi, 1999, vol. 3, pp. 132–134)[1]

At the very beginning, the text establishes a proposition with two statements: "Beijing is the capital of our country" and "It is a beautiful city." The authoritative proposition, justified by itself and allowing no argument or explanation, presupposes that the description that follows is nothing but "beautiful." Then, in the last paragraph, the exclamation "How beautiful Beijing is!" further reinforces the proposition. This is, in turn, connected with the last two sentences about "love" ("We love Beijing. We love our motherland."), thus creating a subject position—a possible world where beauty and love are mingled with motherland. It can be noted that the modality of the text is overwhelmingly strong—that is, the descriptions of what is the case are categorical, not hedged. For example, if we were to change the sentence "Beijing is a beautiful city" into "Some part of Beijing is beautiful," or "We love our motherland" into "We ought to love our motherland," the effect would be completely different. The deliberate choice of the strong modality positions the child reader to believe that what is represented is true, or fact.

Another characteristic pattern observed in the text is that the syntactical relations between sentences are mainly paratactic. According to Fairclough (2002), paratactic syntax is accumulative in its meaning effects, listing, and adding of example to example, and is oriented to appearances and to the range of evidence, rather than to explanations, causes, and effects. It ties in with the categorical and authoritative assertion of truisms, enhancing their rhetorical force through accumulation. In this case, the categorical and authoritative assertion is that the beauty of Beijing is absolutely true through the accumulation of simple descriptive sentences. Through parataxis, the text portrays ancient buildings, parks, freeways, and skyscrapers as equally beautiful. The destruction of cultural heritage and serious pollution of the city are simply omitted. This kind of linguistic choice runs across many other passages that describe the cultural sites and scenic spots of China. Now, let's turn to an example from another perspective:

Yesterday, this was a village.

Life remained the same for ages. Poverty and backwardness was perplexing. Modern civilization was remote and vague.

At the early morning, father was laboring in the fields. In a mist of smoke and fog, mother was cooking at the stove. In the piles of straw, boys were rolling about. At the stream, girls were washing.

Oh, within a few short years that have passed, changes are beyond our imagination....

The highways have replaced the old muddy roads. The tall buildings have replaced the shabby houses. Happy laughter and beautiful songs have filled the children's parks. The colorful lights and pretty fountains have decorated the city like a paradise....

With big lorries, people transport cement and steel. With office briefcases, they negotiate establishing factories with their foreign business counterparts. With the bright lights, they read books in the ocean of knowledge. With beautiful music, they dance and sing songs loudly....

It is the reform and open-door policy that have lent them the wings.... (Yuwen bianjishi, 1999, vol. 6, pp. 128–129)

In looking for links and contrasts between the notions of "yesterday" and "today" described in the text, three patterns are identifiable in the presentation of changes of the "village." One pattern is that the words used to describe or present yesterday portray a negative sense while the words used to describe today portray a positive sense. Consequently, a binary opposition is created, whereby the child reader is positioned to favor "today's world" over that of "yesterday." For example, in the fourth paragraph alone, there are seven concrete nouns (highways, buildings, songs, children's parks, lights, fountains, and city) that are employed to signify different things in "today's world"; these are described with five adjectives (tall, happy, beautiful, colorful, and pretty) that have positive connotations. However, in the same paragraph, for contrast, just two concrete nouns (roads and houses) are used to depict something in the past. Despite the small number, the concrete nouns are modified by pejorative adjectives (muddy and shabby), which manifest negative notion of "yesterday." However, who has brought about the changes from "poverty and backwardness" to "modern civilization"? To answer this question, it is necessary to look at another linguistic use of transitivity. The purpose of transitivity is to construct processes, the participants involved in them, and the circumstances in which they take place.

When we consider the role of the participants portrayed in the text, we can see that there are no agentive participants in what happened "yesterday." The participants are all regulated as mediums who acted, but the activities are deprived of specific goals (for example, "father was laboring", "mother was cooking"). The impression we get from these agentless activities is that the participants are aimless, passive, and helpless. In contrast, the participants in what happens "today" are nearly all agentive, acting on different kinds of things (for example, "people transport cement and steel," "they negotiate establishing factories"). The activities involve not only business, but education and entertainment as well. However, the agent that has brought about the dramatic change is not clear until the sentence that proclaims: "It is the reform and open-door policy that have lent them the wings." The emphatic structure and metaphor used within the sentence attribute the change from "backwardness" to "modern" to government policy. In this passage, as in many other passages in the textbooks, the contrast between China before and after the reform, is designed to get the child reader to understand that without the government, there would be no modern life, and without correct governmental policy, there would be no such dramatic changes from a village of poverty to a modern city.

THE DISCOURSES OF CULTURAL VALUES AND BELIEFS

As shown in table 6.1, 43 out of 148 passages are classified as constructing the discourses of cultural values and beliefs, accounting for 29.1 percent of the texts. The discourses of cultural values and beliefs are found to be constructed from five different perspectives, namely, concentration on, and hardwork in, study; collective spirit; respect for authority (leaders, teachers, elders); modesty; and honesty. These perspectives are, in fact, cultural norms constructed within the textbooks to encourage child readers to learn and obey. In other words, these cultural values are a kind of desired behavior that the government and cultural elites are interested in transmitting to their younger citizens through language education.

The perspective of concentration on, and hard work in, study receives the most attention; thirteen passages fall into this subcategory. These passages are designed to cultivate in children either the value of hard work, or the importance of concentration on study. Next in order is the perspective of collective spirit, which makes up eleven passages. These passages are intertextually related, in terms of theme and orientation, to teach the children that happiness or satisfaction comes from helping or serving others in particular, or society in general. There are seven texts classified as a perspective of respect for authority. The authority that is to be respected is that of government officials, teachers, and elders. However, these kinds of power relations are manifest in many other passages, not through the primary concerns of the texts, but embedded within the linguistic choices. Interrelated with this category is the perspective of modesty, which comprises seven passages. The theme and orientation of these texts denounce arrogance and praise self-restraint. However, hidden in the semantic structures of the texts is the message that the status quo should be accepted and competition or will to change is discouraged. The perspective of honesty makes up five passages. The themes of the texts range from not telling lies, to not accepting what does not belong to you.

One of the texts presents a story entitled "A Kitten Fishing," which contains the themes and orientations of the discourse of cultural values and beliefs:

A Kitten Fishing

Mum cat went to a river to fish with her kitten. A dragonfly came flying around. The kitten was attracted. She laid down her fishing rod to catch the dragonfly. The dragonfly flew away and she did not catch it. When she came back to the riverside, she found her mum got a big fish…. The kitten said, "It is really frustrating! Why doesn't a fish bite my hook?" The kitten's mum said to her, "It is not the reason why the fish doesn't bite your hook. You tried to catch a dragonfly at one time and at another time you attempted to catch a butterfly. How can you catch a fish this way? Don't be half-hearted!"

She listened to what her mum said and began to fish wholeheartedly. The dragonfly and butterfly came again. The kitten

went on fishing as if she did not see them. In a few minutes, she
caught a big fish. (Yuwen bianjishi, 1999, vol. 2, pp. 51–53)

In this story, the kitten initiates a series of actions out of mere interest
or emotion (attraction), rather than thinking or reasoning, and the actions
inevitably result in failure (did not catch a fish). Lexical and syntactic repetition (e.g., come, see, lay down, find, and catch) is enabled by a story-
grammar restatement of macropropositional initial events, internal
response, attempt, and consequence. The kitten's attempts and failures in
contrast to her mum's success (caught a big fish) result in a moral lesson.
The moral lesson is verbalized by the mum cat's utterance, "Don't be half-
hearted." The moral lesson is then further reinforced by the kitten's success
after accepting the advice. Through the interactions between the mum cat
and her kitten, a beneficent pro-social behavior is conveyed: an adult gives
advice, while a child listens to advice. Therefore, this story has a double-
edged moral lesson: On the one hand, the child reader has to think rea-
sonably and concentrate in order to achieve success; on the other hand,
he/she must seek advice or monitoring from an adult, as well as obey them
in order to achieve his/her purpose.

Another story "A Beautiful Rooster," which appears in a different volume,
also presents a moral lesson. The discourse of cultural values and beliefs
occurs here also:

A Beautiful Rooster
       A long, long time ago there was a rooster. He always consid-
ered himself the most beautiful in the world....
       One day, he went out. When he came to a big tree, he saw a
woodpecker. He asked, "Long-beaked woodpecker, can we compare
each other to see who is more beautiful?" The woodpecker replied
coldly, "Sorry, there are worms in the tree, so I will get rid of
them." On hearing this, the rooster walked away proudly. When
he came to an orchard, he saw a bee. He said, "Big-eyed bee, can
you compete with me to see who is prettier?" The bee said coldly,
"Excuse me, the trees are in blossom. I'm busy collecting honey."
At the words, the rooster went away. When he came to a rice field,
he saw a frog. He asked the frog, "Big-bellied frog, dare you compete with me for beauty?" The frog answered, "Sorry, there are
pests in the rice fields, I have to catch them."
       Then he met an old horse with a sack of grain on his back. He
told the old horse his problem with the woodpecker, the bee, and
the frog. He asked the old horse sadly, "Old uncle horse, why did
they refuse to compete with me?" The old horse said, "Because
they know that beauty is not judged by appearance but by how

much you do for others." Hearing these words, the rooster felt ashamed of himself, and no longer competed with others. Instead, he got up early everyday and crowed to remind others to get up early for work. (Yuwen bianjishi, 1999, vol. 3, pp. 117–121)

In this particular story, the rooster is regulated as the initiator of a series of actions, namely asking questions, while the woodpecker, the bee, and the frog play the role of addressees, and the old horse plays a moral judge for their actions. After three failed attempts to engage in a competition for beauty with three apparently ugly-looking counterparts (symbolized by "long-beaked," "big-eyed," and "big-bellied"), the rooster came to the old horse with his problem. The old horse then suggested that "beauty is not judged by appearance but by how much you do for others." Thus, the problem is solved and the moral lesson learned.

The obvious moral is that to show oneself off is not an acceptable behavior, but to help others is. However, there is implicit ideology at work, too. That is, people have to be content with what they have, and do what they are assigned to do. The natural job for a woodpecker is to get rid of worms from trees; a bee to collect honey; a frog to catch pests; and a rooster to crow in the early morning. With this reasoning, child readers are positioned to be modest rather than proud of themselves, study hard rather than play, and accept what is given rather than think creatively. A logic runs through this story, like many others, that everything is naturally ordered and any attempt to change it is doomed to failure.

Discourses of Pro-science and Technology

As shown in table 6.1, 38 passages are identified as constructing the discourse of pro-science and technology. The discourse is constructed from two perspectives. One perspective is to teach child readers to form a scientific attitude and rational mind. The sixteen passages range from Chinese folk stories, to children's poems, to stories of famous scientists in terms of genre. It serves as a springboard from which the perspective of scientific knowledge and modern technologies is developed. The twenty-two passages that are classified under this perspective cover commonsense knowledge of natural phenomena, such as season changes, plants, animals, rivers, and the sun and the earth, as well as modern technologies, such as the telescope, computer, radar, new types of glass, and hydropower plants. These texts are mainly expositions in terms of genre. The theme and orientation of these passages intertextually sing the praise of science and technology, which has brought about a better life for the people. The negative side of modern industry's science and technology is simply omitted.

The following story "New Types of Glass" is a good example in which the discourse of pro-science and technology speaks:

New Types of Glass
Modern science and technology is playing an important role in our life. It has made our life more secure and comfortable. Everywhere we can find it at work for us. Take glass for example. There are different types of glass in service for us.

One kind of glass is called "alarm glass." Built into this glass is a net of tiny metal ware. The net is connected with an automatic alarm by electricity. If a criminal touches the glass, the alarm will be triggered automatically. This kind of glass is used in museums, banks, and jewelry shops. It is also used in buildings where secret documents and information are kept.

Another type of glass can play a function of reflecting the sunlight. If buildings are equipped with this kind of glass, everything can be seen clearly from the inside but the inside cannot be seen from the outside. It can also change the shade of color with the sunlight and regulate the light beam inside the room. So it is called "automatic curtain"….

In the modernized construction, new types of glass are playing an increasingly important role. In the glass development, we will make more wonders. (Yuwen bianjishi, 1999, vol. 6, pp. 94–96)

This text begins with the assertion that science and technology is important and has made our life more secure and comfortable. The repeated use of the inclusive pronouns "we" and "us" in the first four sentences establishes a solidarity relationship between the child reader and the text producer. More importantly, it has set up the presupposition that all people, including the child reader, enjoy the benefits of science and technology without exception.

Having established an unchangeable proposition and authority, the passage lists four different types of glass, which serve "us" (for the sake of saving space, two paragraphs describing two other types of glass are omitted in the above quotation). In each paragraph, a specific type of glass is described; its basic function is provided, and then its uses are defined. For example, in the second paragraph, "alarm glass" is described as functioning as an automatic alarm, which in turn, can stop a robbery. It is used in museums, banks, and so on.

Characteristic of the description and definition in each paragraph is the linguistic means of present tense and passive voice sentence structures. For example, "Built into this glass is a net of tiny metal ware," "The net is connected with…," "It is also used…." By means of these linguistic choices, the text detaches the knowledge it describes from any identifiable human source. The description is given in the present tense, not located in any specific time and space. Rather, it is a universal claim. It seems that all types of glass are developed in China and they are readily available. In addition, this universal claim ties in with the assertion made at the beginning of the text, which positions child readers to believe that they are the beneficiaries of these technologies. At the end of the passages, again using the inclusive pronoun "we," the text positions child readers to believe that they can also help to "make more wonders" if they learn about science and technology. In other words, by building up a version of the world where scientific knowledge and technology can solve all problems and benefit all people, the text tries to persuade child readers to study scientific knowledge and modern technologies as a priority. This version of the world, and the persuasion it evokes, runs through the passages identified in this category. The public discourse of environmental problems, such as air pollution, floods, and shortage of water caused by the recent industrial development in China, never surface in the textbooks.

The Discourses and the New China: A Closed System

The identification of the dominant discourses in this chapter demonstrates how cultural knowledge is institutionally constructed and ordered to impart dominant ideology in Chinese language textbooks. The analysis of these sample texts has disclosed the rules that underlie their ideological positions. The constructed areas of cultural knowledge within the textbooks embody the government's and cultural elites' interests, reify official interpretations and value judgments, and give prominence to certain knowledges while rendering others invisible.

Through intertextual analysis, three discourses are identified to dominate the textbooks, namely, patriotism, cultural values and beliefs, and proscience and technology. These three areas of cultural knowledge receive nearly equal attention in the textbooks, as shown in table 6.1 by the distribution of the number of passages classified in each category. These three areas of cultural knowledge are constructed as a closed system with hierarchical levels, where the identity, interest, behavior, and intersubjectivity of child readers are defined and constrained. Figure 6.1 represents the discursive and ideological relations between the three levels of the closed system.

In this system, each higher level constrains and defines the other. The patriotic discourse at the upper level of the system constructs for child readers who they are and where they live. In other words, the child reader's social identity is positioned and placed by the discourse as collectively fixed with where they live. By deliberately omitting the racial, class, and

Discourse of patriotism
(Who and where)

Discourse of cultural values and beliefs
(How to behave)

⇑
⇓

Discourse of pro-science and technology
(What to learn)

FIGURE 6.1   The closed discourse system of Chinese language textbooks.

gender differences, the discourse portrays all Chinese people as living happily in a unique and beautiful land. The imaginary coherence and richness
of China, its immense geographical size, and symbolic cultural sites are
constructed and used to generate in child readers a sense of pride in, and
love for, the country. Running through these circular identifications is the
logic that if you love the country, you love or support the government,
because it represents the country.

After "a sort of collective one self" (Hall, 1989, p. 69) is established by
the discourse of patriotism, which provides unifying and unchanging
points of reference and meaning, the discourse of cultural values and
beliefs specifies how the child reader should behave socially. Put simply,
the discourse of patriotism provides a cultural context where child readers
and their settings are defined, whereas the discourse of cultural values and
beliefs sets up the social rules that child readers should obey. The social
rules are ideologically selected to position child readers as self-restrained,
confirmative, and obedient citizens; self-assertion, individuality, and personal interests are regarded as antisocial behaviors. After ritualizing and
fixing the rules, the discourse of pro-science and technology informs child
readers of what they should learn. The scientific knowledge and modern
technologies are legitimated in the discourse as modernity in the form of
rationality, which has yet to contribute to the betterment of the country
and people. Therefore, scientific knowledge and modern technologies are
constructed as closely related to a better life and the development of the
country. In other words, having scientific knowledge and modern technologies is not for social mobility or personal enrichment, but for the
country and its people. Thus, the three discourses form a circular system,
with one linking to another. Within this system, social relations and
human subjectivity are prescribed and constrained: Adults retain authority
positions while children require socialization; government officials, teachers, and the elder have power, while ordinary people, students, and the
young have to obey; women take care of the kids while men are concerned

with building the nation. These asymmetrical power relations are ideologically legitimated and constructed as "commonsense" in the textbooks.

At the same time, environmental damage, the widening gap between the rich and poor, and social problems are all excluded in order to better serve the interest of the government and its elites. As Nichols correctly points out, though in a different context,

> "To serve the ideology, representations must be made to appear to be other than what they are. Above all, they must appear to lack these very contradictions that informed their production. They must appear as signs of eternal values—harmony, wholeness, and radiance, a natural and ideal world spun from the representations of an existing social order". (1981, p. 290)

In this way, the textbooks legitimate and transmit the government's and dominant class's version of the world. It is obvious that the world constructed in the textbooks is distorted, if not totally different, from the real world. As described earlier, China is experiencing a rapid transformation from a socialist society to a capitalist society. Along with the transformation, there are many social problems and ideological tensions. However, the discourses constructed in the textbooks stop short of acknowledging in any explicit and useful way that social problems and ideological tensions exist. It is my belief that the distortion, or mismatch, between the discourses and social reality is what has caused the recent crisis of language education (see for example, Liu, 1995; Hao, 2000). The discourses constructed in the textbooks deliberately disengage and estrange students from a reading of the real world, thus leaving them disempowered whenever they are not in school.

I suggest, therefore, that more research is needed to demystify the discourses constructed in the textbooks, rather than the typical focus on linguistic scaling of difficulty or looking for a "best teaching method" in China. Competing texts and discourses of reality should be introduced in language textbooks in order to make explicit different reading positions and interpretations. By critically reading the competing texts and discourses, students can learn to reposition themselves as speakers, readers, and writers so that they become producers of valued cultural knowledge and not merely consumers of textbook "facts." In this way, students will be better equipped to face the tensions, conflicts, and social problems in the real world.

NOTES

This chapter is a partial summary of the author's Ph.D. research, sponsored by the International Postgraduate Research Scholarship at the University of Queensland. The author is grateful to Allan Luke and Victoria Carrington for their stimulating and insightful comments on earlier versions of the chapter.

1. I have translated passages of the textbooks into English to provide examples. For references, however, the original page numbers and their corresponding volumes are given in brackets at the end of the quoted examples.

REFERENCES

Fairclough, N. (2002). *Analyzing discourse: Text analysis for social research*. New York: Routledge.

Hall, S. (1989). Cultural identity and cinematic representation. *Framework, 36*, 69–81.

Hao, D. Y. (2000). *Kecheng yanzhi fangfalun* [Methodology of Curriculum Development]. Beijing: Jiaoyu kexu chubanshe.

He, Q. L. (1998). *Xiandaihua de xianjing: Dangdai zhongguo de jingji shehui wenti* [Pitfalls of modernization: Economic and social problems of contemporary China]. Beijing: Jinri zhongguo chubanshe.

He, X. (1996). *Zhonghua fuxing yu shijie weilai* (shangxia che) [The revival of China and the future of the world (Vols. 1–2)]. Chengdu: Sichuan renmin chubanshe.

Hu, A. G. (1999). *Zhongguo fazhan qianjing* [Prospects of China's development]. Hangzhou: Zhejiang renmin chubanshe.

Lemke, J. (1995). *Textual politics: Discourse and social dynamics*. London: Taylor & Francis.

Liu, F. (1995). *Zhongguo jiaoyu de weilai* [The future of Chinese education]. Beijing: Renmin jiaoyu chubanshe.

Luke, A. (1995). Text and discourse in education: An introduction to critical discourse analysis. *Review of Research in Education, 21*, 1–48.

Naughton, B. (2000). The Chinese economy: Fifty years into transformation. In T. White (Ed.), *China briefing 2000: The continuing transformation* (pp. 11–49). New York: M. E. Sharpe.

Nichols, B. (1981). *Ideology and the image*. Bloomington: Indiana University Press.

Oakes, T. (2000). China's provincial identities: Reviving regionalism and reinventing "Chineseness." *Journal of Asian Studies, 59* (2), 667–691.

Oksenberg, M. (2001). China's political system: Challenges of the twenty-first century. *China Journal, 45*, 21–35.

Price, D. (1992). Moral-political education and modernization. In R. Hayhoe (Ed.), *Education and modernization: The Chinese experience* (pp. 211–237). Oxford: Pergamon Press.

Wang, J. C. F. (1999). *Contemporary Chinese politics: An introduction* (6th ed.). New Jersey: Prentice Hall.

Wang, X. Y. (2002). The post-communist personality: The spectre of China's capitalist market reforms. *China Journal, 47*, 1–17.

Wasserstrom, J. N. & Perry, E. J. (Eds.). (1992). *Popular protest and political culture in modern China*. Oxford: Westview Press.

Xiao, G. Q. (1994). Minzu zhuyi yu zhongguo zhuanxing shiqi de yishi xingtai [Nationalism and ideology in China's transitional period]. *Zhanlue yu guanli, 4,* 21–25.

Yan, Y. X. (2000). The politics of consumerism in Chinese society. In T. White (Ed.), *China briefing 2000: The continuing transformation* (pp. 159–193). New York: M. E. Sharpe.

Yuwen bianjishi. (Eds.). (1999). *Yuwen: Jiunian yiwu jiaoyu liunian xiaoxue jiaokeshu* (1–12 che) [Chinese language readers: Textbooks for six year primary schools in nine years compulsory education (Vols. 1–12)]. Beijing: Renmin jiaoyu chubanshe.

Chapter 7

New Ideologies of Everyday Life in South Korean Language Textbooks

Dong Bae (Isaac) Lee

INTRODUCTION

The processes and practices of economic globalization are often criticized for benefiting rich, industrialized countries, whilst disadvantaging periphery countries. There is substantial evidence that globalization has marginalized the diverse local cultures of periphery countries, though their local cultures partially affect the cultures of center countries (Sardar and Van Loon, 1997). Further, while the global economy increases its influence across borders, the legal and judicial power of individual nations over their internal economies and social and cultural development is reduced. For countries like South Korea, one of the effects of globalization has been the acceleration and extension of Western dominant culture and economic structures. The urban spaces and cultures of South Korea have increasingly come to resemble Western world culture, evidenced in its patterns of consumption, lifestyle, and media (Hahm, 2002).

This is an ideologically complex process involving both powerful holdover discourses and debates, and emergent new patterns. Despite proclamations that the coming of this transnational capitalist culture led to the ostensible end of ideology, the Cold War continues in some areas like the Korean peninsula, Taiwan, and China. At the same time, the forces of globalization have faced resistance from domestic groups, peripheries, and environmentalists. What this means is that continued, unresolved issues held over from both colonialism and neocolonialism in many ways temper the complex ideological responses of South Korea to new conditions.

The responses of school systems and the curriculum to these forces are worthy of close examination. On the one hand, there is a strong push (just as there is in other places) towards a new human capital model, whereby students would be prepared for participation in transnational, corporate, information-based economies. This new version of the human capital rationale has been the cornerstone of educational policy in Hong Kong, Singapore, and indeed, South Korea. On the other hand, there remain complex issues surrounding cultural identity, history, and the postcolonial representation of South Korean society in not only the school curriculum, but more specifically, in textbooks. In this chapter, therefore, I will investigate how South Korean language textbooks cope with global changes, and how they have begun to construct new versions of South Korean students and South Korean culture. My aim here is to try to document the complex ideological mix represented in textbooks around the issues of ecology, consumption, leisure, and, ultimately, national identity and social cohesion.

The Context: New Times in South Korea

South Korea's gross national product per capita was $10,548 (U.S. dollars) in 1996 (Samsung Economic Research Institute, 2000). In that same year, South Korea became a member of the Organization for Economic Cooperation and Development (OECD). As elsewhere in Southeast and Northeast Asia, a large middle class has emerged in South Korea, and its surplus income has changed consumption patterns drastically; this emergent class has acquired new cars and a range of other consumer items, and families go on domestic and overseas holidays. Western-style cultural spaces are ubiquitous in South Korea nowadays, where urban life consists of visits to, for example, McDonald's and Starbucks, shopping malls, simulated environments, theme parks, and so forth. Putting aside, for a moment, issues surrounding the overall distribution of wealth in South Korea, the expansion of the consumer economy, the emergence of an affluent middle class, and the promotion of a McDonalized culture have worked together in the so-called "economic miracle" of South Korea to create new local cultural forms and patterns of life, as it has throughout Southeast Asia. A key problem is how schools and textbooks have taken up the role of systematically introducing children to these new social "realities."

At the same time, South Korea's export-oriented development strategy, which contributed to rapid economic growth, left the rural sector relatively underdeveloped. Consequently, the increasing rate of income disparity between urban and rural areas—industrial and agricultural sectors—has become a serious problem. Additionally, gender disparities are persistent. As an industrial force, South Korean female workers have contributed significantly to the development of the South Korean economy, but they have not been treated as well as their male coworkers. Although the feminist movement is growing in South Korean society, gender inequality and discrimination still exist. Female workers are paid less, and the opportunities for female workers to receive promotions are restricted.

Chaebols (conglomerates) such as Samsung, Hyundai, Daewoo, Kia, and LG have bolstered the South Korean economy, but have also oppressed industrial workers, influenced the economy and politics, and exerted a powerful, self-interested force through the ownership and domination of the mass media. After the economic/currency crisis of 1997, additional multinational companies, such as General Motors and Renault, established their factories in South Korea. In this way, the 1997 crisis both accelerated and exacerbated many of the inequalities of the "new" South Korea—a matter that has contributed to some degree of ongoing political protest and instability.

Furthermore, serious environmental pollution (which has been a central social and geographical problem) has been worsened by corporate-driven and transnational industrialization (Macdonald, 1990). The fact that pollution from major manufacturing areas located on the northeastern and eastern coasts of China has crossed over into South Korean territories by way of prevailing weather patterns complicates matters.

Given these issues, it should not be surprising that a principal corporate and government strategy has been to focus public attention on political conflict and reunification. Ju Young Jung, a South Korean businessman and former head of Hyundai, visited North Korea on 17 July 1998 and started economic cooperation between the two countries by initiating Mt. Kumgang Tourism on 18 November 1998. In 2000, the South Korean president, Kim Dae Jung, participated in a successful summit held in North Korea and agreed to prepare for a peaceful and gradual reunification. Since then, the two Koreas have increased their economic cooperation, and have agreed to reconnect the railways that run between Shinuiju, North Korea (located in the northwest), and Seoul, South Korea (the country's capital), as well as the railways that run between Wonsan, North Korea (located in the southeast), and Seoul, South Korea. As a result of this cooperation, families once separated by the Korean border have been able to reunite.

In these contemporary contexts of rapid industrial growth, a declining rural sector, worker alienation, increasing gaps between rich and poor, increasing problems of pollution, and unresolved and historically vexed debates around reunification, current educational reforms are being undertaken. It is, thus, of interest to analyze how textbooks are engaged in representing and portraying the complex dynamics of the new South Korea.

In what follows, I look at selected narratives taken from textbooks used in teaching Kugö (Korean) to early primary school children (the literal translation of Kugö is "national language"). In South Korea, Korean language textbooks are written and developed by the Ministry of Education (Kyoyukbu). More specifically, they are written by a governmental committee made up of school teachers, governmental researchers, and university lecturers. The committee members design and develop the textbooks, and when the Ministry of Education approves them, they are published by Daehan Printing and Publishing Company (Lee, 2000).

Here, I will examine how textbooks represent and instantiate contemporary ideologies around three key thematics in South Korean education: environmental issues, emergent Western/Northern lifestyles of leisure/consumption, and, of course, the perennial matter of political reunification. I analyze them using various techniques of critical discourse analysis, such as story grammar (Luke, 1988) and particular modes of lexical and syntactic analysis, as described by Fairclough (1995).

Environmental Issues

The economic growth of South Korea was rapid, and was achieved at the expense of the environment. Writing over a decade ago, Macdonald (1990 p. 106) argued:

> South Korea has become one of the most polluted areas in the world. The drive for rapid economic development and the destruction of the Korean War have taken a heavy toll on Korea's environment— particularly in the South, where both population density and the rate of economic growth are higher than in the North. (p. 106)

After Japanese colonization, which ended in 1945, and the Korean civil war in 1953, most poor South Korean people endeavored to escape from severe poverty. As a result, South Korean leaders focused on the rapid growth of the economy without fully considering the side effects of industrialization. If anything, the situation in South Korea has worsened, since Macdonald wrote, accelerated by the "offshoring" of dirty industry by postindustrial countries of the northern and western hemispheres. Advanced countries, such as Japan and the United States, have transferred their pollution-oriented industries to underdeveloped countries like South Korea. In one generation, South Korea's mountains, rivers, and seas have been polluted and destroyed.

National Language 1-1: Reading (Kyoyukbu, 1999), published for grade one, semester one, depicts the negative effects of industrialization in a story "The Songs of Insects":

> *The Songs of Insects*
> 1.   There was a little pond in the forest.
> 2.   There was a tall tree.
> 3.   The sky was blue.
> 4.   The blue sky fell down on the pond.

5.   The white cloud was floating.
6.   A little frog was singing by the pond.
7.   An insect was singing in the tree.
8.   A little frog was telling the insect the story of the pond.
9.   The insect was also telling the little frog the story of the forest.
10. The little frog and the insect were singing together in a friendly mood.
11. People were gathering in the forest.
12. They ate their lunch by the pond.
13. People sang songs and played hide and seek.
14. The little frog hid in the middle of the pond.
15. People threw rubbish here and there.
16. The forest became dirty and the water of the pond became polluted.
17. Now the sky does not fall down any more.
18. Odigatnunji [Where has the frog gone?].
19. The little frog does not answer even though the insect calls it many times.
20. Now the insect has no friends to play with. (pp. 78–81, my translation and my line numbers)

This story places a strong emphasis on green ideology. The surface agent of this story is people (in particular, children), and the object that they have destroyed is nature. What is silent here are the real agents of the destruction of the environment: the multinational companies, such as Samsung, Hyundai, and Daewoo. The story grammar of this passage reads as follows:

> A little frog and an insect (pro-ecology people) (protagonists) → A pond in the forest where the blue sky fell down and the white cloud was floating (setting) → A little frog and an insect made a good friendship (initial event) → People gathered by the pond (second event) → The pond became dirty and polluted and the friendship between the little frog and the insect was broken (consequences) → Pollution destroys insects and animals which live in harmony, and ultimately destroys humans (didactic lesson).

Through this narrative logic, the story depicts the negative aspects of industrialization by pointing to pollution as the cause of ecological destruction, such as was the case in the death of the frog and the pollution of the pond. But the agency behind the problem of pollution is shifted from industrialization to the citizen—in particular, to young children. According to Macdonald (1990), 75 percent of South Korean waste comes from industry. Industrialization, initiated by the South Korean government and multinational companies, has severely damaged the nature and environment of South Korea. However, while the story portrays young readers as agents of pollution (as they throw their rubbish into forests and lakes), it fails to portray multinationals as agents of pollution. The responsibility for pollution is placed on child consumers, not on multinationals and industry. The story also argues that pollution equals rubbish, thus establishing a particular designation of the cause of pollution. Yet even if individuals stop throwing away rubbish, industrial pollution will remain. The text appears to protect the interests of multinational companies and South Korean chaebols by avoiding reference to their responsibility for the pollution.

Lines eighteen to twenty imply that the children made the frog disappear. To where? The Korean expression "*odigatnunji*" in line eighteen, which means "Where has the frog gone?," and "does not answer" in line nineteen suggest that the frog was killed by the pollution. But the story expresses this in a euphemistic way, such as "hid" in line fourteen, "*odigatnunji*" in line eighteen, and "does not answer" in line nineteen.

In actuality, the "people" in the text are affected by the government's economic policies. Why did they gather in the forest? Why couldn't they play near their houses and go for a picnic in the park? As described in the industrial context at the onset of this chapter, most natural spaces in South Korea have been polluted and ruined. Therefore, the "people" have to go to the forest to have a picnic and enjoy nature. But the book only criticizes "people," and does not present the real cause of environmental problems.

What does the little frog symbolize? It could be nature or the environment, but ultimately, it symbolizes human beings. Contemporary environmental crises are universal problems caused by modernization. Beck (1992) points out that the ecological crisis is not "observable, local and personal," but rather, "unobservable, global and impersonal." In "The Songs of Insects," the frog disappears, thus depicting the demise of the environment and perhaps, ultimately, human life. However, this story attempts to place the blame for contemporary environmental crises on everyday people, such as picnickers. In so doing, "The Songs of Insects" absolves conglomerates from responsibility for the environmental crises, even though there is clear evidence pointing to their guilt. This evidence can be seen in phenomena like "the boomerang effect," which describes the process whereby pollution from South Korean companies established in China has blown back into South Korea by way of easterly winds.

In this way, "The Songs of Insects" operates through several similar ideological misrepresentations. The story places the entire responsibility and agency for an increasingly polluted environment upon everyday people and ignores the significant role of systemic, geopolitical, and corporate causality. At the same time, in an almost complementary move, the textbook portrays South Korea as a country that stresses and encourages a lifestyle based on leisure and consumption. This has been a key force in the overall economic formula of a globalized South Korea.

LEISURE AND CONSUMPTION

As the industrial economy shifts towards an increasingly service-based economy, and as a new middle class emerges, the direction of industry throughout much of the world has changed. Initially focused on mass production, industry has recently taken steps to develop major service, information, and tourism infrastructures for the purpose of supporting expanding consumption and leisure activities (Featherstone, 1990). Urban, postmodern South Korea has centered increasingly on cultures of consumption, leisure, and entertainment, and has been spurred on and encouraged by an expanding, powerful, and broadly accessible mass media. In many ways, the theme park is the contemporary expression of this move towards space par excellence. Disneyland-style theme parks are now spreading beyond Japan and South Korea to Hong Kong, China, and Southeast Asia.

The Korean textbook *National Language 2-1: Speaking and Listening* (Kyoyukbu, 1992), published for grade two, semester one, encourages students to discuss their summer holiday plans. The story "Summer Holiday Plans" provides stimuli for the students to contemplate, such as playing ball, snorkeling, and going to a theme park; these stimuli are depicted in the text using illustrations (pp. 92–93).

"Summer Holiday Plans" constructs a world of leisure by presenting simulated spaces and new geographies. The text includes one particular illustration in which a Ferris wheel and a roller coaster occupy part of a theme park (p. 93). In this illustration, children are riding on a dragon-like roller coaster with their mouths open wide and their hands in the air. A young boy is riding on a merry-go-round in the foreground, and a Ferris wheel is turning in the background. The textbook illustrations portray South Korean natural spaces as being replaced by and reorganized for simulated spaces of industrialization and urbanization. This can be contrasted with the rural and traditional landscapes portrayed in textbooks from earlier in the twentieth century (Lee, 2000).

South Korean parents and children often go on picnics to rural areas and by the ocean. *National Language 1-1: Reading* (Kyoyukbu, 1999), published for grade one, semester one, uses an illustration to present a family picnic in an idealistic and imaginary rural area (pp. 38–39). The characters are portrayed as middle-class, urban citizens, and are wearing urban, contemporary clothing. In rural areas, it is common to see farmers working on their farms. What we see here, however, is a definition of South Koreans as urban tourists, visiting a constructed version of the "rural."

By only depicting a cow and the surrounding farmland, the story excludes farmers from the rural place. In this regard, the position from which the story is told is urban-centric. This story constructs rural areas and recreational places from an urban citizen's point of view. Further, water as the illustrated is blue and clean, even though most water in South Korea is polluted, or in the process of becoming polluted.

National Language 1-1: Reading also pictorially portrays a girl's trip to the beach with her father (another type of leisure activity) in a story entitled "Following Father." The conceptual image of the sea is constructed by introducing cohesive lexicals such as the sea, the beach, seagulls, and a boat. It reads:

> *Following Father*
> 1. Eunju went to the sea with [Taraseo] her father.
> 2. She went to the sea by train.
> 3. There was a boat on the sea.
> 4. The sand was shining on the beach.
> 5. There was a cloud in the sky.
> 6. Seagulls were flying …
> 7. Eunju was returning home, following her father.
> 8. She was coming by bus.
> 9. She was talking about the sea with her mother.
> 10. She was talking about blue seas, white clouds, sandy beaches, and seagulls.
> 11. Eunju wants to go to the sea again. (pp. 64–67, my translation and my line numbers)

In this story, no people appear to be on the beach except Eunju and her father. In South Korea, beaches are polluted, but people still crowd around coastal areas, making it extremely difficult to find a beach populated by only two people. The beach in this story is very clean and quiet. In this sense, a romantic, pastoral version of South Korean nature has been presented; again, it is presented as an object of leisure for an urban middle class. The story also uses vocabulary to exaggerate the favorable qualities of the seashore, such as "shining" sand (line four), not "dirty" sand, and "blue seas" (line ten), not "polluted seas." In order to highlight an unpolluted nature, this story uses the repetition of vocabularies: "sea" and "beach" were used a total of eight times; "seagulls" and "sand" were used twice each. The story also contains a gendered meaning: Eunju and her father went to the sea without mother—the implication being that she stayed home because she was a housewife.

As leisure and sports have started to become a part of postmodern society, the perception of sports and exercise has also changed. South Korea has traditionally put less emphasis on physically strenuous sports and games (as compared to Western societies), and more emphasis on socializing for recreation and amusement (Macdonald, 1990). But nowadays, Koreans enjoy most sports, and are often encouraged to exercise weekend mornings. For example, a story "Sunday Morning," which is contained in *National Language 1-1: Reading*, normalizes sports/exercise activities as part of an emergent new urban lifestyle:

> *Sunday Morning*
> 1. Sunday morning, we go to the hill.
> 2. We go to the hill with our father.
> 3. One, two, three, four.
> 4. We exercise.
> 5. We exercise with our father.
> 6. Sunday afternoon, we play soccer.
> 7. We play soccer with our friend.
> 8. We play soccer enthusiastically.
> 9. Sunday evening, we study.
> 10. We study with our sister.
> 11. We study happily. (pp. 30–33, my translation and my line numbers)

Although this text encourages readers to exercise on hills, not many South Koreans have access to such places. This story establishes a mythical universe for student readers, wherein the students' preferential activities are based largely on the timing of their actions. On Sunday morning, they go to the hill and exercise. On Sunday afternoon, they play soccer, and on Sunday evening, they study (see table 7.1).

Physical exercise is stressed in lines one through eight of the story "Sunday Morning." Children go to the hill in the morning to exercise, and play soccer in the afternoon. Yet, the passage regards studying as the most important activity for students to take part in: lines nine through eleven depict children studying, even on Sunday. In order to instill in students favorable feelings regarding study, the book uses words like "happily" in line eleven to positively portray the activity. Education is regarded as an important key for social mobility in South Korea. Among the OECD countries,

TABLE 7.1   Participant roles

Participant (agent)	Process	Circumstances (with whom)	Circumstances (when)
We	Exercise	With our father	Sunday morning
We	Play soccer	With our friend	Sunday afternoon
We	Study	With our sister	Sunday evening

South Korea has the greatest percentage of expenditure on education (Kong, 2002). This text portrays its own use and uptake, focusing on and extolling the virtue of study and reading.

The story "Sunday Morning" uses the homogenizing pronoun "we" ten times, yet the term "we" is often gender exclusive, excluding female characters. For example, in one illustration there are four boys playing soccer, but no girls (p. 32). In other illustrations, only the father, not the mother, is in the mountains with the children (pp. 30–31). "Sunday Morning," like "Following Father," show how the textbooks are gender biased in the exclusion of female characters. This story uses much repetition: "we" was used ten times; "play soccer" and "we study" were used three times each; and "go to the hill" and "we exercise" were used twice each. The pronoun for participants is "we" and "our." In Korean, the generic pronoun "we" refers not only to the children in the narrative, but to the children who read the textbook as well. In this way, the story represents the ideal primary school child.

So far, I have mentioned the general picture of leisure and consumption in South Korea's booming capitalist society. The changing patterns of a culture based on leisure and consumption cannot be completely described without also describing the urban spaces in which most Koreans live.

In *National Language 1-1: Speaking and Listening* (Kyoyukbu, 1994), the story "My Daily Life" constructs postmodern spaces of South Korea (p. 60). The young protagonist in the story comes down with a cold on a Sunday morning. His mother takes him to the hospital, where he reluctantly receives an injection. An accompanying illustration shows the young protagonist in the background being dragged to the hospital by his mother (p. 60). Even though most urban Korean space is occupied by cars (which are parked everywhere), in this illustration there are only a few people and one dog standing in the street, and there are no vehicles to be seen. Furthermore, the same illustration shows three boys playing together in the foreground, while one girl is playing by herself on a swing. Another girl is exiting a nearby bookshop, also alone. In this way, the story suggests a gender separation related to this age group or social cohort.

An issue that is particularly important to most Koreans is that of political reunification. This salient issue is evident in the following story from *National Language 2-1: Reading* (Kyoyukbu, 1991), published for grade two, semester one.

A Story of Balloons
1. Two balloons are floating higher and flying farther. Mt. Kumgang [in North Korea] can be seen. It is very beautiful.
2. "I wish people could see Mt. Kumgang as freely as us," says the blue balloon.
3. "Yes, well, let's pray it will be done,"

4. The red balloon says to the blue balloon.
5. The red balloon and the blue balloon float higher. (pp. 118–119, my translation and my line numbers)

In this story, it can be conceived that "balloons" represent "people," even though the story clearly distinguishes "balloons" from "people." "People," in line two, symbolizes the citizens of South Korea. The story portrays South Korea's hope for reunification and free access to North Korea, and supports the South Korean government's proposal for a South Korea–centered reunification policy.

North Korea, however, proposes a different reunification policy. The textbook *Korean Beginning 1(b)* (Chongryun Sangimwiwonhoi Kyokwaseo Pyunchan Wiwonhoi, 2001), published by the General Federation of Korean Residents (GFKR), the North Korean–affiliated organization of Resident Koreans in Japan (see Inokuchi & Nozaki's chapter in this volume), includes the story "The Reunification Train Runs." (The textbooks used by GFKR schools have been supplied, or strongly influenced, by North Korea.) The story revolves around their political ideology.

The Reunification Train Runs
1. The reunification train runs.
2. Toot toot it runs.
3. All our friends are riding on it.
4. It runs to the South. (pp. 26–27, my translation and my line numbers)

In this story, the reunification train runs towards the South from the North. "All our friends" refers to all citizens of North Korea: they all run to the South for reunification. This obviously supports the North Korean government position. Interestingly, even though both North and South Korean textbooks raise the issue of reunification and support their own government ideology, they silence the cause of the separation, the barriers to reunification, and the way towards reunification from critical perspectives.

CONCLUSION

Contemporary Korean language and literacy textbooks, like all works in this genre, construct a particular version of the moral, social, economic, and cultural orders. I have shown how contemporary South Korean urban lifestyle is constructed. In this version of a contemporary, globalized, modernized South Korea, an ideological blend offering substantive lessons and role models for ecological consciousness, practices of leisure, and consumption can be seen. Underpinning this is a subtle set of metaphoric messages about the virtues of, and imperatives for, reunification. In achieving these particular representations, the selective traditions of these textbooks are replete with particular kinds of representations and omissions.

In "The Songs of Insects," the textbook portrays children, rather than multinationals, as the main agents responsible for destroying the environment. In "A Story of Balloons," the textbook supports the South Korean government position for a South Korean–centered reunification policy. Finally, in the North Korean textbook, "The Reunification Train Runs" supports a North Korean–centered reunification policy. The textbooks focus on urban, middle-class residents who picnic in rural areas, go on holiday trips, and go to the beach, but exclude rural residents or fishery workers. There is also a gender bias in the textbooks in representing who goes to the beach, exercises, and plays soccer. Additionally, despite urbanization and industrialization, textbooks present polluted areas as clean, natural places where citizens go on picnics—as if nature has been preserved.

There are many silences and absences in these narratives. South Korean literacy textbook narratives do not deal with the social realities of the new South Korea: the poor, rural people; the foreign workers; the crime; the social problems, such as housing; the unbalanced development of South Korea's rural and city areas; and the union movement and student unrest—even though all of these often appear in the mass media. The books also omit direct mention of foreign elements such as McDonald's, Pizza Hut, and Coca-Cola, which are commonly found in South Korean cities. At the same time, they tend to sanction and construct an idyllic, modern, middle-class lifestyle for South Korean children. In this regard, the work is representative of some of the unresolved push/pull dynamics around globalization.

In closing, I would like to make several suggestions for the improvement of textbooks. First, the children's genuine and diverse worlds must be integrated into school textbooks and classroom teaching. As this research shows, the children's world is, for the most part, described from dominant adult perspectives. The overall cultural representations, themes, and textual information do not sufficiently portray the children's worlds and interests. This encourages an uncritical acceptance of the adult, normative world, a shift that constitutes adult colonization via pedagogy (Baker & Freebody, 1989). Although the school curriculum and texts cannot be divorced entirely from the needs of society to educate its youth, they can include children's viewpoints and voices to explore issues surrounding school, families, and communities. Given such curriculum and texts, teachers could then go a step further to examine, from critical perspectives, the problems their students face in their daily lives.

Second, the worlds represented in textbooks are those of upper- and middle-class cultures, while representations of the lower-class are omitted. Upper-class children's improved opportunities for social mobility are, in fact, represented as "natural" and normatively preferred in early pedagogy, while the marginalized social classes are further disadvantaged (Whitty, 1985; Wilson, 1990). Such representations can alienate working-class students from schooling. Curriculum and texts, therefore, need to represent different social groups in term of their knowledges, worldviews, and language forms and contents. However, the mere inclusion of underrepresented knowledges may not serve equality and social justice in and through school knowledge. The texts should be written and read critically. It follows that we need to change both the educational content and teachers' pedagogical awareness/approaches simultaneously. For the latter purpose, critical discourse analysis of the sort I have employed to read the textbooks in this chapter can be a powerful tool for change, since it allows teachers to become aware of the power relations represented in textbooks and enables them to teach the texts critically.

REFERENCES

Baker, C. D., & Freebody, P. (1989). *Children's first school books: Introductions to the culture of literacy.* Oxford: Blackwell.

Beck, U. (1992). *Risk society.* London: Verso.

Chongryun Sangimwiwonhoi Kyokwaseo Pyunchan Wiwonhoi [North Korean Japanese Committee for Textbook Publishing] (2001). *Kugö Chogub 1(ha)* [Korean beginning 1(b)]. Tokyo: Hakwooseobang.

Fairclough, N. (1995). *Critical discourse analysis: The critical study of language.* London: Longman.

Featherstone, M. (Ed.). (1990). *Global culture.* London: Sage.

Hahm, C. B. (2002). Clash of civilizations or cultural convergence?: Lessons from Korean history. In Korea Foundation (Ed.), *Korea's interface with the world: Past, present and future* (pp. 354–365). Seoul: Ji Moon Dang.

Kong, J. S. (2002). Korea has the greatest percentage of expenditure on education. *Dongailbo.* Retrieved November 11, 2002, from http://www.donga.com/fbin/output?f=todaynews&code=b_&n=200211110234&main=1

Kyoyukbu [Ministry of Education]. (1991). *Kugö 2-1 Ilki* [National language 2-1: Reading]. Seoul: Daehan Printing & Publishing.

Kyoyukbu. (1992). *Kugö 2-1 Malhaki Dudki* [National language 2-1: Speaking and listening]. Seoul: Daehan Printing & Publishing.

Kyoyukbu. (1994). *Kugö 1-1 Malhaki Dudki* [National language 1-1: Speaking and listening]. Seoul: Daehan Printing & Publishing.

Kyoyukbu. (1999). *Kugö 1-1 Ilki* [National language 1-1: Reading]. Seoul: National Textbook Publishing.

Lee, D. B. (2000). *The ideological construction of culture in Korean language textbooks: A historical discourse analysis*. Unpublished doctoral dissertation, University of Queensland.

Luke, A. (1988). *Literacy, textbooks and ideology: Postwar literacy instruction and the mythology of Dick and Jane*. London: Falmer Press.

Macdonald, D. S. (1990). *The Koreans: Contemporary politics and society*. Oxford: Westview Press.

Samsung Economic Research Institute (2000). *1999 Hankuk Kyoungjeui Hoikowa Kwaje* [The 1999 Korean economy in retrospect and the way forward]. Seoul: Author.

Sardar, Z., & Van Loon, B. (1997). *Cultural studies for beginners*. Cambridge: Icon Book.

Whitty, G. (1985). *Sociology and school knowledge*. London: Methuen.

Wilson, B. (1990). Social outcomes, power and education. *Curriculum Perspectives, 10* (2), 1–9.

Chapter 8

Environmental Education and Development in China

Darren M. O'Hern

The developing world has placed an almost insurmountable amount of pressure on natural resources in the wake of modernization and industrialization. China, sometimes characterized as the largest developing nation in the world, exemplifies the environment versus development dichotomy. In response to the environmental degradation of rural and urban China, environmental education has officially been advocated, but remains underrepresented on practical levels (Stimpson, 1995, 2000; Lee & Tilbury, 1998). How can the seemingly different goals of, on the one hand, economic and social development, and on the other, environmental conservation and sustainable resource use, be reconciled? Where does environmental education fit into China's educational future? What characteristics of the Chinese educational system impede environmental education's full integration and understanding within the curriculum?

This chapter examines the state of environmental education in China and argues for a renewed focus on the environment through changes to the Chinese formal educational system. The first section will outline the environmental conditions that are contributing to a sense of urgency surrounding the issue of development and environmental degradation in China. The second section discusses the conflicting issues of economic and social development, and environmental preservation and sustainable resource use. The third section highlights the current state of environmental education in China and describes the systemic and philosophical impediments to environmental education's full integration within the formal educational system. Lastly, the educational system is evaluated as the best place for intervention in the establishment of an environmentally and ecologically conscious and participatory Chinese populace.

CHINA'S ENVIRONMENTAL DEGRADATION

China's natural resource base and ecosystem health has decreased at an alarming rate in recent years (Zhu et al., 2002; Schafer, 1999; Banister, 1998). This disturbing trend has been attributed to numerous factors, such as the growth of China's manufacturing industries, weak or outdated pollution controls, and increased resource consumption. In particular, the pressures of an increasing population and China's explosive urbanization over the last twenty to thirty years have exacerbated the problems.

Many of China's rural inhabitants practice subsistence agriculture and small-scale industrial production in areas that contain fragile ecosystems, especially in the central and western parts of the country. As the population grows in these regions, marginalized agricultural areas are claimed for residential purposes. The result is deforestation, soil erosion, water shortage, and an overall degradation of the overrun ecosystem (Stimpson, 2000).

China's urban population growth has also put pressure on rural agricultural districts. As urban populations increase due to natural population growth and the relocation of poor migrants in search of employment, urban resources have had to accommodate an increased demand for goods and services. Production in rural agricultural districts, where most of China's food supply is grown, has been unable to keep pace with the needs of expanding cities. The resulting demand has led to intensified agricultural production on land that is depleted of nutrients and expansion of farming into the margins of forests, grasslands, wetlands, and deserts (Banister, 1998). Thus, urbanization in the People's Republic of China has been accompanied by increased soil and water pollution and degradation of rural ecosystems.

The situation in the southern Chinese city of Guangzhou, the capital of Guangdong Province, is indicative of the current environmental crisis. Stimpson (2000, p. 64) outlines the detrimental effects of growth-related activities in this urbanized area:

> Industrialization has led to a problem in disposing of toxic waste from textile, plastic, and electronics industries in Guangzhou. ...
> Urban expansion has resulted in habitat loss and decreasing biodiversity generally in the region. ... Increased demand for food has led to increased use and risk from chemical fertilizers and pesticides in the countryside around Guangzhou. (p. 64)

Unfortunately, this predicament is typical for mid- to large-sized Chinese cities that are embracing the current trends of rapid industrialization and economic growth.

Air quality in urban and rural areas is also an issue which, until recently, has not received widespread attention from China's environmental policymakers. In urban areas, particulates released during the combustion of unwashed coal for industrial, municipal, and household energy needs have drastically lowered ambient air quality. Sulphur dioxide emissions in China's cities, especially in southern China where coal with high sulphur content is burned, rival the world's dirtiest metroplexes. Leaded petrol, industrial emissions, and coal combustion have also created a serious lead pollution problem in urban and suburban China (Banister, 1998).

In rural areas, the indoor burning of biofuels, such as coal, fuel wood, and compost for cooking and heating purposes, has contributed to high indoor air pollution levels. In the colder regions of China, inefficient stoves burn throughout the winter for warmth, thus increasing the indoor levels of fine particulates, gaseous hydrocarbons, and carbon monoxide. These heating and cooking methods contribute to a high incidence of respiratory illnesses and cancers in rural populations (Banister, 1998).

China's soil and freshwater supplies are being polluted due to intensifying agricultural production in rural districts and provinces, and industrialization and commercialization in urban areas. In recent decades, the reliance on agrochemicals for increasing agricultural output has led to the accumulation of heavy metals in many of China's rurally farmed soils. For example, the United Nations Food and Agriculture Organization estimates that China's use of inorganic fertilizer jumped nearly 100 times between 1949 and 1995, an increase of more than 2.5 times the world average. Such application of fertilizers can result in the accumulation of heavy metals in the soil and elevated uptake of heavy metals by crops, thus adversely affecting food quality and safety (Wong, Li, Zhang, Qi, & Min, 2002). The pace of China's industrial growth, especially since 1949, has led to inorganic pollution of lakes and rivers by the release of untreated industrial wastewater. Untreated sewage from sprawling urban neighborhoods has been dumped into rivers and lakes, poisoning ground- and surface-water supplies. In rural and underdeveloped areas, water and food contamination from bacteria, viruses, parasites, and other disease vectors are still commonplace.

Historically, many of the policy decisions that have been made by the Chinese government have contributed to the trend in environmental degradation. For example, during the Great Leap Forward (Chairman Mao Zedong's plan for economic and social development, which took place between 1958 and 1960), the energy needs for "backyard steel furnaces" resulted in increased deforestation and led to soil erosion and stream siltation. Additionally, the systematic expansion of agricultural crops, such as grains, into areas ill-suited for their production resulted in decreased soil fertility and increased land degradation (Banister, 1998). These policies, coupled with the agricultural invasion of forests, grasslands, and wetlands, led to widespread environmental damage and the deterioration of fragile ecosystems.

Today, China's rapid modernization, characterized by unbridled industrialization and urbanization, presents major difficulties for environmental conservation and protection efforts. Pollution from industry has become one of the most recognizable environmental issues in China, but it remains a secondary consideration behind questions of population growth, economic development, and natural resource consumption (Stimpson, 2000). China's environmental situation is compounded by its recent adherence to a development paradigm that calls for massive economic expansion, industrialization without environmental checks and balances, and rapid, not incremental, modernization. Given this predicament, critical questions arise in relation to China's push towards national economic and social development: Is the Chinese situation necessarily pitting environmental conservation and economic development directly against each other? Can China glean lessons from other countries in Southeast Asia that are experiencing similar difficulties in reconciling economic and social development with environmental well-being? To address such questions, which are directly related to China's current social and economic policies, it is helpful to examine recent tendencies in Chinese industrial advancement and the resulting environmental impacts.

Development and the Environment: Oil and Water?

At the advent of the twenty-first century, the gap between states that have industrialized/modernized and those that have not has become nearly unbridgeable and, in many cases, is glaringly obvious. Throughout the 1980s and 1990s, international development schemes adopted by macrolevel development policymakers, such as the International Monetary Fund (IMF) and World Bank, advocated the opening of markets and increased industrialization as effective strategies for modernizing underdeveloped areas across the globe. Accompanying these policies has been the export of manufacturing jobs to underdeveloped countries, where cheap labor costs and relaxed (or nonexistent) industrial controls attract multinational corporations from the postindustrialized world. When such development schemes are translated into practice on regional and local levels, natural resource consumption and degradation often accelerate, and may continue to increase without attracting proper amounts of governmental attention. Indeed, as "modern" economic policies have been adopted and promoted in developing countries across Asia, the balance between industrialization/economic growth, and natural resource usage/degradation has been underemphasized by governments.

During the past two decades, China has become an increasingly active (and more recently, dominant) player in the growth and integration of a universal world system: a process loosely termed "globalization." Participation in, or exclusion from, the process of globalization can vary on local, regional, and national scales, and may occur within one or more of Marginson's (1999) six aspects of globalization: finance and trade; communications and information technologies; international movements of peoples; the formation of global societies; linguistic, cultural, and ideological convergence; and world systems of signs and images. The effects of globalization have become manifest in numerous ways within Chinese society, from cultural and social exchange through the growth of communication technologies, to ideological and political upheaval in the wake of increased materialism and consumerism. However, China's participation in the globalization process has been largely concerned with the intensification of economic exchange in regional and global financial markets and trade relations.

China has witnessed unprecedented industrialization, economic growth, and modernization since the mid 1980s. Industrial output grew more than 12 percent each year between the early 1980s and the late 1990s, with rapid growth rates and substantial investment in large manufacturing firms by foreign sources. By 2001, eleven Chinese firms had been included in the international Fortune 500 listing (Nolan, 2002). State policy also contributed to economic diversification and increased labor productivity during the mid 1990s. In 1992, Deng Xiaoping promoted the adoption of all economic mechanisms that could prove useful in bolstering China's economic strength, regardless of whether a specific mechanism was originally used in a capitalist or socialist system (Liu, Liu, Wang, & Woo, 2001). Yet, as this economic advancement increases in intensity and breadth, environmental considerations have been neglected.

At various intervals throughout China's economic boom, legislation aimed at protecting natural resources and curbing environmental degradation has received popular attention; such legislation "officially" called for the protection of the environment. Nevertheless, many state-sponsored policies and initiatives have lacked practical implementation strategies and full governmental backing. For example, the discharge of municipal wastewater more than doubled between 1981 and 1995, but only 7 percent is treated despite the adoption and promotion of guidelines governing the release of industrial wastewater (Banister, 1998). As this example suggests, China faces a dilemma that seemingly pits economic development and modernization against sustainable resource use and environmental conservation. This dilemma can be summarized as a struggle between entrepreneurship/ consumerism and traditional/modern values that encourage environmental sustainability (Stimpson, 2000).

The tension between economic goals and environmental sustainability is also evident in the struggle over the Yangtze River (Three Gorges) Dam project. Government officials argue that the high-profile dam project, which began in 1994, will bring electricity to rural areas, increased trade opportunities, and a higher quality of life despite the environmental and social impacts, which include the displacement of over one million residents and massive environmental damage from the 420-square-mile (1,100-square-kilometer) reservoir (Ash, 1998). In this case, the cost of modernization and increased productivity will be gross environmental degradation and the "purging" of traditional cultures and livelihoods (Chafy, 1997).

China's balancing act is complicated by its socialist political orientation. Hannum (1999) argues that conflict between the political agenda to reduce class inequalities and the need for economic development poses a serious threat to China's internal stability. This problem is complicated by competition for resources between policies designed to promote economic development and policies intended to expand social opportunities to traditionally disadvantaged groups. In this new era of globalization and economic advancement, national and local leaders must delicately balance the needs of all citizens with the economic and environmental realities facing the country today. Whether or not this balance can be achieved remains open for debate, but China might want to look to its regional neighbors for innovative strategies and policies to help cope with the perceived development-environment tension.

The struggle between the goals of economic development, industrialization, and modernization and the goals of environmental conservation and sustainable resource use has played out in various ways within the Asia-Pacific region over the last two decades. During this period, certain state and nongovernmental organization (NGO)–sponsored efforts have addressed this growing tension. In the early and mid 1990s, Thailand developed and implemented technological programs aimed at developing the nation's renewable energy capabilities, including solar and biomass resources (Sabhasri and Wibulswas, 1992). Broader initiatives, such as the Science Across Asia-Pacific Project, introduced participants to environmental and sustainability issues and sought to raise student awareness of societal interactions by providing opportunities for collaboration between schools and institutions from different countries within the Asia-Pacific region (Southeast Asian Ministers of Education Organization, 1993). Countless other efforts, from grassroots campaigns to national policy mandates, have targeted the ecological ramifications of the region's explosive economic growth. Yet, modernization and industrial considerations have consistently been favored over environmental concerns.

When faced with such daunting situations (internal and external pressures to modernize and compete for regional and global economic superiority; ecological devastation; depletion of natural resources), what can China's political and civic leaders do to ensure the continued growth of

China as a nation without jeopardizing its ecological future? What role, if any, can environmental education play in the conservation and protection of China's natural resources in light of new movements in industrial modernization and economic development? Answers to these difficult and challenging questions may begin to emerge after examining the content and structure of Chinese education and the history of environmental education in China.

Environmental Education in China

China has a rich history of officially promoting environmental protection through educational means. Lee and Tilbury (1998) separate China's developments in environmental education at the policy level into three major phases: an "expert" phase (1973–1982), a "red" phase (1983–1992), and a "sustainability" phase (1993–present). According to these researchers, the "expert" phase was characterized by an assumption that knowledge was paramount in the protection of the environment, and by increasing both public awareness of environmental issues and the distribution of trained professionals in the field, environmental degradation would be halted. During this phase, a science-based, rather than education-based, approach was used for the dissemination of environmental knowledge by technically trained specialists. Teachers were also encouraged to integrate environmental education into daily lessons as a separate and distinct academic subject.

The "red" phase of environmental education development was characterized by a shift in focus from technical expertise and mastery to more social approaches to protecting the environment. Throughout the 1980s—the height of the "red" phase—education concerning the environment and protection of China's natural resources was not viewed as an ethical endeavor, as it may have been in the previous phase, but as a patriotic act and national duty. Government restructuring brought environmental education under the control of the newly formed National Environmental Protection Bureau, which eventually discontinued environmental education's autonomy as an independent subject.

Since the mid 1990s, the "sustainability" phase has been characterized by recognition of the concept and goals of environmental sustainability. The term "sustainability," once unheard of in state discourse on development and the environment, began to appear in official papers and policy documents on environmental education after the 1992 Earth Summit in Rio de Janeiro, Brazil. Since then, increased emphasis on the social environment has helped to redefine environmental education as a discipline that can increase student awareness of the ethical considerations of environmental protection and development.

In the last decade, Chinese governmental policy has, on the surface, reflected a renewed interest in, and dedication to, environmental protection and the advancement of environmental education. In 1992, a revised primary school curriculum was established to facilitate the teaching of environmental science within subjects such as biology, geography, and chemistry. Through this new curriculum, China's State Education Commission has advocated an interdisciplinary focus on education and emphasized the importance of extracurricular activities for increasing student understanding of the environment (Kwan & Lidstone, 1997). Education guidelines, such as *Geography Teaching Outline for Full-time Senior Middle Schools*, released in 1996, encourage active teaching and learning exercises, such as fieldwork and hands-on activities, for dealing with environmental issues and lessons (Lee & Tilbury, 1998). Additionally, the government has allowed foreign teachers and "prepackaged" environmental education programs to enter Chinese classrooms in an attempt to use Western-style teaching methods to increase the spectrum of natural science education taught in schools (Berkovits, 1997).

The amount and purpose of natural science education in Chinese schools varies depending on the grade level involved. In primary schools, educational content that includes environmental principles is intended to promote the development of students' observational skills. At the secondary level, environmental concepts are referenced in biological and geographical studies and are used to enhance critical research and problem-solving skills. In the upper levels of secondary education, environmental science may be formally addressed as a periphery discipline. According to Jiang Xiang of Beijing Normal University's Environmental Science Institute, it is at these levels that students should "cultivate the correct environmental moral and value concepts, grasp the requisite skills of environment, and actively participate in activities in environmental protection" (Kwan & Lidstone, 1997, p. 130).

Although the educational goals of encouraging environmental empowerment and inspiring local and national environmental activism are optimistic, students are unlikely to receive adequate exposure to the environmental content needed to attain such lofty results, mainly because environmental education remains marginalized as a "legitimate," systemwide discipline. Overall, academic subjects that deal with ecological and natural resource–based themes, such as environmental education, remain broadly underrepresented in the formal curriculum and are unlikely to be assimilated within the Chinese educational system for several reasons.

First, the absence of constructive attitudes among educational administrators, teachers, and the general populace has hampered the school- and community-based support that a "periphery" subject such as environmental education needs for successful inclusion into the Chinese educational system. In schools, administrators and teachers generally view environmental education as a short-term subject and show little understanding of its value or importance. One teacher in Hangzhou City indicated that it was "not worth" concentrating on courses that were not included on national examinations, such as environmental education (Zhu, 1995). In nonformal settings, environmental education activities occur sporadically and are often deemphasized by students who give higher priority to subjects in the formal curriculum (Lee & Tilbury, 1998). Furthermore, parents are more concerned with their family's economic security and their children's academic achievements than they are with more intangible issues such as environmental health and ecological sustainability (Stimpson, 2000).

Second, organizational barriers within the formal educational system prevent environmental education from being fully recognized as, and integrated into, a mainstream academic subject. China's formal curriculum is highly centralized and its content is determined solely by the State Education Commission. Such a "top-down" approach to curriculum development and dissemination leads to a highly uniform national syllabus which permits little local and school-based selection of content (Lee & Tilbury, 1998). In such a rigidly controlled educational system, teachers and community members who advocate environmental education are faced with pressures from external sources (the State Education Commission) and internal sources (headmasters and other teachers) to conform to the "standard" curriculum.

Another characteristic of the Chinese educational system that impedes the inclusion of environmental education is the reliance on nationally mandated examinations as the driving force behind all teaching and learning. High-stakes exams, which are given yearly, determine whether or not students will advance a grade level, and are used as the major indicator of a student's potential for advanced study. Societal rewards for examination success, in the form of better-paying government jobs and higher social status, reinforce student perception about the importance of exam preparation (Zhu, 1995). In a system entrenched in the accumulation of credentials and paper results (what Dore [1976] referred to as "The Diploma Disease"), the integration of subjects that are not represented in the formal curriculum or on governmentally designed examinations (such as environmental education) may be viewed as counterproductive for student preparation and classroom instruction.

Additionally, the integration of environmental concepts and problem-solving skills into standard subjects is rarely attainable due to a lack of adequate teaching materials and resources. Lee and Tilbury (1998) indicate that senior middle school geography textbooks neglect the role of individuals in environmental conservation and decision making, and fail to support social participation in environmental improvement. Additionally, they point to the lack of local references in teaching materials as an obstacle to reducing the abstract nature of the environment and promoting personal change.

Finally, teachers in China are ill-prepared, in terms of both usage of appropriate instructional methodologies and mastery of environmental subject materials, to independently bolster environmental education in school settings. Several researchers (Stevenson, 1987; Corral-Verdugo, Frias-Armenta, & Corral-Verdugo, 1996; Russell, 1999) have argued that approaches to environmental education that encourage students' critical thinking and problem-solving skills are more effective in promoting an environmentally responsible agenda than instructional styles that rely on the direct transmission of fragmented knowledge to students. In Chinese classrooms, teachers are reluctant to incorporate environmental issues into an already overloaded syllabus and are primarily concerned with student performance on examinations and coverage of the prescribed curriculum. To accomplish these goals, instructional methods revolve around the "teacher as giver of knowledge" paradigm and play down student-centered activities and interactions (Berkovits, 1997). Conversely, the objectives of environmental education, as outlined by Stevenson (1987, p. 73), include:

> … the intellectual tasks of critical appraisal of environmental (and political) situations and the formulation of a moral code concerning such issues, as well as the development of a commitment to act on one's values by providing opportunities to participate actively in environmental improvement.

Thus, environmental education involves student introspection and individual determination of proper responses to environmental issues or crises—tasks that are not easily accomplished in an educational setting where limited environmental knowledge is handed down through a rigid and highly formalized curriculum. In addition, teacher education programs often incorporate a reductionist and instrumentalist approach to building skills and fail to include sufficient training in environmental education or ecological concepts and principles (Stimpson, 2000). Overall, Chinese educators seem more concerned with the transmission of exam content and the reinforcement of student passivity than they do with developing students' critical understandings of natural, social, and cultural environments through the use of "transformative" approaches to education.

Today, the environmental education movement in China faces a daunting challenge. Organizational impediments within the educational system and conflicting attitudes towards the role and purpose of environmental education serve as major obstacles to its integration into the formal and nonformal educational sectors. Furthermore, current policies and practices reinforce educational priorities that could marginalize subjects emphasizing social development and civic participation, such as environmental education. As China continues to develop economically and blossom as an industrial giant, its educational system not only trains Chinese students to compete in the global marketplace, but could function as a key "entry point" for confronting and reducing the tensions between "production and pollution."

THE ROLE OF EDUCATION

Can Chinese education rise to the challenge of not only raising the ecological literacy of its citizens but encouraging the development of contextually specific strategies for sustainable, environmentally friendly economic growth and modernization? Is it possible, given the systemic and ideological constraints mentioned above, for China's formal educational system to be amended to not only include, but embrace environmental education and activism? These challenging questions cannot be answered easily, and proper consideration of their implications would entail a thorough reexamination of the role and purpose of education in Chinese society today.

The structural and curricular characteristics of China's contemporary state educational system were heavily influenced by Deng Xiaoping's social and economic restructuring policies, which took place during his tenure as the de facto leader of China from 1976 until his death in 1997. When Deng implemented the "four modernizations" (defense, agriculture, industry, and science), state development polices began to heavily favor economic growth and modernization through the acquisition of foreign technologies. These guidelines helped to shape the goals and purpose of Chinese education and continue to influence educational policy today.

The current educational situation in China, where the goals and priorities of the formal system of schooling reflect those of the greater society, is not a unique one. Educational sociologists have debated the role of schooling in society for decades, and maintain that the contemporary purpose of education is to transmit cultural knowledge, skills, and values to students (Stevenson, 1987). Through this process of transmission, a select group of individuals is granted the opportunity to develop the curriculum and standards by which the formal educational system is governed, thus reinforcing an insular set of beliefs and values. In China, this process translates into a managerial view of education and a curriculum that underscores technological and economic superiority through teacher-centered learning and instruction. Indeed, it currently appears that the main purpose of education in China is to provide the state with individuals who are prepared to enhance China's economic, technological, and industrial progress. This is evident in the high value attached to proficiency in the "hard sciences" (such as chemistry and physics), the use of high-stakes national examinations as the primary determinant for upward mobility and economic success, and the spread of vocational and technical schools.

At present, on both regional and global scales, China's drive towards technological advancement and economic prominence consumes state social politics and planning. In an atmosphere where "modernization" is paramount, how can China's growing environmental crisis be addressed in a manner that alleviates the perceived "development versus environment" tension? In his discussion of the "culture of progress," Chafy (1997) argues that Western notions of progress are embedded in the models of development that currently influence macro-level policies in many developing nations, including China. He further recognizes the need for unconventional models of development that strive for social and environmental sustainability and challenge "deep-seated" ideologies about progress and modernization.

The strategies that are currently used to evaluate China's economic and social progression employ such Western-influenced paradigms and depict development as a linear process. In order to confront this culture of Western-defined progress, new roles will need to be conceptualized for established state institutions. Chafy envisions education as representing a key entry point for restructuring and reshaping the ideological beliefs that, when translated into practice, contribute to the environmental dilemma China is currently facing. However, for Chinese education to be utilized as an agent of change, the formal curriculum content must become realigned with the concepts of sustainable consumption, ecological connectivity, and environmental preservation.

These ideological changes in education will prove difficult for China, just as they have for many other state education systems in both the developed and developing world. Since the advent of instrumental views of education, Western educational systems have reinforced functional and informational learning oriented towards socialization and the attainment of vocational goals that disregard the challenge of sustainability. If education is to be embraced for the purpose of creating an ecologically literate population and a sustainable future, the dominant educational paradigm must be altered to incorporate the goal of "transformative" learning (Sterling, 2001). In this regard, the educational systems of industrialized countries are no more advanced than those of developing countries.

As China has adopted and instated a more Western approach to education, the educational status quo has not recognized the difficulties involved in reconciling the ideological and philosophical paradoxes that exist within the Chinese system. Instead, educational policymaker rhetoric continues to tout the importance of environmental education to the future of China. Educational ministers and curriculum designers have consistently recognized the need for effective environmental planning to coincide with the greater goals of Chinese development, but they are reluctant to make changes to the established curriculum that would effectively raise environmental consciousness and activism in students. Environmental education is seen merely as a tool for information diffusion and the explanation for government initiatives. As Stimpson (2000) has pointed out, the official perspective on environmental education, which is lacking in critical dimension and overreliant on technocratic solutions to environmental problems, "is predominantly *about* the environment rather than *in* and *for* the environment in any meaningful way" (his emphasis, p. 72).

If amendments to the formal curriculum are to take place, changes will not only need to address the goals and uses of environmental education in light of rapid environmental degradation, but must also acknowledge the inconsistencies between rural and urban areas within the educational system itself. In the late 1980s and early 1990s, educational policy statements recognized the rural-urban disparities in economic development and proposed educational initiatives that aimed to universalize compulsory education across China. However, such political statements failed to bring about substantive reforms of urban- and suburban-centered curriculum. During this period, the rural curriculum focused on offering suitable training for students who would not further their education upon graduation from primary, middle, and high schools. This policy reflected a declining level of priority being placed on urban-rural educational equity, and fostered the vocational and technical orientation of rural schools (Hannum, 1999). Hence, children from rural families were restricted in their educational opportunities, which, in turn, hindered their potential for upward social mobility.

Despite the difficulty the Chinese educational system has had in reconciling these systemic and content-based issues, recent educational policies and programs have made moderate advances in the inclusion and acceptance of environmental education content. Extracurricular school activities, also known as the "second classroom," have shown promise for promoting environmental education and community-oriented environmental programs by increasing student and parental participation in environmental workshops and exhibits. In fact, many schools, acknowledging the importance of local environmental issues, have developed a "social environmental education" approach through extracurricular activities such as beautifying school premises, local tree planting, and informal workshops on forestry and pollution (Lee & Tilbury, 1998). Additionally, NGO-sponsored programs, such as the Environmental Educators' Initiative for China, have addressed issues such as teacher training in environmental education and instruction of environmental content in school and community settings (Shi, Hutchinson, & Yu, 2000). However, as promising as these programs appear to be, the formal educational system continues to impede school- and community-based environmental education efforts as policymakers struggle with the emphasis of environmental issues within the context of modern Chinese education.

Concluding Thoughts

If education that is both pro-environment and pro-sustainable development is to thrive in an educational context that focuses its attention primarily on student enrollment and exam performance, rather than the social development and civic participation of its students, widespread philosophical, curricular, structural, and practical amendments to China's formal education system must be explored. First, instructional philosophies and methods that engage students' critical thinking and evaluative skills must replace the traditional teacher-centered and textbook-based methodologies. Teacher education programs often create educational climates that are inhospitable for the development of skills and attitudes needed by future environmental educators. Teachers emerge from such programs using direct inculcation as the standard method for transmitting environmental values and "facts" to students (Stimpson, 2000). Changes to these long-held instructional paradigms would enable teachers and students to critically examine contemporary relationships between rural and urban populations, the environments in which they live and work, and how China's economic development impacts these spaces.

Second, China's educational content should be amended to fully include environmental education as a legitimate, interdisciplinary content area. Indeed, Zhu Huaixin's (1995) recommendations echo the need for such widespread and comprehensive action:

> from now on, Chinese primary and secondary education should … try to infuse environmental education into the moral, intellectual, physical, and aesthetic education, in order to offer society qualified people with environmental understanding and awareness. (p. 107)

These changes in the content of Chinese education would need to coincide with structural reformations to the formal system itself. For example, centrally constructed, nationally administered high-stakes examinations should be deemphasized as the primary determinant of student capability, and replaced with assessment strategies that incorporate more comprehensive and contextually influenced variables of student potential and achievement.

Lastly, China's educational policymakers must hasten and expand upon the few "successful" environmental education initiatives that have been promoted through nonformal school- and community-based programs and NGOs. However, systematic evaluation and expansion of such sporadic projects may not be enough to allow China to begin reconciling its predicaments of declining environmental health and an environmentally ambivalent populace. As the notion of "shared environmental responsibility" has spread through regional discourses on economic, social, and political development, China must look to the numerous cross-national initiatives that address the Asia-Pacific's common environmental problems, lack of adequate environmental instruction, and general ambivalence towards the issues of development and sustainability. By tapping such efforts for strategies and expertise, Chinese policymakers and educators may begin to develop environmental education efforts that thrive across the vast nation and challenge conventional treatments of environmental issues at state, regional, and local levels.

There is an unquestionable need for a renewed focus on environmental education in China. However, the future of environmental education is uncertain. China's educational leaders must not only establish sound means for the formal integration and nonformal expansion of environmental education, but must also address the delicate balance between economic development, social development, and the environment. China's immediate future is critical, for, if educational content and practice are not amended to promote environmental conservation and protection, the inhabitants of China's rural agricultural provinces and sprawling metropolitan areas will soon find their natural resources and ecological systems devastated.

NOTES

I would like to extend thanks to Robert Stevenson and Greg Dimitriadis, University at Buffalo, for their guidance and time; to Yu Wang and Shengjun Yuan for their helpful comments; and to my wife, Jessica, for all of her encouragement.

REFERENCES

Ash, J. (1998). Damming the Yangtze. *Forum for Applied Research and Public Policy, 13* (3), 78–84.

Banister, J. (1998). Population, public health and the environment in China. *China Quarterly, 156,* 986–1015.

Berkovits, A. (1997). China's revolution in education: A bold attempt to tame the environmental dragon. *Wildlife Conservation, 100* (1), 44–50.

Chafy, R. (1997). Confronting the culture of progress in the twenty-first century. *Futures, 29* (7), 633–648.

Corral-Verdugo, V., Frias-Armenta, M., & Corral-Verdugo, B. (1996). Predictors of environmental critical thinking: A study of Mexican children. *The Journal of Environmental Education, 27* (4), 23–27.

Dore, R. (1976). *The diploma disease: Education, qualification and development.* Berkeley, CA: University of California Press.

Hannum, E. (1999). Political change and the urban-rural gap in basic education in China, 1949–1990. *Comparative Education Review, 43* (2), 193–207.

Kwan, T., & Lidstone, J. (1997). Environmental education in China: National policy interpreted on local level. *Forum for Applied Research and Public Policy, 12* (4), 129–132.

Lee, J., & Tilbury, D. (1998). Changing environments: The challenge for environmental education in China. *Geography, 83* (3), 227–236.

Liu, G., Liu, X., Wang, L., & Woo, W. (2001). China's new horizon: Challenges and opportunities for WTO membership. *China Economic Review, 12* (2–3), 103–106.

Marginson, S. (1999). After globalization: Emerging politics of education. *Journal of Education Policy, 14* (1), 19–31.

Nolan, P. (2002). China and the global business revolution. *Cambridge Journal of Economics*, 26, 119–137.

Russell, C. (1999). The three T's: Approaches to environmental learning. *Pathways: The Ontario Journal of Outdoor Education, 12* (2), 4–6.

Sabhasri, S., & Wibulswas, P. (1992). Thai energy sources and related environmental issues. *Energy Policy, 20* (6), 522–527.

Schafer, H. J. (1999). Development policy cooperation with China in the environmental sector: Principles and focal areas. *International Journal of Environment and Pollution, 12* (1), 34–42.

Shi, C., Hutchinson, S. M., & Yu, L. (2000). Moving beyond environmental knowledge delivery: Environmental Educators' Initiative for China. *Environmental Education and Information, 19* (3), 205–214.

Southeast Asian Ministers of Education Organization. (1993). *Science across Asia-Pacific.* Poole, England: BP Educational Service.

Sterling, S. (2001). *Sustainable education: Re-visioning learning and change.* Devon, England: Green Books.

Stevenson, R. (1987). Schooling and environmental education: Contradictions in purpose and practice. In I. Robottom (Ed.), *Environmental education: Practice and possibility* (pp. 69–82). Geelong, Victoria: Deakin University Press.

Stimpson, P. (1995). Environmental education in China: The context. *International Research in Geographical and Environmental Education, 4* (1), 85–89.

Stimpson, P. (2000). Environmental attitudes and education in southern China. In D. Yencken, J. Fien, & H. Sykes (Eds.), *Environment, education and society in the Asia-Pacific: Local traditions and global discourses.* New York: Routledge.

Wong, S. C., Li, X. D., Zhang, G., Qi, S. H., & Min, Y. S. (2002). Heavy metals in agricultural soils of the Pearl River Delta, South China. *Environmental Pollution, 119* (1), 33–44.

Zhu, H. (1995). Education and examinations—a major constraint hindering environmental education in the People's Republic of China. *International Research in Geographical and Environmental Education, 4* (2), 106–107.

Zhu, Z., Deng, Q., Zhou, H., Ouyang, T., Kuang, Y., Huang, N., & Qiao, Y. (2002). Water pollution and degradation in the Pearl River Delta, South China. *Ambio, 31* (3), 226–231.

Chapter 9

School Knowledge and Classed and Gendered Subjectivities in South Korean Commercial High Schools

Misook Kim

INTRODUCTION

As in most countries, vocational high school students in South Korea are unjustly marginalized, and represented in contradictory terms. On one hand, dominant discourse maintains that vocational high school students should be proud of themselves: proud to be unskilled or semiskilled workers, and proud of their contribution to national economic development. On the other hand, once the discourse moves away from national economic issues, vocational school students, as compared to academically successful college-track students, are more likely to be represented as "dull," "not college material," "troublemakers," "uncultured," and "quick at figures" (implying burned out).

Given such contradictory representations, how do vocational schools function in forming their students' subjectivities and their responses to such subjectivities? As Apple (1979) cogently points out, schools not only process people, but knowledge as well. Schools differentially give legitimacy to various types of cultural resources, and differentially qualify people to access more legitimate knowledge and positions of power by using their own criteria and ritual. These school practices are closely related to existing asymmetrical social relations. In this chapter, I will analyze how schools regulate students and school knowledge, and how students produce meanings about school knowledge and their sense of self in relation to schooling. Data in this chapter were collected in ethnographic research on two commercial high schools in South Korea.

THEORETICAL FRAMEWORK

According to Althusser (1971), the subject and its imaginary relationships are constituted through an ideological mechanism of interpellation. Althusser implies that interpellation is not a univocal process, yet he does not elaborate upon it. In this regard, Therborn's (1980) conception of the contradictory nature of the interpellation process is useful. According to Therborn, ideologies subject individuals to a particular social order that "allows or favours certain drives and capacities, and prohibits or disfavours others" (1980, p. 17). Through the same process, subjects retain capacities to qualify such ideologies by specifying them and modifying their range of application. Therborn makes another important point: To reproduce a certain social organization, there is a basic correspondence between subjection and qualification, and there is "always an inherent possibility" of a contradiction between the two (p. 17).

Therborn's insightful conception allows room for the possibility of human agency and for the more contradictory and complex nature of subjectivity. However, he does not provide a sophisticated mechanism whereby subjects qualify, challenge, and transform the ideologies responsible for their constitution in specific historical conditions. Here, we need to look at the positions of poststructuralists, since they suggest more sophisticated views about how meaning systems construct and reconstruct various positions of subject. Poststructuralists conceive ideology (signification) as a matter of arbitrary meaning fixing based on discursive power. In discursive fields, meanings are fixed temporally and always locally contested due to the inherently unstable effects of language and unconscious desire (Weedon, 1987).

Regarding subject construction, they argue that a certain subject is qualified through differentiation and exclusion, which creates de-authorized "others" and distinguishes the subject from its constitutive outside. For, meaning is made through overt or covert contrast, whereby a positive definition depends on the negation or repression of something represented as antithetical. The oppositions become hierarchical, where one term is dominant and the opposite term is subordinate. Fixing the process of oppositions conceals the fact that things presented as oppositional are interdependent, rather than derived from inherent antithesis. In this way, the meaning of social difference is culturally represented and these representations organize asymmetrical social relationships in a particular way (Scott, 1986; Butler, 1992).

From a poststructuralist viewpoint, challenges to relations of power can arise from the very subject position such relationships make available, and from the very particular technical forms of power. In this contestation, the subjects' local, disqualified, and disorganized knowledge, emotions, and experiences become a central source of resistance against domination (Henliques et al., 1984; Knights & Vurdubakis, 1994).

SETTING: TWO PRIVATE COMMERCIAL HIGH SCHOOLS IN SOUTH KOREA

The educational system in South Korea is a six-three-three-four system: six-year elementary schools, three-year middle schools, three-year high schools, and four-year colleges and universities. Due to difficulty in collecting students, the Ministry of Education let vocational high schools select their students before academic high schools; their selections were based on middle school grades. However, the number of vocational high school students has decreased, as most students want to go to academic high school and then college.

The data used in this chapter are based on an ethnographic study of two private commercial high schools in South Korea: a mixed-gender commercial high school and an all-girls commercial high school. Both schools are located in a small city in midwestern South Korea. The great majority of students from both schools came from lower-class families; their parents being poor farmers (42.1 percent at the mixed school, 46.2 percent at the all-girls school), manual workers (20.0 percent and 21.2 percent respectively), individual service workers (14.7 percent and 10.6 percent), low-status clerical workers (11.6 percent and 6.7 percent), and small-shop owners (10.6 percent and 12.5 percent). In both schools, there were no students in my research classes whose parents had professional jobs, such as doctor, lawyer, businessman, or professor. I observed two sophomore classes at the mixed school (one male and one female class) during the second semester of 1991, and two senior classes at each school for the entire 1992 academic year. In order to collect data, I employed observation, semi-structured and open interviews, and document analysis.

BECOMING COMMERCIAL HIGH SCHOOL STUDENTS

Commercial high school students and teachers divided formal school knowledge into two groups: "commercial" (major) and "general" (humanities) subjects. Commercial subjects included commercial practice, commercial calculation, general business, marketing, business law, accounting, trade, typing, bookkeeping, and computers. General subjects consisted of ethics, literature, history, social studies, mathematics, science, music, home economics, Korean, Chinese characters, Japanese, and English.[1]

Students tended to regard commercial subjects as "important," and general subjects, minus English, as "less important." The students' general perception that commercial subjects were more important was grounded on two main elements: the dominant representation of the commercial high school, and the practical needs of the students (employment).

The importance of commercial subjects was taken for granted because (in the words of the students) "we attend a commercial high school," or "we are commercial high school students," or "we are going to be clerical workers." Preconstituted meanings (what commercial high schools are, and what social positions commercial high school students are qualified for) often become the inferential bases that lead the students to identify with the pre-constituted relation (Butler, 1992).

While the institutionalized definition of a commercial high school student managed to construct the students' identities, even before students attended a single class the schools strongly acted in maintaining this dominant representation. The schools did this by their inner mechanisms, such as organizing curriculum, instituting rewards and punishment, and regulating meanings in everyday school lives. For instance, students were forced by their formal curriculum to spend twice as much time on commercial subjects as on general subjects because commercial subjects were given more weight in evaluation. During the morning and evening meetings, homeroom teachers often advised students to attain formal qualifications as soon as possible by working hard on commercial subjects throughout their high school years, especially during the first and second years.

Another reason that students perceived commercial subjects as more important was because they were closely related to the students' practical needs. To be recommended for a good job, the students had to have good grades on their written examinations. Because school recommendations for employment were given based on grade point averages,[2] and because commercial subjects were more heavily weighted in grading, students felt a need to work harder on commercial subjects.

Two kinds of examinations taken in both schools became crucial in hierarchically defining students and qualifying them for recommendations. There were regular examinations set up by the teachers, and mock examinations set up by other institutions. The examinations set up by other institutions were called "mock" because they simulated real employment examinations given by companies and public workplaces; school authorities regarded these exams as "more objective." Both examinations were taken twice a semester and included commercial subjects, English, and common sense. The students did not put much weight on common sense because it required minimal effort. Thus, in terms of trying to achieve good grades, commercial subjects and English were strategically more important for the students to concentrate on. The written employment examination in English was a particularly critical test to get high grades on because most commercial school students regarded English as either the most difficult subject or an abandoned subject.

In the mixed-gender and all-girls schools, as in most schools, meritocracy based on written examinations was used as a central technique for regulating students and establishing school authority. Students in both schools were differentially qualified for employment recommendations based on their school grades. The schools classified, qualified, and punished students by their own developed ritual, namely, examinations (Foucault, 1979).

Technical Qualification and Its Meaning Regulation

The mechanism of objectification, in which students are presented as quantified objects, was reinforced by another requirement of companies: technical qualifications. Of the commercial subjects, abacus calculation, bookkeeping, and typing were seen as the most essential because a certain level of formal qualifications in these areas was necessary for all who wanted to apply for clerical work.

As in many countries, typing qualifications in South Korea were gender specific. Though both the girls and the boys were required to take a typing class by the Ministry of Education, since most companies did not require men's typing skills, the boys did not take the typing class or skills seriously. They just took the typing class once a week to complete the formal requirement for graduation and have the basic skills needed for any office job.

Not surprisingly, the boys' typing qualifications were far inferior to those of the girls. In the mixed school, only one-fourth of the boys had second- or third-level typing skills, as compared to five-sixths of the girls. In the all-girls high school, the typing qualifications tended to be a little higher, and more girls (nine-tenths) had the same degree of qualifications. From the girls' point of view, it was taken for granted that typing was a basic requirement for employment.

Teachers of the three subjects said that the process of acquiring such qualifications did not demand "brains," but "hands." According to the teachers, those who were skilled with their fingers tended to acquire the qualifications faster. My observation of these classes supported the teachers' argument to some extent. As I wrote in my field notes:

> Commercial calculation teacher came in the classroom. He put an attendance book on the desk. He said, "Let's begin. Take your abacus." After adjusting his stopwatch, which was dangling on his neck, the teacher of commercial calculation [abacus calculation] ordered, "Start." The students busily moved their fingers on the abacuses. The teacher did not mention in detail what to do, but the students did something. After a while, the teacher simply said, "Stop." The students quickly put their hands under the desks. A number of girls were still touching the abacus. The teacher let

them stop touching the abacus. The teacher looked around the class and said, "Are you ready? Let's do multiplication and division. Start." He slowly walked around his students, while looking at the stopwatch. There is no noise at all but the sounds of abacuses. The teacher's job was to look at his watch, push the stop button, and give a very short command without any kind of detailed explanation. The students mechanically follow the directions. During the commercial calculation class, the students did nothing but practice on an abacus over again and again. The bell rang. The teacher said, "All right, let's finish it." With the command of the chairperson, the students bowed to the teacher and said unanimously, "Thank you, sir."

In the commercial calculation class, students practiced addition, subtraction, multiplication, and division. The content and order of the class was so highly ritualized that the teacher did not give any detailed account of the practice, and the students did not ask about it. All they needed was practice to increase or maintain their speed and accuracy. The teachers of commercial courses often told students, "You are commercial high school students. For you, speed and accuracy are most important. You have to deal with numbers efficiently. You will use numbers most frequently in the workplace."

The dominant representation of and the naming of commercial high school students forced these young people to identify themselves with the subject's already established category. The category of commercial high school students simply did not work as a description of a certain image. Rather, it was a part of regulatory practice—its materialization was compelled. A student's body had to be publicly and visually qualified. To be a "real" commercial high school student, one was expected to have a certain degree of formal qualifications. The teachers frequently told their students, "You don't get them [qualifications] yet. Are you a real commercial high school student? Who on earth believes you are a real commercial school student?"

The degree to which the students disciplined themselves when dealing with numbers and letters had to be assessed by other public institutions. The public institutions gave them qualifications differentially according to their degree of speed and accuracy. Although vocational qualifications were assessed by a local agency, those qualifications were not regarded as "real ones." The central state authority (the Ministry of Commerce and Industry) endowed the "real" qualifications. Thus, teachers suggested that students pursue the more authentic qualifications given by the state authority, even if they were more difficult to acquire. However, acquiring qualifications did not mean the students were finished—even after attaining qualifications, students had to practice typing, abacus, and bookkeeping on a daily basis because "Our hands get hardened if we don't practice everyday."

Although attaining qualifications for abacus, bookkeeping, and typing required considerable practice, time, and money, these skills are not typically utilized in the workplace. Automation and computerization of office work in large companies make such skills almost useless—only very small and non-computerized offices require them. Teachers and students alike knew that the qualifications for abacus and bookkeeping were not necessary to do real work.

If technical qualifications are not utilized in workplaces but are required for job entry, how do schools get their students to obtain them? To meet such a contradictory situation, both schools commonly stressed to students the importance of showing industriousness in their lives beyond the formal and numerical qualifications. According to them, companies demanded qualifications not because they wanted those skills, but because they wanted someone who was industrious, conscientious, and positive-minded, no matter what the situation called for. Many students similarly said, "I know that those skills are not used so much at workplaces. However, I hear that companies think that those who have good qualifications are sincere and work hard in school." The numerically evaluated, but rarely utilized, qualifications became a kind of symbol to measure a future worker's potentiality as a docile body.

In this way, commercial high schools encouraged their students to be industrious and have a positive attitude, rather than call into question the problematic process of obtaining qualifications and employment. In order to secure student compliance with the school message, the school organization selectively mobilized meanings so that they made good sense to the students, but stayed within the operations of asymmetrical power. Precluding the possibility of an alternative, or disqualifying the alternative, achieved the regulation of meaning.[3] The schools did not lead students to reconsider the problematic tendency of recruitment and think about alternatives. Instead, they emphasized the importance of morality and respect for the established order.

In fixing, normalizing, and naturalizing the meaning of qualifications, school organizations tried to perform a variety of disciplinary measures. Teachers in both schools frequently checked how much their students' qualifications improved, and categorized students according to those who got higher qualifications and those who did not. Homeroom teachers wrote in detail in their pocket notebooks about their students' progress in technical qualifications; based on this knowledge, teachers judged students normatively (i.e., an industrious or lazy student, a good or bad student). The teachers still tended to evaluate the students' quality based on their qualifications, all the while knowing that they were hardly used at the workplace.

The schools' process of meaning making and discipline in regards to qualifications largely worked. The majority of students transformed themselves in, and through, the school's dominant ideological operation. For students, at the very least it was necessary to get qualifications out of material interest, because the qualifications were required for employment. Additionally, many students had feelings of security and "freedom from teachers' nagging" by having those qualifications. However, their efforts to attain qualifications were not imposed simply by external enforcement. The process of obtaining qualifications gave them a sense of achievement, thereby creating internal enforcement as well. Many students said they felt proud when their qualifications improved; they felt their sense of competence and achievement grow. Some students devoted themselves to acquiring such high qualifications that they went far beyond the requirement levels of companies. These students' efforts certainly stemmed from their own material interests in placing themselves in a more favorable position in an uncertain labor market. However, this was not the only reason they did it. They did it because it gave them a sense of achievement and self-dignity. The sense of competence, achievement, and satisfaction felt by the students, to some extent, helped the commercial school's smooth operation.

The school's regulation to maintain the dominant meaning systems of knowledge was not always consistent, however. For instance, though teachers played a prominent role in encouraging students to become accurate and speedy technicians, students who followed the teachers' advice were criticized for their ability to deal with numbers quickly. According to the teachers, commercial high school students lacked a general capacity to understand the world because they were too engaged with the simple operations of numbers and letters. General subject teachers more frequently gave such criticism, but even the commercial course teachers had negative opinions about commercial courses and their students' thinking ability. A calculation teacher in the mixed school said:

> This is totally skill training, although abacus develops the students' sense of number…. These kids just do ordered jobs. They lack creativity and application. It is difficult to communicate with them. They do not read many books. It is a serious problem.

In their formal classes, students did not seriously call into question commercial knowledge. Instead, they chose to either conform to the teachers' directions or keep silent. But the overt acquiescence did not mean that students completely accepted school knowledge without conflict. The students, who neither called into question what they were learning nor rejected learning commercial knowledge in the formal classes, more freely and clearly expressed hidden, ambivalent feelings or skeptical views about commercial knowledge during my interviews. For instance, Sun-Young, a female, stated:

> I hate all subjects, which include the letter of commercial or business. Those subjects make me feel like a calculator, which has

no feeling or thoughts. I've found myself to get more calculative. I hate myself.

On one hand, students felt a sense of competence when they found they were getting quicker at numbers and getting qualifications. On the other hand, they did not like the calculative element that this brought to their personality. To learn commercial knowledge for employment meant to lose valuable humanity, which was considered to be less calculative and more "noble" in nature. They also felt that they had lost their purity as students who were supposed to be free from the adult world and its working places. Some teachers said just as much in their private conversations. According to them, commercial high school students' quick sense of numbers led them to "get burned out more quickly" than "academic high school students who are not yet contaminated by the dirty social world." Because a vocational high school student had faster access to the adult world as a full-time worker, they were not "pure" students. In this sense, the dominant representation of a normal student was highly class embedded.

SELECTIVE INTERNALIZATION AND CONTESTATION

Since qualifications given for abacus and bookkeeping were not useful in the workplace anymore, students' subjective investment seemed to decline regarding these subjects. Many teachers said that their present students' qualifications were not as good as those of former graduates. Some teachers explicitly complained about their students' "declining quality" in private conversations. One male teacher stated:

> The students of today do not work hard to get qualifications. You know, the former students did not do that. There were many students who had top class qualifications in abacus, bookkeeping, and typing. But now there are only a number of students who have the first-class qualifications. The quality of students is getting worse and worse day-by-day.... They have a rotten mind ... I don't know where the world is going.

However, students severely opposed the teachers' views that the quality of students was getting worse. A female student named Yoon-Soo said:

> Why should we work hard and pay lots of money? It is not related with our quality. You know, getting qualifications just needs practice and time. My friends go to other private institutions like beauty schools instead of getting the useless qualifications.

School authority was secured precariously. There was a gap between normality, emphasized by official school discourse, and actuality, performed by the students. Based on their cost-benefit analysis, many students felt it was necessary to invest in a proper degree of effort to obtain qualifications. Some students decided to learn skills according to their own life plans, like beauty or heavy-industry skills, and ignored the school's encouragement to get qualifications.

Furthermore, the unused, but essential, formal requirements for obtaining office work caused some students to seriously question their schools and companies. Eun-Joo, a female student, commented:

> They don't care about us. Companies only care about getting hard workers, like an ox. The school is crazy about how many students they put in the workplace, wherever they are.... We have to work hard to death, paying lots of money for the private lesson teachers, only to get these useless qualifications. Why don't they let us get really useful skills? Newspapers and TV always make a great fuss about academic school students and their abnormal school lives. They don't mention about our hard lives. It's so unfair. We are the same people as them.

The fact that this girl was very critical about the unreasonable and unfair practices of school and society did not mean that she totally rejected the dominant ideal image encouraged by the schools. Rather, she wanted to be an example as a means of resistance. Eun-Joo stated:

> I am going to work harder, succeed, and have a happy home life. By doing so, I will show them that people who do not go to college are able to make it. And I don't want to be scolded or looked down upon by virtue of being a commercial high school student. So I am very careful in behaving consciously, especially outside school [smiling].

General Subjects: Exclusion and Ambivalence

General subject teachers (and sometimes even commercial subject teachers) regarded commercial high school students as having a "lack of culture" and a "lack of basic academic ability and motivation." According to the teachers, students' lower academic abilities and lack of motivation discouraged "normal teaching." Thus teachers had to lower their teaching levels in order for the students to follow the class.

Another reason teachers lowered their teaching levels (either on their own accord or on the advice of colleagues) was because they were supposed to keep from stigmatizing their students. They praised the students for good educational results as well as for engaging in smooth relationships with their teachers. Stigmatizing acts could cause contestation from the students, thereby undermining the legitimacy of the commercial high school itself. Thus teachers were encouraged by school administration to let students feel some sense of competence and pride about themselves and their school. Teachers could complain about their students' lower abilities and lack of motivation in the staff room, but they were not supposed to do so directly in front of the students. However, teachers did not always obey the school taboo. Consciously or subconsciously, they revealed frank feelings about their less-able students, thereby hurting their students' self-esteem.

Finally, teachers argued that the students' strong concerns about employment prevented them from spending a lot of time studying general subjects. The teachers' hard work often turned into disappointment or frustration because of their students' predominant concerns for getting qualifications or preparing for employment examinations. General subject teachers said, "They do what they need immediately and they think things fall right before their noses. They won't do something for the long-term future." However, although general subjects were not directly connected with marketable skills or qualifications, commercial high school students felt that they could not ignore them entirely because they comprised fifty percent of school examinations. In order to get a good grade point average and have a chance at being recommended for "a good job," commercial school students had to maintain good grades even in general subjects.

Subjects did more than play an important role in students' grade point averages and employment possibilities. The subjects also symbolized explicit status and prestige in South Korean society, where school systems were characterized as having a strong degree of insulation between academic and vocational school systems. The commercial courses, which were viewed as "important" by commercial high schools, occupied much lower social status outside the schools. On the other hand, general courses, which were seen as "relatively unimportant" by commercial high schools, occupied higher status outside the schools. These inverted hierarchical meanings caused commercial high school students to have complex and contradictory feelings towards both commercial and general subjects.

Here, the teachers' subtle or explicit criticism of students seemed to increase the students' complex feelings towards commercial and general knowledge. The following observation note shows this well:

It was an English class in the mixed school…. Ms. Seo let students whose attendance numbers contained today's date (Sept. 6th, thus, 6, 16, 26, 36, and 46) read one sentence and interpret it. A student whose attendance number was 36 finally finished reading a sentence, but she could not translate it into Korean.... Ms. Seo put her textbook down on the desk and talked to students. "Look. You have to be more concerned about proper pronunciation and know the exact meaning of English words. Otherwise, your colleagues or your boyfriends will humiliate you. You know, one graduate told me that she was so embarrassed because she could not understand the English joking of company people. She regretted not having studied English hard enough." The students quietly listened to her continue. "And please read classic literature whenever you have time. You can buy a pocket edition with a small amount of money or borrow it from the public library if you can't afford it. Instead of only watching TV on weekends, read classic novels too." A female student said in a less confident voice, "It is too boring and hard." "Yes, it is," other students backed her up. Ms. Seo said in a firm tone, "Why on earth do you guys choose only the easy way? You first have to correct such a problematic attitude. With that attitude, how could you tell your children to read good books or study hard? They will also defy you because you are ignorant mothers." Students silenced.

Regarding this kind of criticism from teachers, some students complained that they had no time to engage in cultivating proper cultural taste because they had to take private lessons to get technical qualifications quickly, and other students complained that reading classic novels was boring. But many students quietly listened. Indeed, a great majority of the students felt a sense of inferiority in general subjects. The students thought that spending a lot of time studying general subjects meant going to college and attaining higher status, while less study of those subjects meant employment, no college, and attaining lower status.

The following statement by Kyung-Ran, a female student, clearly shows the students' complex and contradictory feelings towards general subjects:

When teachers of mathematics, Korean, and English teach us without sincerity, I think in my mind that they just kill time. Academic high school students study them to death, don't they? Rather, they have tutors to help them learn more because they don't think it is enough to learn only in school. But we are learning so poorly even in school. I think I am getting farther away from going to college, as I am living this way.

Actually, it was not very difficult to find general subject teachers saying in their classes, "You don't need to study this part unless you have a plan to go to college," or, "It is too difficult for you. Let's skip it," or, "I won't ask you this question on the following examination. You don't need to study it. I just told it for your information." Here, the problem is that the students' uncomfortable feelings towards general subjects increased when they thought that the humanitarian teachers were not working hard enough. Students felt that many teachers did not educate them well because they were not going to college. The teachers' less-serious attitudes towards teaching made the students feel ambivalent, mistreated, and negative about their chances of going to college.

However, even though commercial high school students had a sense of inferiority in general knowledge and were critical about their general subject teachers' less-serious attitudes towards teaching, it did not mean that the students admitted the usefulness of school knowledge in their real lives. In my interview with Eun-Young, she stated:

> I don't think that higher achievers should have a priority in having recommendations. I've screwed up my school life. But, you know, I had a pretty good reputation when I worked as a part-time worker [at a fastfood store in a bus terminal]. Those who study hard at school don't necessarily become good workers. School knowledge is mostly useless and irrelevant to doing real work. My friends who got jobs in companies or factories say so.

I asked, "Then, what is important?" Eun-Young replied, "To be kind and to make people feel good and to work hard."

As in commercial subject classes, students did not directly challenge the legitimacy of school knowledge in general subject classes. Their frank views were expressed either in private conversations with friends or in my interviews after class. Many students valued the external merits of schooling (credentials) much more than learning knowledge itself. As Eun-Young expressed, most of the students did not admit the relevance of school knowledge in their practical lives. Using their real work experiences and the work experiences of friends, some students called into question the meritocratic principle being applied in the distribution of school recommendations. Even more, some student radically challenged the arbitrary hierarchy between academic and commercial skills. For example, Min-Ju, a female student stated:

> Well, they say what we do all day long is just pounding typewriters or an abacus, or calculating the amount of the profit and loss. Yes, that's true. And we might not know about academic knowledge as much as they do. So what? Then, can they type as fast and accurately as we can? Can they adjust the accounts as quickly as we do? They can't. It's so unfair.

CONCLUSION: SOCIOSYMBOLIC DIFFERENTIATION AND SCHOOLING

Reproduction theorists (e.g., Bowles & Gintis, 1976; Bourdieu & Passeron, 1977; Bernstein, 1975; Kuhn & Wolpe, 1978) have argued that the school curriculum embodies hierarchical forms of knowledge. This view is valid in some important ways in my study. The two South Korean commercial high schools functioned as a mechanism for instituting patterns of social differentiation, operating not only through the content of knowledge, but also through the regulation of its distribution and interpretation. Learning different knowledge did not mean simply acquiring different skills; it meant social and symbolic differentiation. Whether or not, and to what extent, the students learned substantial knowledge was not a big issue. Rather, the types of knowledge they were supposed to learn, the types of high schools (academic or vocational) they went to, and the social positions they were entitled to after graduation, defined an individual's social value.

The present study suggests that schools actively create and maintain social differentiation, rather than counter it. Based on their own criteria (such as examinations or course requirements), the two schools in my study decided who was adequate for advancement into the higher status of knowledge and higher social positions, and who was better suited for learning narrowly defined technical knowledge. The commercial high school students' exclusion from high-status academic knowledge, and their inclusion in vocational knowledge meant that they were excluded from positions of control or dominance in society In other words, the distinction made by the schools between two categories of knowledge was used to allocate many commercial high school students to lower socioeconomic status and conditions in the future.

It should also be noted here that the social distinction by which the two commercial high schools differentiated the students worked rather ideologically in the sense that they tried to produce certain kinds of subjectivity with respect to existing rules, desires, or pleasures. They did not help the students develop the skills that would make them employable and mobile in a society stratified according to class and gender. What the teachers taught in the commercial high schools was largely out-of-date, and the employers' demands to develop practical skills could not be undertaken because of the school's poor financial situations. Apparently, schools' practices were focused on student attitudes (such as diligence, obedience, responsibility, cooperation, punctuality, honesty, and accuracy), and the category of commercial high school students did not work as a simple expression of a certain image. Rather, it was a part of regulatory practice—it compelled students to materialize it by showing a proper studenthood, which in turn helped reproduce dominant class and gender relations.

The present study suggests, however, that earlier reproduction theorists overstated the implications of the theory. The reproduction process—the process of transformation from concrete individuals (young people) to concrete subjects (for example, commercial high school students as low-status laborers or second-class citizens)—is not likely to be achieved smoothly in practice. The subordinate groups (female students in my case) did not simply internalize the hierarchical categories of subject—they contested it in a number of ways. The symbolic ordering process of subjectivity in commercial high schools was achieved in a complex, precarious, and contradictory way. The commercial high school students' contestations of the relations of power in schools was grounded on the very subject positions and on the very forms of ruling extant in specific sociohistorical circumstances. Thinking about the relationship between school knowledge and subjectivity needs, therefore, to be situated within its specific educational context where histories, hierarchies, tensions, and struggles co-exist and often conflict each other.

Notes

This chapter is a revised version of a paper originally published in South Korea. See Kim, M. (1999). Sang-go-saeng-doe-gee: Hak-gyo-ji-sik, sa-hoe-jeok-sang-jing-jeok-cha-beul-wha, joo-chae-sung-heung-sung [Becoming commercial high school students: School knowledge, socio-symbolic differentiation and subjectivity formation]. *Kyeo-yook-sa-hoe-hak-yeon-goo*, (1), 103–129.

1. Mixed-gender and all-girls schools had several subdepartments, such as information processing, trade, accounting, and commerce departments. Depending on which subdepartment students belonged in, they learned somewhat different commercial subjects.

2. For female students, appearance was also a crucial factor in their employment. However, the emphasis on appearance resulted in young women's sharp contestation. See Cho (2000).

3. Commercial school teachers in Seoul asked the Ministry of Education to reform commercial high school curriculum. They asked for the abolishment of qualifications for abacus, bookkeeping, and typing; they asked the Chamber of Commerce and Industry to keep businesses from requiring such qualifications; they suggested that commercial high school students be taught more appropriately in order to meet the information period. However, it was not accepted. At the end of the 1990s, companies stopped requiring qualifications for abacus and typing. Instead, they asked applicants to low-status official positions for qualifications in information processing.

References

Althusser, L. (1971). *Lenin and philosophy and other essays*. (B. Brewster, Trans.). London: New Left Books.

Apple, M. W. (1979). *Ideology and curriculum*. Boston: Routledge and Kegan Paul.

Bernstein, B. (1975). *Class, codes and control: Toward a theory of educational transmission*: (Vol. 3). London, Routledge and Kegan Paul.

Bowles, S., & Gintis, H. (1976). *Schooling in capitalist America*. New York: Basic.

Bourdieu, P., & Passeron, J. (1977). *Reproduction in education, society and culture*. London: Sage.

Butler, J. (1992). *Bodies that matter: On the discursive limits of sex*. New York: Routledge.

Cho, M. K. (2000). Bodily regulation and vocational schooling. *Gender and Education, 12* (2), 149–164.

Foucault, M. (1979). *Discipline and punish: The birth of the prison*. (Alan Sheridan, Trans.). New York: Routledge.

Henliques, J., Hollway, W., Urwin, C., Venn, C., and Walkerdine, V. (1984). *Changing the subject: Psychology, social regulation and subjectivity*. London and New York: Methuen.

Knights, D., & Vurdubakis, T. (1994). Foucault, power, resistance and all that. In J. M. Jermier, D. Knights, and R. N. Walter (Eds.), *Resistance and power in organizations*. London: Routledge.

Kuhn, A., & Wolpe, A. M. (Eds.). (1978). *Feminism and materialism: Women and modes of production*. Boston: Routledge and Kegan Paul.

Scott, J. W. (1986). Gender: A useful category of historical analysis. *American Historical Review, 91* (5), 1053–1075.

Therborn, G. (1980). *The ideology of power and the power of ideology*. London: Verso.

Weedon, C. (1987). *Feminist practice and poststructuralist theory*. Oxford: Blackwell.

Chapter 10

Identity Conversion, Citizenship, and Social Studies

Asian-Australian Perspectives on Indigenous Reconciliation and Human Rights

Michael Singh

INTRODUCTION

Governments do more than produce or capitalize on crises by inventing policy improvisations to make interventions in civil society. Throughout time they have conducted campaigns for legitimizing themselves and their policies through appeals for the reproduction of a populist national identity wedded to the state. The racist project of building a Whites-only Australian federation, which was initially protected by the United Kingdom, and then by the United States, also involved the mobilization of identity "conversion strategies" (Bourdieu, 1984) to produce White Australians who were adverse to the admixture of all non-Europeans, immigrants, and Indigenous people (the Aboriginal and Torres Strait Islanders) alike.

The doctrine of *terra nullius*, which was in place in Australia for over two hundred years, held that this country was an empty land awaiting British invasion and colonization. To put the doctrine of terra nullius into effect, Indigenous people were removed by the Australian Federation from their lands, and generations of Indigenous children were effectively stolen by the federation to be converted into White Australians. The Indigenous Land Rights struggles began with the resistance wars fought by Indigenous warriors, and in 1992 Eddie Mabo won a High Court case that ruled that Indigenous Australians did, under British law, have the right to Native Title. As a result of this case, Indigenous Australians could in effect now own or lay claim to much of the land claimed by the British Crown during colonization and controlled by the governments of the federation.

The Reconciliation Movement is a citizens' movement that has created opportunities for Indigenous Australians to recount the legacy of colonialist hatred directed against them, enabling them to publicly reclaim their humanity and a sense of dignity. It aims at Indigenous and non-Indigenous Australians coming to an honest understanding of their shared history, a commitment to building cooperative partnerships, and a recognition of the rights of Indigenous people(s) (see Australian Human Rights and Equal Opportunity Commission, n.d.). Opposed to the Reconciliation Movement is the White Nation Movement led by Anglo fundamentalists such as Pauline Hanson, whose policies were enacted by the current Howard government in the years since 1996. The Howard government's failure to respond adequately and appropriately to the Reconciliation Movement has in turn generated the rise of the Reparations Movement.

This chapter provides an analytical interpretation of interviews with informed and active Australian citizens about their reconciliation with Indigenous Australians. Interviewees in this study identify themselves as representing the complex and differentiated admixture of Asian Australians. The interviewees are conscious that, as Asian Australians, the cost of their conversion to White Australians is their rejection of Indigenous Australians. Even after the centenary of federation, the colonialist legacy of White Australia politics sustains a problematic relationship between Indigenous and Asian Australians. However, it is argued that such "funds of community knowledge" may supply social studies education with material to explore and help dissolve the technical and arbitrary political divisions that separate Indigenous and Asian Australians (Moll, Amanti, Neff, and Gonzalez, 1992; Singh, 2001b).

CONVERSION STRATEGIES AND SOCIAL STUDIES EDUCATION

Taking up Pierre Bourdieu's (1984) ideas on "conversion strategies," this chapter tests their currency, value, and contemporary relevance in thinking through innovations in social studies education in the face of White Australia politics. Through various changing "conversion strategies," Anglo fundamentalists are armed with the power, privilege, and framework necessary for identifying who is worthy of being regarded as a "White Australian," and determining how "White Australian-ness" is viewed. Without the federation's sociocultural "conversion strategies" producing the distinguishing identity of "White Australians," there could not have been a vision for forming a "White Australia." The Anglo fundamentalists are opposed by cosmopolitan Australians who employ counterstrategies to accumulate new forms of social, multicultural, and economic capital so as to take local advantage of current developments in global restructuring. With the end of the post–World War II, anti-Asian, "populate or perish" immigration program in the 1970s, the non-European presence in Australia has grown, enhancing the power of those who have struggled against Anglo-fundamentalist protectionism to advance a sense of cosmopolitanism grounded in the Australian social and historical context.

This strategic redefinition of cosmopolitanism as contextually located moves beyond idealized imaginings of cosmopolitanism as a worldwide, altruistic human community blessed with peace and standing in opposition to the nation-state (Robbins, 1998). Here then the idea of "Australian cosmopolitics" is meant to signal a desire to transform Anglo-fundamentalist nationalism, through the repudiation of regressive parochialism, into a worldly politics with a multiplicity of transnational attachments that necessarily remains embodied in the drama and seductions of the nation-state. "Australian cosmopolitics" acknowledges the specifics of time and space in which people are located as well as the complexities inherent in the stretching of their worldly belonging in terms of conscious, emotional loyalties as well as invisible connections and interdependencies. In contrast to altruistic imaginings of a free-floating cosmopolitanism, this linking of the nation-state and cosmopolitanism invites a critical orientation to both.

This struggle can be explained in terms of "conversion and reconversion strategies" (Bourdieu, 1984, pp. 125–168), whereby Anglo-ethnics and Other Australians "cash in" their investments in the monocultural capital represented by White Australia politics in preference for the complexities of Australian cosmopolitics. By means of different and contested conversion strategies, people consciously or unconsciously seek to protect or enhance their cultural capital by positioning themselves within the power structures of White Australia politics, or the alternative tradition of Australian cosmopolitics. The success of these conversion strategies depends on the changing power relations between Anglo fundamentalists and cosmopolitan Australians as much as on the broader global changes. The volume and composition of multicultural capital, as well as the role of the federation, are key instruments for its production. These struggles make evident the boundaries and barriers created by White Australia politics, which need to be moved.

Tom Nairn (2002) argues that in the United Kingdom, despite the collapse of the fabric of "Great" Britain, there is still an unshakeable obsession to reproduce the historical vestments of the nation's long-past, world renowned leadership and power. Of course, from time to time the people of the United Kingdom have been subjected to a conversion process, whereby their sense of national identity has been politically readjusted to suit the state's efforts. Through these efforts the state can redeem its imaginings of continued "greatness." These conversion strategies include appeals to unshakeable nostalgia, the dispersal of xenophobia over asylum-seekers, and orchestrated efforts to "put the 'Great' back in Britain" (Nairn, 2002, p. 17). They also include reasserting Protestantism as the core of British national identity—by conflating ethnocentrism with religion, the people of the United Kingdom are assured that their religion makes them the chosen people with a semisacred identity. The United Kingdom invests much into its claims of an exceptional heritage, and opposes any possibility of it being "little" rather than "great,"—that is, of England being an ordinary republican nation-state. This is especially manifest in its dogged refusal to establish a modern written constitution. A sense of British-ness is being prolonged, with public leaders "finding themselves able to go on only by reconfiguring the present with overpowering templates drawn from the past" (Nairn, 2002, p. 16).

Extrapolating from Nairn's (2002, p. 10) argument that Britain's public leadership has "yet to liberate itself politically from recollections of a former life," it can be observed that in Australia, the Howard regime, threatened with ordinariness and marginalization in a neoliberal world, seeks to redeem White Australia politics through a crusade against Muslim asylum-seekers and Muslim nations (Indonesia, Afghanistan, and Iraq) in order to rekindle its fading light among increasingly cosmopolitan Australians. Much of the rest of the world does not take the Australian struggle to win converts to White Australian-ness very seriously. This is because the federation's bipartisan leadership is unwilling to engage in the difficult work of building the nation and its national identity anew. In Australia, as in the United Kingdom, there is a need to establish an enlarged democratic state where interethnic constituencies can work towards a new civic cosmopolitanism which accords with a restructured world. By establishing an enlarged arena for democratic practice, Australia's leadership could make the formation of interethnic alliances possible. This would be much more appropriate for these times, when Anglo-ethnics can no longer escape the admixture of non-European Australians and the emergence of new voices and political leaders from their ranks.

Elsewhere, I have explored the similarities between the orientation of Australia and the United States to the project of nation building, and how they have both privileged Anglo-ethnics and sought to exclude Other races (Singh, 2001a). Given the parallel trajectory of these nations, research from the United States into identity conversion strategies provides useful insights for social studies educators in countries with similar histories, insights which can be tested locally. For instance, Gabriel (1998) argues that in the United States, class, property ownership, and assimilation into Anglo-ethnic culture play an important part in shaping the inclusion of different ethnic groups into the category of Whiteness, its power, and its privileges. On the question of Black-Jewish relations in the United States, Cornell West (1993, p. 71) observes, "black anti-Semitism and Jewish anti-black racism are real." However, despite being a despised and degraded people, and despite a rich tradition of progressivism, Jews, like other

European immigrants to the United States in the nineteenth century, "for the most part became complicitous with the [U.S.] American racial caste system" (West, 1993, p. 72). Media of every kind, including social studies textbooks (Elson, 1964), played a role in forming Whiteness and coalescing Anglo-fundamentalist interests by demonizing and stereotyping Other races.

The experiences in the United States and the United Kingdom suggest that Asian Australians may convert to solidarity with White Australia politics, so as to attain acceptance among Anglo fundamentalists (Singh, 1999). Part of the price for doing so includes the relegation of Indigenous Australians to the lowest caste. However, the "solidarity" produced by Asian Australians and Anglo fundamentalists under these conditions is inherently unstable. The conversion of Asian Australians to the values of White Australia politics does not guarantee them protection from, or the erasure of, routine anti-Asian racism, discrimination, and harassment (Singh, 1996), nor does it compensate for the costs involved in the denial of their ethnicity, language, or civic rights (Gilroy, 2000).

It is here that social studies education may contribute through its well-established role of developing in students the competencies a cosmopolitan democracy requires of informed and active citizens (Singh and Moran, 1997). McLaren (1997) encourages practices that make direct connections between students' learning experiences and democratically inspired social movements using knowledge-creating pedagogies. Working from a commitment to enlarge communal understandings through democratic encouragement of different knowledges, Feinberg (1993, p. 176) argues for the enrichment of social studies education "through the inclusion of multiple voices and different cultural experiences."

The data presented in the following sections are derived from research investigating Asian Australian perspectives on White Australia politics. This research addresses what, at times, seems to be the fraught relationship between White Australia politics and the legitimacy of Other Australians having a voice in the affairs of their country. During the course of the interviews, participants raised, of their own volition, the need for reconciliation between Indigenous and Asian Australians, and also argued the need for Asian Australians to support the transnational struggles of Indigenous Australians for human rights. In giving voice to the perspectives of Asian Australians on these issues of citizenship and history education, pseudonyms are used.

RECONCILING INDIGENOUS AND ASIAN AUSTRALIAN CITIZENS

White Australia politics expresses itself by its disavowal of Indigenous ownership of Australian lands, its denial of Indigenous dislocation, and the suppression of the history of Indigenous colonization. White Australians have the exclusive privilege and power of claiming entitlement to the land and its history. The promise of exclusive possession was the basis for the founding of the federation in 1901. In the creation of a Whites-only Australia, "the fantasy was that the entire territorial space of Australia was to be for one race only, the white race" (Ang, 2001, p. 128). Nevertheless, reconciliation between Indigenous and Asian Australians is integral for the future of Australian cosmopolitics, as expressed by Kim Ong in one of the interviews:

> What I'm so troubled about these days, as an Australian, as a politician, as an Asian Australian, is that there has been no significant movement from the more established European migrant communities, or from the Asian Australian communities, to take a pro-active role in the process of reconciliation with Indigenous Australians, the real owners of this land. If we, as Australians, cannot even acknowledge the first owners of this land, then what hope do we have for achieving reconciliation among the rest of us?

The dream of reconciliation seems irrepressible. There are community leaders who are eager for social studies education to enrich Asian Australian students with multiple Indigenous voices, knowledge claims, and their cultural practices (Feinberg, 1993). Study of the related history of injustice experienced by Indigenous and Asian Australians under White Australia politics may help to create empathy and alliances (West, 1993). However, the power and seductions of Anglo fundamentalism means that there can be no guarantees. As Kim Ong puts it:

> To date I have not seen many Asian Australian leaders or groups speak with the Indigenous Australians. They need to say, "We are in this together. We are Australians together. We acknowledge your suffering in the past. The experiences of the Chinese during the Gold Rushes tell us a little of the harshness and the discrimination that have occurred over a much longer period to Indigenous Australians. We, as Asian Australians, know a little of what it's like. We want to share this past suffering with you. We also want to acknowledge and to claim with you that together we are Australians. We want to join hands with Indigenous Australians to forge the shaping of this, our country.

The identification of Asian Australians with Indigenous Australians has little to do with their non-European backgrounds, and runs against the

Anglo-fundamentalist desire to keep them separate, because challenging any alliance might maintain the focus on Anglo-fundamentalist interests and concerns (West, 1993). Both Indigenous and Asian Australians have interrupted the moral and economic certainties Anglo fundamentalists felt they were exclusively entitled to; this compounds the doubts and insecurities faced through the intensifying practices of globalization, which, in Australia's case, means an increasing Asian presence and an increasing engagement with Asia, often despite political desires for it to be otherwise. There is only minimal recognition of the need for dialogue among non-European Australians, the objects of White Australia politics. Without reference or deference to the dominating power of Anglo fundamentalism, non-European Australians are only now slowly beginning to ask what postcolonialism, multiculturalism, Asian literacy, and globalization might mean for Australian cosmopolitics. There is a desire for Asian and Indigenous Australians to jointly investigate not only their shared sociopolitical experiences, including those made manifest since 1996 by the White Nation Movement, but also the distinctive claims of Indigenous Australians as the original inhabitants of this land. For example, Yee states as follows:

> I took a group of Chinese Australians to Cherbough, an Aboriginal settlement. We met a woman whose surname was Lau; she traced it back to her grandfather, who was a seaman from China. Some of the first Chinese gold miners in Australia married Aboriginal women. That's why throughout northern Aboriginal communities there are connections with the Chinese (and the Japanese). That's one reason why Chinese Australians need to know more about the Aboriginal Australians and their culture and philosophy. It would be very useful for Chinese Australians to meet Indigenous Australians, to get to know and understand them, and to form productive working relationships.

The White Australia project of biological assimilation through the sponsored "breeding out" of Indigenous Australians by absorption into Anglo-ethnic communities was challenged by those Indigenous Australians who married Indonesians, Malays, Chinese, Japanese, or Pacific Islanders (Anderson, 2002). Not surprisingly, there are Asian Australians who want to understand Indigenous Australians as they see themselves, and Asian Australians who want to see themselves as they are seen by Indigenous Australians (McLaren, 1997). Students could explore the knowledge behind each group's perceptions of the Other so as to establish what it means to be an Indigenous or Asian Australian. Extending this further, the exploration of the knowledge claims behind each group's perceptions of the "Other" will help to establish what it means for each to be cosmopolitan Australians. Kau explains in an interview:

> In 1998, during the "Pauline Hanson" debates, it was the first time Aboriginal people were working with the Chinese Australians. They would sit together, have regular meetings, and work out strategies against racism. I have been here for more than twenty years and that was the first time I witnessed such cooperation between the Aboriginal and the Chinese Australians. Previously there was very little understanding between the two groups. The Chinese Australians simply do not understand the Aborigines. They probably have the same misunderstanding about Aborigines as do Anglo-ethnics.

Given the potential for creating an interethnic, cosmopolitan consciousness, social studies education could help Indigenous and Asian Australians become aware of how White Australia politics have oppressed Other Australians (West, 1993, p. 53). For Indigenous and Asian Australian struggles against White racism to have any ethical credibility, it is necessary for students from both backgrounds to learn how and why they might condemn any instance of racist vilification. Indigenous and Asian Australian students need to know that interethnic collaboration will gain them enhanced moral strength to combat Anglo fundamentalism, White Australia politics, and racism of any kind (West, 1993). Thus, it is important for social studies educators to introduce Asian Australian and Indigenous Australian students to their shared histories (Feinberg, 1993). This means providing opportunities for students to incorporate jointly created knowledge and symbol systems into representations of Australian cosmopolitics. As Kau puts it:

> A good thing to come out of this, was a better understanding of the Aborigines, their history, their ways of living and their languages, as well as the British colonization of Australia. Aboriginal speakers told us about the Stolen Generation. These were things we had never heard before.

Social studies education can develop students' competencies for undertaking this community-building work and the collaborative, participatory processes through which common goals are developed (Feinberg, 1993). Social studies education can be part of the structures that need to be mutually maintained and nurtured to create Indigenous and Asian Australian communities that produce shared knowledge and symbols of their histories and futures. Anhzaq comments,

> The way the Howard government has dealt with so-called "Aboriginal issues" is appalling. This country has moved to

welcoming people from different walks of life and different nationalities, different countries, but it can't give justice to the people who were here first. I find myself, as an Indian Australian, more accepted, more tolerated and welcome in this country than the Indigenous people. That I have been given a fairer go than Indigenous Australians worries me greatly.

Despite Anglo-fundamentalist pessimism about the possibilities of shedding White Australia politics, social studies educators might find it useful to have their students explore the historical and contemporary bonds between Indigenous and Asian Australians (West, 1993). Anhzaq argues that it is no longer necessary, if it ever was, for Anglo-ethnics to be the sole conduit that brings together the admixture of Other Australians. In doing so, she hints that the passivity of Indian Australians may reflect their internalization of White Australia politics and their acceptance of its stereotypes about Indigenous Australians, despite this being inconsistent with their collective experience. Anhzaq states,

> Reconciliation is a huge issue that we have to deal with. I haven't seen many Indian Australians in the forefront of this movement. I see Jewish Australians meeting to debate the issues. To a large extent Indian Australians take a back seat. Comments are made in their dining rooms but they don't speak their minds publicly as much as they should. Those Indian Australians in the business need to be influencing the government to prioritize reconciliation.

The fallacious idea of *terra nullius* expressed the willful disregard of Indigenous Australians, and a racist conception of them as less-than-human. The exclusion or elimination of all non-Europeans made the formation of the federation and conversion of White Australians possible. Some Asian Australians are making alliances with the Reconciliation Movement, linking themselves directly to social issues facing Indigenous Australians (McLaren, 1997). Anhzaq sees the Reconciliation Movement as providing strategic sites for students to investigate and calculate the structural and conjectural relations between Indigenous and Asian Australians. She is aware that the reproduction of White Australia politics involves actively convincing Asian Australians to see reconciliation as an Indigenous issue, not an issue for all Australians. As she puts it:

> Reconciliation is a major issue for the well-being of this country— so that all Australians, no matter where they come from, can feel that they are an equally valued part of this society. Every ethnic group would benefit from reconciliation because its concepts and

the principles are far reaching. For this reason, Indian Australians should put more effort into reconciliation; it is much more than an "Aboriginal issue." It is about the reconciliation of Anglo Australians with people from many different ethnic groups to ensure all have an equal footing and an equal stake in the development of this country. I would love to see Indian Australians play a greater role in reconciliation. However, they tend to not want to create too many waves, just in case there is a backlash.

The unsettling positioning of Aboriginality within the ambiguities of White Australia politics has even caused scientists to attempt to incorporate it into the construction of White Australian-ness by configuring Indigenous Australians as dark, distant relatives or archaic Caucasians (Anderson, 2002). To dissolve the arbitrary divisions between Anglo-ethnics and Other Australians, reconciliation cannot be regarded as a matter for Indigenous Australians alone. Asian Australians can also facilitate debate about reconciliation, as Oh-rev expresses:

> More than multiculturalism being under threat it's the Black/ White relationship that's not going anywhere fast. Reconciliation needs much work. Wave the flag, sign the book, make friends with people you meet, but do not just nod in acquaintance.

Some Asian Australians have embraced reconciliation because of their opposition to White Australia politics, the politics which has distorted and delimited their positioning within the federation (Gilroy, 2000). They too, are experiencing the confusion and the emotional discomfort, however, when learning to participate in the official "Welcome to Country" ceremony, where they come to know the expectations that Indigenous people's ancestral spirits have of visitors to their lands. After the disturbing embarrassment of being made to feel like a stranger who was politely invited into what Indigenous people still see as their country, there comes the discrete reminder that White Australians have shown little respect for Indigenous peoples, their land, and their beliefs. Slowly, the symbolic significance of this welcoming ritual dawns. The assumption of Australia as being *terra nullius*, an empty land awaiting British colonization and occupation, is no longer the law of the land. Asian Australians feel as if their full inheritance as Australian citizens was denied. However, that feeling is something they seek to address and resolve. As Oh-rev puts it:

> If we can't get the "Australian House" in order, then all the other things that we do are just a bit of the gloss. We tell people in

Indonesia, East Timor, Irian Jaya, India, and Pakistan how to manage their affairs. But we are not in a position to do that while we still have unresolved issues in our own backyard.

The Reconciliation Movement is a struggle by Indigenous Australians, in collaboration with non-Indigenous Australians, for the reappropriation of their resources, which are the material structures of cultural production. The movement also represents a battle for collective control over one's own future socioeconomic development. For Asian Australians the focus is not guilt, but a concern about making "a fair go" practical. While the media has played a key role in making Asian Australians, such as Yee, aware of Indigenous concerns, social studies education can also provide important knowledge and skills. As Yee puts it:

They don't really know about Aborigines and reconciliation. They learn some things from the media. Even from the news they learn about the marches and demonstrations over Land Rights. They know about it but they are not equipped by the media to act on this information.

Social studies educators could show students how marches, rallies, collective action, and media reports about these events provide important rituals for interethnic community building. These events allow for a sense of affiliation with "Others" and the celebration of the coming together of Asian Australians with Indigenous Australians. Oh-rev states,

When the "Mabo decision" hit the headlines, it became important to understand Australia's multilayered history. It's very sad that reconciliation did not happen in time for the centenary of federation. It would have been a very historic moment. That at the end of a hundred years the federation still has this issue unresolved is a sign of failure. Why, in a hundred years, could this problem not have been resolved?

In giving their perspectives and sharing their knowledge on Asian Australian relations with Indigenous Australians, these informed and active Australian citizens allude to the strategies of White Australia politics to secure converts. While unable to return to the past power relations, and unable to destroy the non-European Indigenous and immigrant presence, Anglo fundamentalists seek to dominate and expropriate the dynamic power of the emerging Australian cosmopolitics. Through inciting fear and anxiety around the uncertainties and insecurity created by neoliberal globalism, they struggle to reestablish the ideology of White Australia politics. While the interviewees acknowledge that Asian Australian ignorance towards the plight of Indigenous Australians is not unlike that of Anglo-ethnics, the role of Anglo-fundamentalist conversion strategies in structuring this forgetfulness is evident. Likewise, there is recognition of Australia's racialized caste system, and a troubled admission that not only does it exist, but it positions Asian Australians ahead of Indigenous Australians in its racist hierarchy and the relative degrees of tolerance Anglo fundamentalists exercise over Indigenous and Asian Australians. Nairn comments on the double consciousness and the strategic advantages that immigrants, with the appropriate social, economic, and cultural capital, can make of it in the following terms:

> [They] have a mixture of distance from and enterprising curiosity about their [new] country, which conveys certain advantages. They can perceive and exploit aspects of [their] new home culture more readily than many [Anglo fundamentalists]—for whom this matrix remains taken for granted, a matter of "instinct" (often incurious) rather than for access and manipulation. Though clearly important in commerce and business, the immigrant edge probably counts for most among intellectuals. (Nairn, 2002, p. 99)

The dominating ideas of White Australia politics shape the terms of reference for Asian Australian participation, thinking, and arguments. It affects their views of themselves as informed and active citizens, and influences the framing of their views and relations with Indigenous Australians. In a relatively poor position for organized and knowledgeable resistance, Asian Australians are acknowledged as being in danger of "seeing themselves completely through the dominating definitions" provided by White Australia politics (Bourdieu, 1984, p. 146). The Anglo-fundamentalist stories of Indigenous Australian poverty as being a "natural" function of their cultural differences, rather than injustices perpetuated by or with the knowledge of the federation, have made serious inroads into the imaginings of Asian Australians. Some appreciate that their conversion to the Anglo-fundamentalist caste system comes at a cost: the silencing of Indigenous and other Asian Australian knowledges, borne out of the fear of resentment politics. Asian Australians might very well plead, "Indigenous Australians, please do not leave us home alone with Anglo fundamentalists!"

However, the sense of communal togetherness produced under these conditions is inherently unreliable, especially given that the price for it includes conformity to the dominating norms of White Australia politics. Thus, Asian Australians can gain "enhanced status in exchange for the assertion of their White racist credentials," specifically by relegating Indigenous

Australians to the lowest caste (Gabriel, 1998, pp. 122–154). As Anglo fundamentalists are able to convert Asian Australians to their cause, they are then able to play up the divisions among those who constitute Other Australians and solidify the distinctions important to maintaining the White racist hierarchy. Of course, in accepting this bargain, Asian Australians cannot expect Indigenous Australians to support them when Anglo fundamentalists mobilize their anti-Asian racism, as they regularly do.

Annexing Asian Australians to Anglo-Fundamentalist Struggles against Indigenous Human Rights

Starting to become aware of the plight of Indigenous Australians, some Asian Australians now feel very strongly that reconciliation is integral to Australian cosmopolitics. Apparently the federation could not imagine a future reconciliation, and so felt it had nothing to lose by alienating Indigenous Australians—at least until the nation's leadership changed. The federation's determined opposition to genuine reconciliation, evident in its attacks on the Mabo Native Title decision and its ignoring of the report of the Stolen Generation, means that the focus has now shifted to reparations. These Asian Australian interviewees are eager for the federation to act constructively to ensure that relevant human rights issues are addressed. This suggests hope for engaging Asian Australians in furthering the interests of Indigenous Australians. It is important for newly arrived immigrants to be provided with accounts of Australian history from the standpoint of Indigenous Australians. Otherwise, there is the possibility that Asian Australians will believe that the marginalization of Indigenous Australians is a result of their unconstrained choice, or rooted in their cultures. This could easily lead segments of the Asian Australian population to oppose the reconstruction of government welfare programs for Indigenous Australians in terms of reconciliation and reparations. As Chen states,

> Originally we thought that this was a White Australian country. As we learned its history, we found it was the Aboriginal's country. They are now displaced people. Some Anglo Australians want to shut their mind to these events. They want everyone to forget it. They are living in a foolish man's paradise by trying to ignore this history. Deliberate forgetfulness is not the way to reconcile the situation.

"White blanket" histories (Smith, 1980) preserve the triumphantalist view of White Australia politics as the only way to build the federation and deny Indigenous Australians the right to mourn. Indigenous Australians cannot be expected to celebrate events that, for them, signify the destruction of their cultures. Reconciliation sees national events as combining mourning with celebration. For all Australians, Australia Day can mourn the British colonial invasion, and celebrate the reconciliation that has yet to be achieved. The federation's refusal to apologize for the suffering it caused Indigenous Australians is an expression of its power (it does not have to do so), and a reflection of its fear of humiliation: fear of being shamed for its deliberate efforts to rid itself of the admixture of Other races; fear of being of equal status with the Indigenous Australians, who are still in Australia. Whether it is seen as an act of cowardice or an act of hostility, the federation's refusal to apologize also compounds the original wrongdoings. A real act of contrition would give Indigenous Australians rights and meaning in Australian history, including rights to the language in which it is to be discussed and a new public meaning in the collective past (Lakoff, 2000). These negative, shameful aspects of the federation's history are part of the project of building Australian cosmopolitics. As Wang puts it:

> There is no single Asian Australian view. They, like all Other Australians, are subject to inherited ways of thinking and current propaganda. Compassionate Asian Australians are concerned about Indigenous Australians, a people who have been robbed, their social structure destroyed, their children taken away from them. I am very saddened by this state of affairs. I am ashamed of how we—as a public, as a government—treat Indigenous Australians.

The virtuous qualities of Australian cosmopolitics could be represented if the federation would formally sanction expressions of sorrow and remorse through symbols. For instance, black armbands are important symbols of mourning in Australian cosmopolitics. Che states,

> I would like to see all Australians being able to say, "Yes this is the way our nation was formed. We have good things and bad things in our history. We take pride in all the good things and we show our regret and sorrow for all the bad things." We need to publicly recognize that all of this is our heritage.

Recognizing the significance of the Stolen Generation means acknowledging the modes of governance that allowed this "final solution." Such memory work is important for our collective appreciation of White Australia politics, which, once again, seeks to harness converts for a Whites-only Australia in the service of Anglo fundamentalism (Gilroy,

2000). The brutality of the Federation's White Australia politics has left residual challenges to be addressed. Che goes on to state,

> Making oneself a part of Australia's multicultural heritage includes taking on responsibility to Indigenous-Australians. This includes a willingness to say "sorry" for things that may not have been done by us, perhaps because we were in another country at that time. But this is a part of Australia's heritage, which is what we want as Australian citizens. We must learn how to take the good and the bad of Australian history as part of our heritage.

The inability of "White blanket" histories to recall the experiences of Indigenous Australians leaves Anglo fundamentalists unable to mourn. However, the federation's political leaders seem to be afraid that historical recollections might implicate them in White Australia politics, and create an opportunity to dissolve such politics. Yet, as Che puts it,

> The Indigenous Australians are displaced people. This was their country before British colonization. You just can't ignore that by saying, "It was done by our forefathers and we had no hand in it." We have benefited from the work of colonization; we cannot ignore that. We have to recognize that.

It is true that Phillip Ruddock did not invent the wheel, and it is doubtful that John Howard, the politician, owns a chariot. However, this in no way stops the federation from making an official apology to Indigenous Australians for the continuing legacy of past wrongs and paying the reparations that are now overdue. To again quote Che,

> Some people say you shouldn't apologize to the Indigenous Australians because "migrants" would be offended, as they weren't here then. That's not my view. That's not fair. It's telling me that I'm only "part Australian." Why shouldn't I, as an Australian, have a right to this country's heritage—the good and the bad? Surely that is my responsibility as an Australian citizen.

By paying lip service to human rights, the federation can use laws, such as mandatory sentencing, to covertly target Indigenous Australians. In one interview, Ahlan Walker states,

> Many people who are imprisoned through mandatory sentencing seem to be Aboriginal Australians. If you commit a white-collar crime then it is different: three years for a billion-dollar fraud; but if you steal biscuits, that is another thing altogether. This law is targeted at a certain group. What they are doing is incarcerating

Aborigines instead of looking at the cause of the issue and working out how to fix the real problems.

These Asian Australian interviewees are aware that by adopting fragments of White Australia politics, especially by making outsiders of Indigenous Australians, they can gain a measure of acceptance in the dominating Anglo-fundamentalist culture. Just as for the Irish and the Jews in the United States, for Asian Australians to convert to "White Australians" helps them define themselves as not being outsiders, thereby gaining them relative acceptance by the dominant groups. This can involve annexing Asian Australians into the stories of White Australia politics, so as to bind them to Anglo-fundamentalist battles against Indigenous human rights. Anglo fundamentalists create the impression that conversion to White Australianness is within the reach of Other Australians, despite the exclusionary significance of White Australian-ness. This places Asian Australians in a dilemma:

> The result is often an inability to choose sides. That is, to decide between making the best of the hulk, or opting more frankly for a democratic replacement. Were the latter a popular movement, with mass support and any prospect of taking over the system, there would probably be no contest here. (Nairn, 2002, p. 105)

The White Nation Movement cannot admit to being racist. The impression of accessibility, and the legitimacy it seeks to create, would fail if it could not rely on the complicity of a few Other Australians. Converts to White Australia politics deceive these Other Australians into becoming imitations of Anglo fundamentalists and consumers of their monoculture rather than producers of Australian multiculturalism. However, in the eyes of the dominating Anglo fundamentalists, these converts frequently betray themselves by the manner and mode of their "mistaken identification and misrecognition"—their mistaken beliefs that they have acquired about being White Australians (Bourdieu, 1984, p. 327). These informed and active Australian citizens understand that who and what counts as a "White Australian" changes over time for different sociohistorical reasons for various groupings of Other Australians. From this, we can see that social studies education has an important role in counteracting the changes that occur through the range of official and unofficial identity conversion strategies the interviewees have identified. Social studies education has a place in pointing to:

> The transcendence of blood relations, not [a] retreat back to them: the construction of civic nationalism, rather than the reiteration

of ethnicity, or mythologies of ancestry and belonging. ... the pressures of a common fate are forcing such political transcendence. (Nairn, 2002, p. 158)

No doubt, some Asian Australians feel that they owe their place in the federation to the dominating Anglo-fundamentalist interests. They live with the fear of not fulfilling the numerous and changing expectations imposed by the demands of Anglo fundamentalists, as well as the awareness of not being quite White, let alone possessing all the dispositions needed to become White Australians. Here they discover a new sense of unworthiness. The paternalistic patronage they receive from Anglo fundamentalists, in the name of White Australia politics, expresses a concern to protect them from any chance of conversion to cosmopolitan Australians. Nevertheless, the "annexation strategies" (Bourdieu, 1984, p. 304) used by these Asian Australians enable them to use their solidarity with Anglo fundamentalists as a bargaining tool. Having converted to membership in the dominating fraction, in order to profit from this appropriation they also see themselves as the vanguard for transforming the ethical dispositions of Anglo fundamentalists. In this, they are able to make a virtue of that which the pragmatism of White Australian politics makes a necessity.

CONCLUSION

The evidence presented in this chapter indicates the ambivalent cultural power of White Australia politics in the relations between Indigenous and Asian Australians. There is an acknowledgment that Asian Australians are subject to, and subjected to, the solicitous conversion strategies of White Australia politics, even among those who desire to acquire the skills to be otherwise. These particular Asian Australians reject the offer of a "White blanket" history through which to lay claim to their Australian heritage and within which to locate their trajectory as informed and active citizens. For social studies education, this adds credence to efforts to build critical analyses of White Australian politics, and to relate Indigenous, European, and Asian Australian perspectives on the federation's history to the dominating accounts selectively created and sanctioned by Anglo fundamentalists. Pedagogically this suggests that social studies education can use student-as-researcher projects to access the funds of community knowledge, and provide students with the concepts to analyze this information.

Social studies education has sought to promote multicultural education and studies of Asia as modest counterconversion strategies to give students a distinctive sense of Australian multicultural citizenship, a renewed relationship with Asia, and a cosmopolitan consciousness. Social studies education also approaches the problems of dissolving the political divisions that separate Indigenous and Asian Australians through pedagogies that favor the admixture of Other Australians via interethnic communities of interest. By drawing on these "funds of knowledge," social studies education can contribute to the exploration and dissolution of the technical and arbitrary political divisions that separate Indigenous and Asian Australians. In particular, social studies educators can introduce Asian Australians and Indigenous Australians to their shared histories and provide opportunities for them to map shared expectations of civic entitlements. Social studies educators can contribute to the replacement of White Australia politics with Australian cosmopolitics by actively challenging the former's exclusions in order to make good the latter. Certainly, social studies education provides opportunities for students to imagine anew the Australian federation's future trajectory. Through pedagogies that make constructive use of culturally different funds of community knowledges, social studies education can make a useful contribution to reconciliation between Asian Australians and Indigenous Australians.

NOTES

Thanks to the interviewees who participated in this study; to Michael Apple for his insights into the relevance of the work of Pierre Bourdieu, and also to Linda and Benjamin, as always, for their time which enabled work on this project. An earlier version of this material appeared in Singh (2001a).

REFERENCES

Anderson, W. (2002). *The cultivation of Whiteness: Science, health and racial destiny in Australia.* Carlton South (Vic.): Melbourne University Press.

Ang, I. (2001). *On not speaking Chinese: Living between Asia and the West.* London: Routledge.

Australian Human Rights and Equal Opportunity Commission. (n.d.) Social Justice and human rights for Aboriginal and Torres Strait Islander peoples. Retrieved December 6, 2004, from <http://www.hreoc.gov.au/social-justice/info-sheet.html>.

Bourdieu, P. (1984). *Distinction: A social critique of the judgment of taste.* Cambridge, MA: Harvard University Press.

Elson, R. (1964). *Guardians of tradition: American schoolbooks of the nineteenth century.* Lincoln: University of Nebraska Press.

Feinberg, W. (1993). *Japan and the pursuit of a new American identity: Work and education in a multicultural age.* New York: Routledge.

Gabriel, J. (1998). *Whitewash: Racialized politics and the media.* London: Routledge.

Gilroy, P. (2000). *Between camps: Nations, cultures and the allure of race*. London: Penguin.

Lakoff, R. (2000). *The language war*. Berkeley: University of California Press.

McLaren, P. (1997). *Revolutionary multiculturalism: Pedagogies of dissent for the new millennium*. Boulder: Westview Press.

Moll, L., Amanti, C., Neff, D., & Gonzalez, N. (1992). Funds of knowledge for teaching: Using a qualitative approach to connect homes and classrooms. *Theory into Practice, 31* (2), 132–141.

Nairn, T. (2002). *Pariah: Misfortunes of the British Kingdom*. London: Verso.

Robbins, B. (1998). Actually existing cosmopolitanism. In P. Cheah & B. Robbins (Eds.), *Cosmopolitics: Thinking and feeling beyond the nation*. Minneapolis: University of Minnesota Press.

Singh, M. (1996). Teaching against racisms: Developing multicultural perspectives. In R. Gilbert (Ed.), *Studying society and environment: A handbook for teachers*. Melbourne: Macmillan.

Singh, M. (1999). Changing uses of multiculturalism: Asian–Australian engagement with white Australia politics. *Australian Educational Researcher, 27* (1), 115–130.

Singh, M. (2001a). The admixture of indigenous and Asian Australians: Funds of community knowledge, social studies education and the dissolution of White Australia politics. *Delta: Policy and Practice in Education, 53* (1&2), 123–137.

Singh, M. (2001b). The centenary of federation: Learning from past mistakes to prevent future wrongs. *Teacher Learning Network, 8* (1), 3–6.

Singh, M., and Moran, P. (1997). Critical literacies for informed citizenship: Further thoughts on possible actions. In S. Muspratt, A. Luke, & P. Freebody (Eds.), *Constructing critical literacies: Teaching and learning textual practice*. Cresskill, NJ: Hampton Press.

Smith, B. (1980). *The spectre of Truganini. Sydney*. Sydney: Australian Broadcasting Commission.

West, C. (1993). *Race matters*. Boston: Beacon Press.

Chapter 11

Fastening and Unfastening Identities

Negotiating Identity in Hawai'i

Gay Garland Reed

INTRODUCTION

Different times and circumstances may elicit different responses to the question, "Who are you?" This is because identity is relational, contested, contingent, negotiated, produced, manipulated, and multiple (Rohrer, 1997). Parker Palmer (1997, p. 15) writes, "[i]dentity is a moving intersection of the inner and outer forces that make me who I am." His definition reflects a poststructuralist view of identity as contingent, situated, and unfolding. Indeed, poststructuralist theory has helped reconfigure essentialist views of identity (Supriya, 1999). Although unfamiliar identity categories open up a space for rethinking identity negotiation, because of the powerful nature of categories there is always a pull toward essentialization, even when the categories are new or configured in unfamiliar ways. Categories are often highly magnetic and reductionist—once created, they draw individuals into their narrow definitions and entrap them.

This chapter focuses on identity negotiation in Hawai'i, a geographic context where mainland U.S. categories are not normalized and where social and cultural arrangements elicit different patterns of identity construction and negotiation. The cultural and ethnic identity markers that dominate the discourse of the U.S. mainland and center around Black, Latino, and White are not dominant in this geographic space. The chapter begins with a discussion of background and framework of the study, and proceeds to analyze some of the ways that identity is fastened, unfastened, and refastened in this cultural space. First, it discusses local identity and the question of who fits and who does not, and why this is the case, by exploring the *haole* (White) identity, and locates it in relationship to local identity. Second, it discusses what it means to

183

be *hapa* (mixed race), and the unique way that the hapa identity is constructed and negotiated in Hawai'i. The final section focuses on the politics of names and demonstrates how naming practices in Hawai'i reveal the intersection of gender, ethnic, geographic, generational, and cultural identities.

Background

Hawai'i is seen as a cultural anomaly in the United States. The state's physical distance from the U.S. mainland is, in some ways, a metaphor for its cultural distance. Statistics taken from the 2000 U.S. census reported Hawai'i's population as follows: 41.6 percent Asian, 9.4 percent native Hawaiian and Pacific Islander, 24.3 percent White, 7.2 percent Hispanic/ Latino, 1.8 percent African American, and 0.3 percent American Indian and Native Alaskan. Hawai'i has the highest percentage of Asian and Pacific Islanders in the United States. The significance of this percentage becomes clearer when it is compared with the 1999 estimate of California's Asian and Pacific Islander population at 12.2 percent (the second-largest percentage in the U.S.), and of the general U.S. population at 4.0 percent. A statistic that is of particular relevance to this chapter is the percentage of people who identify themselves in the category of two or more races. In Hawai'i, this percentage is 21.4 percent, as compared with 2.4 percent in the U.S. mainland according to the U.S. census of 2000.

Hawai'i is a state where everyone is a minority, and there is a distinct local identity that marks insiders from outsiders. The ethnic makeup of Hawai'i includes a lower percentage of Blacks, Whites, and Hispanics than the U.S. mainland (Nakaso, 1998), and means that different cultural, historical, social class, and linguistic variables need to be considered in the discussion of identity. Although Hawai'i cannot serve as a cultural template for other places, it can provide insight into how diversity and identity are constructed. The complex identities that people in Hawai'i have negotiated for decades, and the ways that they have chosen to notice and accommodate them, can be instructive for people in places where identity appears to be less overtly multidimensional. This is true even in areas where the identity tapestry looks significantly different because local conceptions of identity raise serious challenges to the norms of other societies.

The Framework of the Study: Fastening, Unfastening, and Refastening Identities

The present study evolved over a period of four years (1997–2000). Initially it was not a formal inquiry, but a collection of insights from class writings, conversations, and interactions. As significant themes related to identity negotiation in Hawai'i began to emerge, I posed questions to the pre-service and in-service teachers who studied with me and they became willing cultural informants. I followed up with formal interviews when I needed clarification and additional input. Although they represent a very diverse group of locals (people who grew up in Hawai'i) and nonlocals (people who grew up outside of Hawai'i), they are mostly female, mostly local and of Asian (Japanese, Chinese, Filipino) descent, and all studied or taught at the University of Hawai'i at Manoa. The ethnic diversity of the undergraduate student population is revealed in the College of Education's ethnic profile for fall, 1999: 25 percent Japanese American, 20 percent Caucasian, 12 percent Hawaiian/ part Hawaiian, 9 percent Filipino American, 15 percent Asian Pacific Islander, 2 percent Chinese, and 10 percent mixed ethnic background.

In my search for a metaphor to serve as a framework for analyzing identity negotiation in Hawai'i, I have chosen to use an image of fastening and unfastening identity. Like all metaphors and models it has its limitations, but as a heuristic device, it provides a language for this analysis. Identity fastening is defined here as the work that individuals do to claim insider status for themselves and for others. This definition suggests that although identities are sometimes fastened by laws and conventions, they are also negotiated. They are fastened by the categories that we have available, and by the ways that we submit to those categories and subject others to them. Sometimes we intentionally fasten identity to create group solidarity or configure a way to belong.

Identity unfastening occurs in multiple ways and might be perceived as either constructive or destructive from the standpoint of the individual. Identity unfastening often happens when individuals move from one cultural context into another, where the norms and rules for membership are different. In the case of colonization, the fastened identity of the colonizer is imposed on the fastened identity of the colonized, who, in turn, experience the threat of identity unfastening. In the case of the immigrant adopting a new national identity, the process of unfastening and refastening identity may sometimes be voluntary, sometimes involuntary, but almost always disorienting. Further dimensions of this metaphor will be explored as it is applied to the instances of identity negotiation discussed in this chapter, but it should be noted that the process is never unidirectional. Fastening and unfastening usually occur simultaneously and in multidimensional ways.

Cultural Context and Local Identity

Some historical background is useful in establishing the context of ethnic identity formation in Hawai'i. Early work on the social context of Hawai'i notes that Hawaiians were largely indifferent to race until annexation by the United States. After annexation, mainland conceptions of race were partially introduced in the census practices of Hawai'i (Lind, 1955). If the United States is taken as the larger unit of analysis, and Hawai'i considered a unit within this larger unit, we see layers of cultural dominance. Karena, a teacher of Japanese/Okinawan descent who grew up in Hawai'i and describes herself as "local," notes that while she is part of a dominated culture relative to the United States, in Hawai'i she is part of the dominant local culture. Her perception of this situational dominance is an important insight that has implications for social cartography because it marks some people as both insiders and outsiders and acknowledges the complexity of social stratification in Hawai'i.

The dominant culture is sometimes difficult to assess. Depending on the situation, and depending on the power relationships at the moment, it fits somewhere along the continuum of "mainland" to "local." "Mainland" refers to the dominant American culture and is largely defined by European values and styles of interaction. In this case, the term "local" suggests the Polynesian and Asian values and interactional styles of generations of Hawai'i residents, but the definition is subject to debate. Jon Okamura (1981) argues that the notion of "local" has become a symbol of the common identity of people who have an appreciation of the quality and style of life in the islands and who have therefore attempted to maintain control over the future of Hawai'i and its communities. "Local culture" as popularly referred to in Hawai'i means the shared lifestyle, behavior, values, and norms. The pan-Asian American identity never took hold in Hawai'i because, as Okamura (1994) argues, the salience of local identity as a group identity marker was too significant. Part of this was due to the uniqueness of the Hawai'i experience, which included a plantation culture characterized by waves of immigrants from China, Japan, Korea, the Philippines, Puerto Rico, and Portugal who came to work in the sugar cane fields. Dora, a teacher at a private school in Hawai'i who describes herself as "local-Chinese-Filipino," writes about her experience as an "Asian American" at an Ivy League school:

> From the very beginning, I resisted the Asian American label when I got to school. I stayed as far away from the Asian American Student Association as I could in my first two years. I had nothing in common with these people. Most of the Asians on campus were Chinese or Korean sons and daughters from wealthy immigrant families who came from states like California, New York, New Jersey and Texas. I was different. I was a fourth generation Chinese-Filipino from Hawai'i. I was a descendant of plantation workers. Along with being half-Filipino, I was certainly one of the darkest-colored Asians and one of the few Filipinos on campus. (Dora, class writing, 1997)

Dora expresses a sense that categories are waiting to claim individuals. She indicates that identity fastening can happen against one's will and despite one's resistance. Even though she seems to fit the criteria that her mainland Asian American classmates employ to define her as an insider, she carries another set of identity criteria that place her in another identity space. For Dora, whose roots in Hawai'i go back four generations, and whose plantation history and mixed ethnicity identify her as "local," the designation "Asian American" as it is constructed on the mainland is not salient. Dora has a generational mentality that differentiates her from her second-generation classmates and she prefers to describe herself by her ethnic background (Chinese- Filipino) and by her connection to Hawai'i (local).

"Local" and "nonlocal" are terms that represent two pan-ethnic groups which are differentially related to the geographic space of Hawai'i. Journalists Creamer and Infante (1995) write that it is common in Hawai'i to divide the world into "local" and "nonlocal"; the process of discerning where people fit into this dualism, and the process of checking their local authenticity, begins as soon as people meet. Using the language of identity fastening to describe this process, we might say that when individuals meet, they employ a set of identity filters that fasten each other into one category or the other. The first identity filter is visual: Does the individual look as though (she or) he has Hawaiian/Polynesian, Japanese, Chinese, Filipino, Puerto Rican, or Portuguese ethnic roots? The next identity filter is the question, "What school you went?" This question refers to the high school that a person attended, and separates those who grew up in Hawai'i from those who did not. This is because it places them geographically, and it places them linguistically. Hawai'i Creole English (HCE), or pidgin as it is commonly designated, is another identity marker that separates locals from nonlocals; although not all locals speak it, most can understand it. Hawai'i author and playwright Darrell Lum enshrined the school identity filter in the title of his dissertation, *Local Genealogy: "What School You Went?" Stories from a Pidgin Culture* (1997). This simple question is a powerful identity fastener that links the individual to the local genealogy and provides opportunities for connectedness. It is equivalent to asking, "How are we connected?"

Other filters that separate local from nonlocal are conceptions of time and affiliation. A temporal order that is shared by a group often becomes a distinguishing factor that separates insiders from outsiders, thus establishing group boundaries and solidarity (Zerubaval, 1981). In terms of local culture, this temporal order is partially expressed by the term "laid back." "Laid back" refers not only to an orientation to time, but to an attitude of acceptance and focus on affiliation. A distinction that is often noted between mainland culture and local culture is the emphasis on individualism verses communitarianism. Drawing from Asian and Pacific cultures, local culture tends to stress harmony, group membership, conflict avoidance, centrality of the family, and a preference for the middle way (Kuroda, 1998). Nonlocals, particularly haoles (but also Asian Americans) from the U.S. mainland, discover that the cultural characteristics that helped them to become successful in other settings are seen as maladaptive in island culture, where a different set of norms and expectations predominate. Calling attention to oneself, focusing on personal advancement, and developing a strong sense of individual identity are all maladaptive in local culture.

Aside from the use of Hawai'i Creole English, there are noticeable differences in the use of language in Hawai'i as compared with the mainland U.S. Rules about what counts as acceptable discourse are sometimes quite different. For example, mainlanders sometimes view local terminology and ethnic joking as racist. In Hawai'i, the term "Oriental" carries none of the negative connotation that it does on the mainland, so when people from Hawai'i use this term on the mainland, they are surprised to be reminded of their "political incorrectness." People tend to refer to each other most often by their ethnicity: "That haole guy," or "that Japanese lady."

Haole is a Hawaiian word that refers to foreigners but is used in common parlance to designate Caucasian. For the most part, Caucasians are an undifferentiated group in Hawai'i. The pan-ethnic category of Caucasian, or haole, is often mis-designated as an "ethnicity" in common parlance when listed with other ethnicities like Chinese, Japanese, and Filipino. People of Portuguese descent in Hawai'i are exempted from the haole category because of their unique position in the plantation social structure under the White plantation bosses.

In his 1941 dissertation on the Portuguese in Hawai'i, G. A. Estep's interviewees help to explain why Portuguese are not haole. They suggested that it was a matter of difference in language, customs, and, most importantly, economic status. A teacher who describes herself as "fourth-generation Madeiran" writes that, "Being Caucasian, in my understanding, was being haole, and I wasn't haole. I was Portuguese and I was local. Still today, as an adult, people often tell me, 'Oh, you're Portuguese. I thought you were a haole'" (Carla, class writing, 1995).

In her study of postmodernism and community, Gail Furman (1998) discusses the necessity of the "decentering of whiteness" as a prerequisite for creating the kind of postmodern community that she envisions. In some respects, but certainly not in every social context in Hawai'i, the comments from Estep and Carla, and the comments that follow, suggest that "Whiteness" has been decentered, if not deprivileged.

Avtar Brah (1996) notes that cultural differences are constituted within the interstices of sociopolitical and economic relations. This is another aspect of the haole experience in Hawai'i, where Whiteness and European cultural roots are associated with a legacy of cultural, political, social, and economic hegemony. Some of the negative feelings directed towards

Caucasians have come as a result of their historic role as conquerors and oppressors of Native Hawaiians, and later of the generations of workers who came to work their plantations. In contemporary Hawai'i there is a stigma attached to being haole, and characteristics associated with this designation include loud, talkative, insensitive, "in-your-face," "me-first," miserly, and wealthy. Evan, a local second-generation Filipino teacher working on the island of Kauai once explained that "[t]here are 'haoles' and there are 'haole haoles.' I got good 'haole' friends, but you don't wanna be around a haole haole" (class discussion, 1998). In this statement, Evan makes a distinction between haole as a somewhat neutral racial designation and haole as a term that is historically situated and saturated with all of the negative stereotypes that characterize Whites in Hawai'i. And even though haoles are the outsiders in the local/nonlocal duality, there are shades of haole that intersect with shades of local, which makes the picture far more complex than the simple duality suggests. Dora, the "local-Chinese-Filipino" teacher, writes:

> Sometimes, to my chagrin, I had to admit that my boyfriend was haole or White. In fact, all the men I had ever dated were haole. But this one was different, he was local haole and he understood my language and my history and my home. He was in some ways more "local" than I'll ever be. He attended a public high school, and later Windward Community College, the University of Hawai'i and Kapiolani Community College. He was an artist who could express Hawai'i in more creative ways than I could ever do. He was an avid surfer, hiker, and free diver. (Dora, class writing, 1997)

Dora begins her discussion with a sense of shame at having a haole boyfriend, then elaborates on how he is really more local than haole and even more local than she is. She unfastens his haole identity, and carefully and methodically fastens his local identity. Many of the identity markers that define "local" identity are expressed here: an understanding of local language and history, attendance at a public high school and an array of tertiary institutions in Hawai'i, and a strong connection to place through a love and respect for the land and the ocean. Nevertheless, a sense of local history and reverence for place do not really substitute for plantation roots. Since the ethnicity of Dora's boyfriend precludes a claim to authentic local lineage, Dora draws on the wider rubric of local identity to explain how he is connected to Hawai'i and to claim him as local. It is indicative of local culture that such explanations are acceptable. We might say that he is exempted from the haole designation by attending to the rules of what it means to be local. Dora, the local gatekeeper, is unfastening his haoleness by allowing him to slip toward local.

Haole is more than simply being White. It is historically and economically situated and encompasses a variety of cultural behaviors and sensibilities, and a particular interactional style. Haole identity can be unfastened, but it takes work. In this scenario it took the work of the boyfriend to attend to the rules of local culture, to behave in certain ways, and to cultivate local sensibilities. It took the work of a local gatekeeper like Dora to stretch the concept of "local" to encompass him.

Ruth Frankenberg (1993, p. 6) writes: "(n)aming 'whiteness' displaces it from the unmarked, unnamed status that is itself an effect of its dominance. Among the effects on white people both of race privilege and of dominance of whiteness are their seeming normativity, their structured invisibility." In the context of Hawai'i, the naming of Whiteness (haoleness) helps to remove the status of normativity and structured invisibility—"In Hawai'i you get called on your haoleness, you are confronted with your race" (Rohrer, 1997). Suddenly, ethnic recognition determines interaction (Whittaker, 1986).

When identity is normalized and invisible, it is experienced as unfastened by cultural insiders. When it is noticed and named, it suddenly becomes fastened, and it takes conscious effort to unfasten it. In this section, we considered the ways that local, nonlocal, and haole identities are fastened and unfastened in the process of identity negotiation in Hawai'i. In the next section of the chapter, *hapa*, or mixed ancestry, will be considered.

"*Hapaness*": Ambiguous Ancestry

Another aspect of local identity that sets Hawai'i apart from other places in the United States is the attitude towards people of mixed ancestry. As noted earlier, over 21 percent of Hawai'i's population identify themselves as being of two or more races. In Hawai'i, *hapa* usually refers to Asian and Caucasian mix. To be of mixed race in the United States has generally been highly problematic. Much of the literature on biracial identity discusses self-esteem problems and marginality (Lyles, Yancy, Grace, & Carter, 1985). According to the research, dual racial and cultural identity negatively affects normal ethnic socialization and produces developmental problems for biracial children (Herring, 1995). People of mixed racial background are often rejected by members of both of the racial groups that make up their heritage.

Terms used to describe people of mixed race, like "half-breed" and "half-caste," are negatively charged. There is a sense that if you are not of one race you are "nothing," or at best, "half." The social construction of the mixed-race status in the United States has led to identity estrangement for people who see themselves not as "both this and that," but as "neither one nor the other." Up until the 2000 census, people were always forced to select one box or another. For persons of mixed race, the result was the official denial of some part of their ancestral identity, and a sense that "mixed" was somehow less. For people of mixed Asian and White ancestry who grew up in the United States, experiences differed depending on geography and physical characteristics. Children who could "pass" as White, or who blended in because they seemed to fit into one of the ethnic categories of their peers, had different experiences than children who looked more "exotic" and whose facial features tended to resemble the non-White parent.

The situation in Hawai'i is quite different. Part of the acceptance of *hapaness* in Hawai'i must be attributed to patterns of intermarriage that have characterized Hawai'i's ethnic landscape since the early 1800s. Writings by C. E. Glick (1992) on patterns of intermarriage in Hawai'i suggest that there are three historical stages:

1. Nearly all incoming persons are male and they intermarry (with Hawaiians).
2. More females arrive and intermixture is discouraged.
3. Americanization, loss of parental influence on offspring, marital choice, and increased intercultural marriage takes place.

Glick says that all groups are currently at the third stage, which seems to be generally true, although young people continue to encounter parental displeasure at dating outside of their ethnicity. Nevertheless, the statistics indicate that parental influence on marital choice is decreasing. To get a sense of how these numbers have progressed over time, and a more specific look at intermarriage patterns by ethnicity, see the table below. Figures from data compiled on eight ethnic groups during the years of 1912 to 1953 indicate that the rate of interracial marriage steadily increased over time.

We should be cautious in analyzing this data because of the flexibility of the term "interracial," which also seems to mean "interethnic" in this table. If people tend to use these terms interchangeably, this may partially explain why the census data from 2000 indicates such a high percentage of mixed-race individuals. If the local convention is to collapse race and ethnicity, then people may self-identify as mixed-race when they really mean mixed-ethnicity. It should also be noted, however, that interethnic marriages could sometimes be even more problematic than interracial marriages when the partners came from historically antagonistic groups like Filipinos and Japanese or Japanese and Korean. Nevertheless, this data suggests a long history of interethnic and interracial marriage, which helps to explain the relatively positive view towards hapa children. In other words, hapaness was normalized by island attitudes and historical ethnic intermixing.

TABLE 11.1.   Interracial marriages as percentage of all marriages in Hawai'i, 1912 to 1953

	Outmarriages (%)				
	1912–1916	1920–1930	1930–1940	1940–1949	1950–1953
Hawaiian					
Grooms	19.4	33.3	55.2	66.3	76.7
Brides	39.9	52.1	62.7	77.2	78.0
Part-Hawaiian					
Grooms	52.1	38.8	41.0	36.9	39.6
Brides	66.2	57.7	57.9	64.2	58.0
Caucasian					
Grooms	17.3	24.3	22.4	33.8	35.6
Brides	11.7	13.8	19.7	10.2	14.7
Chinese					
Grooms	41.7	24.8	28.0	31.2	41.0
Brides	5.7	15.7	28.5	38.0	42.5
Japanese					
Grooms	0.5	2.7	4.3	4.3	7.4
Brides	0.2	3.1	6.3	16.9	17.6
Korean					
Grooms	26.4	17.6	23.5	49.0	68.0
Brides	0.0	4.9	39.0	66.7	72.3
Filipino					
Grooms	21.8	25.6	37.5	42.0	42.0
Brides	2.8	1.0	4.0	21.0	30.0
Puerto Rican					
Grooms	24.4	18.6	29.8	39.5	48.4
Brides	26.4	39.7	42.8	50.3	59.0
Total	11.5	19.2	22.8	28.6	31.0

Source: Adapted from Lind (1955).

More recent data from the *State of Hawai'i Databook* indicates that in 1996, 46.5 percent of the marriages in Hawai'i, where at least one of the partners was a resident, were interracial. This number is slightly higher than in 1992 when the percentage was 45.7. Allen Awaya, Professor of Education at the University of Hawai'i, is not of mixed race himself, but looks ambiguous enough to be an "Asian mix." He says, "During my lifetime [he was born in 1948] it was always better to be hapa rather than just one race because hapa people were seen as inherently more attractive. I think it was also partly because it meant that you were removed from the immigrant status. You weren't just 'fresh off the boat'" (Awaya, interview, 1999). His statement might be taken as a privileging of Caucasian physical characteristics—as a movement away from recent immigrant status—revealing another dimension of identity negotiation from foreign to less foreign.

Identity negotiation was somewhat different for Paul, a man of Okinawan/Caucasian ancestry who grew up in the mainland U.S., as he recalls incidences in which ethnicity was an issue. In his stories, it is not hapaness that is the issue, but being part Japanese. In fact, he notes that he does not look Japanese, but actually more Latino. His friends in the southern California town where he grew up were mostly Mexican, so he says that he "fit in" because his ethnicity was masked by his appearance. During his senior year of college, he adopted his mother's family name as his middle name to outwardly express the Okinawan part of his ethnic identity.

The need to express the "wholeness" of ethnic identity when it is masked by appearances arose in a conversation with Lamar, a university student in his early twenties: "On the mainland I am just Black, but I'm really part Cherokee, too." His decision to mention this suggests that he is aware that in the geographic space of Hawai'i, one could be both—that identity need not be fastened in the way that it is on the mainland, and that there is a different repertoire of identity markers from which to draw.

The term *hapa* also coveys a sense of the "local" because so many of Hawai'i's children are of mixed ancestry. When questions of ancestry arise in university classes, students appear to feel a sense of pride in listing their heritage, particularly if it includes five or six ethnicities.

As valued as hapaness is by the dominant culture in Hawai'i, the most important thing for children is to fit with their peers. Children seem to feel best when their identity is fastened in ways that show that they belong. This feeling is expressed by Marilyn, a high school teacher of Okinawan descent who is reflecting on the construction of her identity over time:

> One of my earliest school memories is as a first grader, in tears after school, asking my mother if I was "hapa" or "Portagee" as a classmate had insisted I was. Wasn't I Japanese, I anxiously questioned. Most of my playmates were and I didn't want to be different. As I grew older, the unspoken message from teachers and friends was that I was lucky that I looked like a blend. In some ways I suspect that it was an advantage. Since others were not immediately certain of my ethnicity, I was not labeled and boxed so very easily and was possibly given a nanosecond of added attention. (Marilyn, class paper, 1999)

Marilyn reveals layers of identity negotiation and positions herself over time in relation to a fluctuating norm. As a child, looking Japanese was of prime importance in a setting where most of her playmates were Japanese. Later, her ambiguous hapa looks permitted her more latitude in fastening identity.

Andy, a hapa pre-service teacher whose mother is from Minnesota and whose father is local Japanese, notes how his ambiguous identity permits him to operate in different spaces: "Having a Japanese last name makes me feel more like a local boy. I'm White enough that I can sneak into hotel pools unnoticed [although I] was born and raised eating *saimin* and rice." In this case, "Whiteness" has two possible interpretations: Andy may be referring to the Whiteness of being part Caucasian, but he also may be referencing the "Whiteness" of Japanese nationals. When Japanese nationals visit Hawai'i, their "Whiteness," as compared with local Japanese, is a mark of their "foreignness"—their nonlocal identity. While Whiteness offers the temporary privilege of a tourist, it is also marks the nonlocal outsider.

Like the earlier analysis of local, nonlocal, and haole identities as relational, contested, and negotiated, hapa identity in Hawai'i is embedded in a historical context. Identity is negotiated within the shared structure of intelligibility which operates in particular times and in particular cultural spaces. Similar contingencies must be considered in naming practices, which are discussed in the next section.

CULTURAL AND POLITICAL DIMENSIONS OF NAMING PRACTICES

An individual's name is a public as well as a personal identity marker. It is the means by which we are fastened to a particular ethnic or cultural heritage. In the United States, names are less apt to be social class markers than they are in Europe. However, in every community there are family names that are associated with the power structure. Aspects of personal identity that are marked with a name are gender, nationality, and ethnic origin. We speak of girls' names and boys' names and frequently use ethnic designations to describe them, such as, "She has a German name," or "That's a Korean name." Personal names also reflect the dreams and aspirations of parents for their children, or represent a historical continuity with people who have gone before them.

We are all aware of immigrants whose names were arbitrarily changed by unsympathetic immigration officers who found their names difficult, unwieldy, or "too foreign." Likewise, there are stories of insensitive teachers who assume the prerogative of refastening identity by giving their "foreign" students new names for similar reasons. This may be done partly to fit the child into a new social context, or partly for the teacher's own convenience because her or his own identity is so tightly fastened. Seminal events in an individual's life, such as immigration, force them to take on new identities as a means of being accepted in their new setting, as well as of adapting to a new environment. As people shift from one geographic space into another, they sometimes opt, of their own accord, to borrow the identity markers of their new geographic spaces and adopt names that make them seem "less foreign." Such overt identity shifts may take on a sense of urgency when historical events demand a public declaration of one's identity. Cynthia Kadohata writes in her novel, *The Floating World,* that her grandparents, who attended school in Hawai'i when World War II broke out, were forced to change their names before they could enroll. "Satoro, Yukiko, Mariko, Haruko, and Sadamu became Roger, Lily, Laura, Anne, and Roy" (1989, p. 2). In some cases, Japanese families made the choice to change their names as a public statement of their patriotism to America. Most second-, third-, and fourth-generation Japanese in Hawai'i have a Western first name, a middle name that marks their gender and ethnic identity, and a family name that reflects their ancestral origin.

These designations reflect the historical and geographic situatedness of naming practices and are reflective of Palmer's definition of identity as the moving intersection of inner and outer forces. In the processes described above, the push was towards assimilation and the ideal of a more Eurocentric and homogenous vision of collective identity. Another dimension of naming that is discussed below embraces a somewhat different notion of geographic situatedness—one which points away from the Eurocentric aspects of American culture, represents a different approach to identity refastening, and emerges from the Hawaiian renaissance.

The history of the suppression of Hawaiian language and culture in schools parallels the suppression and patterns of deculturalization that took place in other times and other places. One aspect of the revival of Hawaiian arts, culture, and language is the recognition that Hawaiian culture is the "host culture." Families who have no Hawaiian ancestry show their respect and affinity for Hawai'i and its culture by giving their children Hawaiian names. It is not unusual to see the addition of a Hawaiian middle name. For example, a name like David Hiroki Kalani Sato is very much "in style" for third- and fourth-generation youth of Japanese ancestry. This use of a Hawaiian middle name conveys a sense of place and cultural affiliation, and reveals how naming practices can refasten identity in ways that reflect cultural affinity that is not reflected in ethnic heritage. In this case, the addition of a Hawaiian name might also provide some generational information since this practice was not common among second-generation Americans of Japanese descent.

Up to this point, this discussion has placed a special emphasis on local Japanese. It should be noted, though, that people who study Hula and/or Hawaiian language in Hawai'i are often given a Hawaiian name regardless of their ethnic background. While in class or even outside, their cultural affiliation and commitment to this aspect of their identity can be so powerful that they choose to use this name, or a shortened version of it, as their primary designation—even if they claim no Hawaiian ancestry.

What these naming practices suggest is that cultural affiliation is a powerful identity marker that may not be revealed through ethnic or national identity. Furthermore, contemporary naming practices in Hawai'i indicate a movement away from emphasizing European American identity. Finally, they underscore a consciousness of the multiplicity, contingency, and intersectionality of identity.

Concluding Thoughts

The Hawai'i case provides some insights into the ways in which identity is negotiated in a changing social, historical, and cultural context. The examples that are cited in this chapter suggest that local, nonlocal, and haole terminologies are imprecise and flexible—that they are historically situated, continuously contested, and partially rule-driven. They sometimes depend as much on the cultivation of sensibilities and attitudes as they do on ethnic heritage and history. Their salience is derived from the meanings which insiders and outsiders infuse them, and from the work that insiders and outsiders do to fasten, unfasten, and refasten identity.

Attitudes toward hapa identity in Hawai'i are partially determined by the long history of interethnic and interracial marriage. This temporal dimension is supported by critical mass. Another reason for the normalization of hapa identity is due to large numbers of hapa children placed in the framework of a host culture which paid little mind to race until Caucasians arrived.

The section on naming practices shows how naming is an intentional means to publicly fasten or refasten identity. This section shows how ethnic and national identity may be different from cultural identity, but that all can be claimed in a name. All three sections point toward a model that decenters Whiteness by making it less invisible, less privileged, and less central.

Identity fastening, unfastening, and refastening are continuously done to us and by us. They are part of the ongoing identity negotiation process. Clay, who is second-generation Chinese, was born in San Francisco. He is unwilling to claim his "Chinese" identity because he does not speak Chinese and has only a marginal sense of what it means to "be Chinese." In other words, he does not fit the notion of "Chinese" that he carries around in his own head. But at the same time, he realizes the power of physical characteristics as identity markers in the larger society, and worries that he is being fastened into an identity that doesn't fit:

> One's ethnicity needs to be acknowledged and respected, but not pigeonholed. When I look in the mirror each day I see that I am Chinese. Other members of American society also, I think, react to the person they see when they see me. They won't mistake me

for a white or black person. Sometimes the most painful realization in discovering your own personal identity is not all members of your ethnic background may treat you well or with kindness and respect. In fact, there may be hostile rejection from the "group" if there's a difference in politics or social values. That's when I need to connect with others who are more aligned with the person I am inside and not just focus on the outside. (Clay, class paper, 1998)

Clay has learned that society takes the outer characteristics of a person and translates them into some truth about that individual's inner reality—as if gender, race, and ethnicity are a kind of coding system that reveals some ultimate truth. He knows from experience that this practice often leads to cases of mistaken identity. Clay's comments, like those made by others discussed in this chapter, caution against the narrow and limiting ways in which identity is fastened.

Since identities are always being negotiated and are always under construction, the stories in this chapter represent only a few of many possible iterations and instances; yet, the voices of these informants are useful in recontextualizing and reorienting us to our taken-for-granted categories. They enable us to unlock meanings as they reveal and illuminate the complexity of identity negotiation in Hawai'i.

A number of the examples of identity construction that are discussed in this chapter point toward a repositioning of Whiteness and Eurocentric culture away from the center. The narratives of identity construction and negotiation that weave the identity tapestry of Hawai'i problematize and decenter Whiteness by making it less invisible, as well as less central, to the group narrative. This is due to a number of factors that include: the absence of an ethnic majority, the legacy of colonization, the heightened awareness of ethnic and cultural difference, and the ways in which diversity is managed in Hawai'i through ethnic humor and accommodation. Cultural differences in Hawai'i seem to align Asian and Pacific Island groups in collective contrast to U.S. mainland values and interactive styles. All of these factors converge to force self-reflection and a critical examination of Whiteness (McIntyre, 1997).

Notes

Special thanks to those informants who generously shared their stories and perspectives. An earlier version of this material appeared in Reed, G. G. (2001). Fastening and unfastening identities: Negotiating identity in Hawai'i. *Discourse: Studies in the Cultural Politics of Education, 22* (3), 327–339 (see http://www.tandf.co.uk).

REFERENCES

Brah, A. (1996). *Cartographies of diaspora: Contesting identities*. (College of Education data, 2001.) London: Routledge.

Creamer, B., & Infante, E. (1995, February). What does it mean to be local? *Honolulu Advertiser, 12* (1).

Estep, G. A. (1941). *Social placement of the Portuguese in Hawaii as indicated by factors in assimilation*. Unpublished thesis, University of Southern California, Los Angeles.

Frankenberg, R. (1993). *White women, race matters: The social construction of Whiteness*. Minneapolis: University of Minnesota Press.

Furman, G. C. (1998). Postmodernism and community in schools: Unraveling the paradox. *Educational Administration Quarterly, 34* (3), 298–328.

Glick, C. E. (1992). Interracial marriage and admixture in Hawaii. In M. P. Root (Ed.), *Racially mixed people in America* (pp. 239–250). London: Sage Publications.

Herring, R. D. (1995). Developing biracial ethnic identity: A review of the increasing dilemma. *Journal of Multicultural Counseling and Development, 23*, 29–38.

Kadohata, C. (1989). *The floating world*. New York: Viking Press.

Kuroda, G. (1998). Public opinion and cultural values. In M. Haas (Ed.), *Multicultural Hawaii: The fabric of a multicultural society* (pp. 131–146). New York: Garland Press.

Lind, A. W. (1955). *Hawaii's people*. Honolulu: University of Hawaii Press.

Lum, D. Y. H. (1997). *Local genealogy: "What school you went?" Stories from a pidgin culture*. Unpublished dissertation, University of Hawaii at Manoa.

Lyles, M. R., Yancy, A., Grace, C., & Carter, J. (1985). Racial identity and self- esteem: Problems peculiar to biracial children. *Journal of the American Academy of Child Psychiatry, 24* (2), 150–153.

McIntyre, A. (1997). *Making meaning of whiteness: Exploring racial identity with white teachers*. Buffalo: State University of New York Press.

Nakaso, D. (1998, August 31). Hawaii doesn't fit mainland mold. *Honolulu Advertiser*, (1).

Okamura, J. (1981, Spring). Aloha Kakaka Me Ke Aloha `Aina: Local culture and society in Hawaii. *Impulse*, 54–56.

Okamura, J. (1994). Why there are no Asian Americans in Hawaii: The continuing significance of local identity. *Social Process in Hawaii, 35*, 161–178.

Palmer, P. (1997, Nov./Dec.). The heart of a teacher: Identity and integrity in teaching. *Change*, 15–21.

Rohrer, J. (1997). Haole Girl: Identity and white privilege in Hawaii. *Social Process in Hawaii, 38*, 140–161.

Supriya, K. E. (1999). White difference: Cultural constructions of white identity. In T. K. Nakayama & J. N. Martin (Eds.), *Whiteness: The communication of social identity* (pp. 129–148). Thousand Oaks: Sage Publications.

Whittaker, E. (1986). *The Mainland Haole: The white experience in Hawaii*. New York: Columbia University Press.

Zerubavel, E. (1981). *Hidden rhythms: Schedules and calendars in social life*. Chicago: University of Chicago Press.

Chapter 12

The Question of Identity and Difference

The Resident Korean Education in Japan

Hiromitsu Inokuchi and Yoshiko Nozaki

INTRODUCTION

Resident Koreans in Japan (Zainichi Kankoku/Chosenjin) have been the largest minority group in Japan for the last fifty years, constituting approximately half of Japan's entire noncitizen population in the 1990s.[1] During the colonial period, a large number of Koreans migrated to Japan to become part of the labor underclass. Some were physically coerced, and others were forced to do so for economic reasons. In post–World War II Japan, the Japanese government forced Resident Koreans either to become Japanese nationals (legal citizens) or to retain their Korean nationality by remaining "aliens" with limited legal and civil rights. Resident Koreans have fought against the Japanese government's oppressive social policies for years. One of the most important sites of their struggle has been education, to ensure that their youth would maintain, or develop, their identities as Koreans.

In the area of Japanese studies, a volume edited by Changsoo Lee and George De Vos (1981) was the first attempt to address the issues of Resident Koreans. Since the 1990s, new perspectives have emerged that regard the study of Resident Koreans as a significant site from which to examine Japan's multiculturalism, or lack thereof (e.g., Fukuoka, 2000; Ryang, 1997, 2000; Weiner, 1997). Although these studies have underscored the issues of Korean ethnic identity and education as crucial, few have explored the history of Resident Korean education as a case through which questions of curriculum and pedagogy may be considered (e.g., do minority students need to be taught their own language, history, and culture? Do students of the majority group need to understand the heritage of minority groups? If so, what kinds of approaches need to be developed?).

Some educational research has looked at Resident Koreans and their school performance, and implicated the legacy of colonialism as a factor in their academic failure (e.g., Ogbu, 1987). This research, however, with a somewhat narrow focus (i.e., academic achievement), does not adequately examine the complex history of the oppression Resident Koreans have faced and the social, political, and educational struggles they—sometimes with the support of Japanese educators and citizens—have carried on in the postwar period. These struggles have been postwar, postcolonial in nature, rather than part of the colonial legacy per se; thus, postcolonial perspectives are essential to any study that would attempt to comprehend them.

The present study critically examines the postcolonial politics of curriculum and teaching in the educational struggles of Resident Koreans. In particular, it examines the relation of power to education (Apple, 1982) and of identity and difference to educational struggles (e.g., Apple, 1999). Joan W. Scott (1988) argues that the operation of power depends on the construction of a ground of difference (involving a set of binary categories), and that, in turn, any challenge to the power must come from a ground of difference. This study examines the exercise of power in constructing the category of Resident Koreans, and the ways Resident Koreans have challenged that power from various grounds of difference.

EDUCATION AND OPPRESSION: EARLY EFFORTS OF KOREAN MINZOKU SCHOOLS, 1945–1950S

Japan officially colonized Korea in the period 1910 to 1945, during which time Koreans became Japanese imperial subjects (i.e., Japanese citizens). However, while the imperial state granted them *some* civil rights,[2] they nevertheless faced discrimination and prejudice. The number of Koreans migrating to the Japanese archipelago ("mainland") increased steadily during the colonial period (approximately 40,000 Koreans had come to live in Japan by 1920, and approximately 626,000 by 1935). The migration took place primarily for economic reasons, because Japan's colonial policy severely impoverished Korea (Morita, 1996). In addition, during the late 1930s to 1945, a large number of Koreans were taken to Japan by force to work in mines and factories (i.e., as wartime forced labor). By 1945, the Korean population in the Japanese mainland had increased to over 2,100,000.

In 1945, Japan surrendered and Korea declared its independence. Within a few years, many Koreans left Japan, but in 1950 more than 600,000 still remained. Meanwhile, questions concerning the legal status of Koreans residing in Japan—in particular, questions of nationality and citizenship—were put on hold. For example, the voting rights of Korean males were suspended after December 1945. The Allied forces (primarily

U.S. forces) occupying Japan officially stated that Koreans, as the people of a former Japanese colony, "were to be treated as 'liberated' [i.e., non-Japanese] nationals in cases not involving military security," but that it "would be necessary to treat them as 'enemy' [i.e., Japanese] nationals in some cases" because Koreans had been Japanese imperial subjects (Lee, 1981, p. 63, see also Kashiwazaki, 2000). While Japan's Alien Registration Law of 1947 classified them as aliens, another government document considered them Japanese nationals until such time that a peace treaty could be concluded.

Soon after Japan's defeat, Koreans remaining in Japan sought Korean *minzoku* education—an ethnic education aimed at preserving their children's Korean identity (the term "minzoku" has multiple meanings, such as an ethnicity, a people, and a nation)—and they began to build their own Korean minzoku schools. The League of Koreans in Japan (Choren, hereafter LK), was the largest organization of Koreans in Japan at that time; it built 541 elementary schools, 7 junior high schools, 8 high schools, and 22 schools for post-high-school education by October 1947. The schools reclaimed the Korean cultural heritage that had been so severely suppressed by Japanese colonialism. The schools developed their own curricula and educational materials, which emphasized Korean history and geography. In addition, all classes were taught in Korean, Japanese colonialism and its assimilationist ideas were criticized, and Korean nationalism was promoted in its place.

Li Dong-sun, who taught at a Korean minzoku school around the time, later wrote about the joy experienced by Korean students who transferred to his school:

> Any child, every child starting the school asked teachers as follows: "Don't we have to go to Japanese schools any longer?" When the teacher(s) answered "You don't have to," the children altogether cried for joy. They were now free to use the language of their own country without either the fear of prohibition or feeling of constraint by others [i.e., Japanese teachers and students]. Where their ethnic tradition was not disdained and where they did not have to hide that they were Koreans, even though it was a poor school, it was like a heaven. (Li, 1956, p. 70)

The Allied forces occupying Japan did not view the development of Korean minzoku schools in a positive light, however, because the LK was strongly influenced by the (Japanese) Communist Party. The Japanese government, along with the occupation forces, then ordered the schools to comply with Japanese school regulations or be closed. Koreans mounted a strong resistance to the order. In 1948, the U.S. military violently repressed resistance in the Kobe area, declaring martial law and arresting more than one thousand Koreans in a single day. One Korean student was shot dead by the Japanese police in Osaka. In November 1949, Korean minzoku schools were officially closed, though some schools were incorporated into the local public school systems, and some remained open as nonauthorized schools (Ozawa, 1973).

THE KOREAN WAR AND THE CONTINUED EFFORTS FOR KOREAN ETHNIC EDUCATION IN THE 1950S

The Korean War of 1950–1953, and the subsequent military tension between the North and South, made it difficult for Koreans in Japan to return to their homelands. They were also legally recategorized in these years. The revised Nationality Law (effective in 1950) retained the patrilineal *jus sanguinis* principle (according to which the descendants of immigrants are aliens, even though they are born in Japan, unless they apply for naturalization).[3] The San Francisco Peace Treaty (signed in 1951 and effective in 1952) restored Japan's full sovereignty and dealt yet another blow to the Koreans. Just before the treaty became effective, the Japanese government suddenly announced that the people of Japan's former colonies (e.g., Koreans) were to lose their Japanese nationality. Koreans in Japan, who had technically been Japanese nationals, had now become Korean nationals residing in Japan (i.e., Resident Koreans) (see also Inokuchi, 2000; Kashiwazaki, 2000). In addition, the Alien Registration Law of 1952 required them to be fingerprinted every three years and to carry a registration card at all times. The law applied to all foreign residents residing in Japan, but in practice, it was a means to control Resident Koreans. Such treatment was also clearly demeaning, because up until that time only criminals had to be fingerprinted.

During this time, the majority of Korean parents transferred their children to Japanese schools. The number of students who received any kind of Korean ethnic education decreased significantly from thirty-five thousand in 1949 to little more than seventeen thousand in 1952 (Ozawa, 1973). Only about forty Korean minzoku schools remained, and they operated without the permission of the Japanese government. In some regions, Japanese schools established special classes to provide limited ethnic education to Resident Korean students, but for the most part, these classes operated as extracurricular activities. In 1952, there were seventy seven classes of this kind in thirteen prefectures (including Osaka, Kyoto, Shiga, and Kanagawa).

Notable in the 1950s was that after the closure of Korean minzoku schools in 1949, some local governments took over the operation of some of these schools, making them public. In these schools, Korean teachers were either replaced by Japanese teachers, or (re)hired as contracted, untenured staff. However, the essence of Korean ethnic education (e.g., Korean as the language of instruction) was maintained. In Tokyo, for example, fifteen elementary schools, one junior high school, and one high school came to be part of the public school system run by the Tokyo metropolitan government. However, the metropolitan government decided to close these schools after 1952. The decision invited strong protest from both Japanese and Korean teachers, as well as parents, but the schools were closed by the police force in violent fashion in 1955. Elsewhere, a few public Korean minzoku schools continued to operate until 1965.

The early postwar efforts of Korean minzoku schools and the oppression they experienced demonstrate that power works effectively by legally constructing a ground of difference (Resident Koreans as noncitizens in this case). The Japanese state was willing to construct a difference and use its force to suppress the educational desires and opportunities of a minority group. However, Resident Korean educational struggles did not cease. In the following sections, we would like to examine three approaches to Resident Korean education: the North Korean minzoku schools (schools operated by the General Federation of Korean Residents), a minzoku education classes for Resident Korean youth in Japanese schools, and a curriculum for all from the standpoint of Resident Koreans. All have been developed in subsequent years, and all suggest the complexity of the issue of identity (and difference) in curriculum and pedagogy.

"We are North Korean Nationals": GFKR Minzoku Schools

The General Federation of Korean Residents (Chosoren, hereafter GFKR), founded in 1955 and closely affiliated with North Korea, criticized the earlier actions of Resident Koreans. It argued that they should stay away from Japanese politics because they were not Japanese nationals. In its view, they were North Korean "oversea nationals" (*kaigai komin*). The GFKR declared its agenda as follows:

> We shall strengthen the unity and integration of six hundred thousand fellow Koreans residing in Japan, as nationals of Democratic People's Republic of Korea, defend various democratic rights and democratic minzoku education, [and] secure our proper rights of living. (the GFKR Declaration of 1955, cited in Ozawa, 1973, pp. 419–420)

The specific purpose of GFKR education included minzoku education with Korean as the language of instruction, abolition of leftover colonial ideas and feudalistic customs, and overcoming illiteracy (Ozawa, 1973). The GFKR launched a campaign to revive the Korean minzoku schools that had been suppressed in the early postwar years, and gained strong support from the North Korean government, which sent large amounts of funding, scholarships, and educational materials. The school curricula were explicitly North Korea–centric, with the primary aim of educating students to become good citizens of North Korea by following the principles of socialism (see also Ryang, 1997).

In the late 1950s and 1960s, the GFKR worked hard for the legalization of its schools. The schools were gradually authorized by the local governments as "miscellaneous schools." For example, in 1968 the Tokyo metropolitan government authorized the Korean University of Tokyo (established in 1956), despite strong objection by the Ministry of Education. The "miscellaneous schools" status was not equal to that of formal, accredited schools, but nonetheless gave them a legal basis. By the early 1970s, most GFKR schools were authorized as "miscellaneous schools."[4]

The GFKR schools faced a number of difficulties, however. For example, being legally defined as "miscellaneous schools" meant that they were not accredited and, as a result, they were not regarded as satisfying all of the academic requirements. The option of becoming accredited was never really a consideration, since it meant eliminating Korean history, geography, and language classes (e.g., S. Park, 1992; Ozawa, 1997). Consequently, students had limited choices for higher education institutions, because technically, they could not have a high school diploma, which was a basic qualification for university admission. Japanese national universities (which were directly controlled by the Ministry of Education) did not accept their applications, though some private and public universities did.

The GFKR schools also faced serious financial difficulties due to their "miscellaneous school" status. Not only did the Japanese government refuse to provide any financial assistance (which all other Japanese private schools received), but its patrons were also disallowed tax-deductible status for donations. Resident Korean parents sending their children to the schools bore the financial burden.

In the mid-1980s, approximately half of the private, prefectural, and city universities came to accept Korean minzoku school students' applications, though the Ministry of Education allowed no national universities to do so. In 2003, however, the ministry changed its policy regarding university admission of graduates from "miscellaneous schools," and allowed each national university to set its own criteria of admission. As a result, nearly 70 percent of national universities were willing to consider students from the Korean minzoku schools as legitimate candidates for admission in the spring of 2004. These developments have been positive, but increased active recruitment of Korean minzoku school graduates would be desirable, for the graduates of the Korean minzoku schools bring with them valuable cultural experiences and knowledge that have not been inculcated in Japanese higher education institutions.

Currently, the GFKR owns a school system consisting of eighty-three elementary schools, fifty-six junior high schools, twelve high schools, and one university (as of 1993, about 10 percent of Resident Korean children were attending those schools).[5] In the meantime, GFKR schools have experienced a decline in enrollment (e.g., I. Park, 1995). Many Resident Koreans seem to have come to prefer not to associate themselves with North Korea, especially after the mid-1980s, when North Korea's oppressive regime was widely reported. In some respects, however, the decline is a result of the continuing prejudice and xenophobia against Koreans among the Japanese. Resident Korean parents worry about the harassment GFKR students have experienced.

Yang Chin-ja, a Resident Korean mother, recalls wondering whether she should send her child to a GFKR school or a Japanese school. She is a graduate of GFKR schools, but chose to go to a Japanese university because she became critical of GFKR schools. As a mother, she thought that it would be better for her daughter to attend GFKR schools, but she also worried about the harassment her child might face. As she put it,

> The biggest anxious thought I had about deciding to have my child enrolled in the Korean school was, in fact, "if something like the 'chogori ripping incident' might happen again."[6] If something happens in North Korea and if it has a bad influence upon the international society, especially if it becomes a cause of direct threat to Japan, it would be Korean school students who would become the first targets of harassment [by some Japanese]. (Yang, 1995, p. 130)

Many Resident Korean parents have also avoided GFKR schools because they want their children to escape the disadvantage of not having "high school diplomas." Some parents feel their children need to acquire the knowledge and skills necessary to succeed in Japanese society. As parent in Ryang's study (1997, p. 149) states,

> Chol-i [son's name] is to be a man of [the] twenty-first century. ... He has to survive in Japan, has to be made fit for this society. He needs knowledge and skill to do so. Chongryun [GFKR] schools are not, I am afraid, made for this, which is fair enough; I do not ask Chongryun schools to do everything. I will continue to pay local branch fees and participate in the organization as much as I can; I'll continue to be sympathetic and supportive. But Chol-i's future is his, not mine. Because he is interested in becoming a physician, we have to give him our support. (p. 149)

The GFKR minzoku schools' North Korea–centric curricula approach thus underwent a critical reexamination, and in the early 1990s the curricula was changed to be less oriented toward North Korea and to be more adaptive regarding contemporary Japanese society.

The experience of GFKR minzoku schools gives us some insights into the question of identity (and difference) in curriculum development. Resident Koreans who defined themselves as North Korean overseas nationals can been seen as those who fought to remain "Korean," to remain "different." Their form of collective identity was strong, and they were able to create a space for their version of minzoku education. They have suffered from explicit discrimination by Japan's educational policy, however. The recent decline in enrollment in GFKR schools indicates that the dominant society is still intolerant to difference. The latest change of GFKR school curricula also suggests that the North Korea–centric approach, no matter how important it has been, may not accurately reflect the Korean Residents' wishes, and the needs of their youth, today.

KOREAN NAME AS "REAL NAME": KOREAN MINZOKU EDUCATION CLASSES IN JAPANESE SCHOOLS

As already noted, after 1952 Koreans residing in Japan were classified as aliens. The Ministry of Education decided to admit Resident Korean students to Japanese public schools as a "favor," and adopted a firm assimilationist educational policy. The law defining compulsory education did not apply to Resident Koreans, so the official admission list did not include resident Korean children. The Resident Korean parents were required to sign consent forms stating that they would not complain about school policy.[7] The Ministry of Education did not (and still does not) allow schools to provide special classes for Korean history and language during regular school hours.

No matter how assimilationist the Japanese public schools were, an overwhelming number of Resident Korean children attended them. In Japanese schools, Resident Korean students were supposed to be treated the same as Japanese students. This meant that their difference was totally ignored in an official sense, while overt and covert prejudice and discrimination against them continued. Many of them were ashamed of their families' poverty-stricken lifestyle, but they tended to think it was because they were Koreans. Schools with large Resident Korean student populations often faced serious delinquency problems.

In the mid-1960s, the Osaka City Education Board, responsible for a student body with a large number of Resident Korean students, established a council called Shigaikyo, the Osaka City Research Council for the Problem of Foreign Children Education.[8] The council, made up of school administrators, tended to see Resident Korean students as the cause of the problem (Nakayama, 1995; Kishino, 1985). In the early 1970s, the position of the council was criticized by many Resident Korean groups as well as progressive Japanese teachers. In their view, the problem was Japanese schools and society, which did not offer educational opportunities for Resident Koreans. Some teachers facing Resident Korean students began to explore ways to develop a Korean minzoku education within the Japanese (mostly public) schools. The minzoku education movement promoted the teaching of the Korean language, history, music, and dancing, and helped connect Resident Korean students to each other.

In most cases, minzoku education programs were run as extracurricular activities, such as after-school classes.[9] Instructors for these classes were often Resident Korean volunteers, and some schools later hired full-time Resident Korean teachers. Some schools that were located in communities with a large Resident Korean population invited Resident Korean parents and grandparents to take part, and were very successful in providing opportunities for learning about Korean culture and history. This extracurricular approach was by no means sufficient and was typically regarded as exclusively for Resident Korean students, though there were a few (rare) cases in which some Japanese students and parents joined the activities.

Many teachers involved in the minzoku education movement believed that the students needed to affirm their identity as Koreans and develop their self-esteem. The most important practice of minzoku education classes has been to encourage students to use their Korean names ("real names") and overcome the identity dilemma (Kishino, 1985).[10] Many Resident Korean students hid their ethnic origins by using a Japanese alias, primarily out of fear of being subjected to prejudice and discrimination.[11] The teachers believed that as a result, many of them experienced a dilemma of ethnic identity: In order to be proud of themselves, Resident Korean students would need to assert themselves as Korean and affirm their identity as Koreans; but by identifying themselves as Korean, it would be impossible for them to avoid the stigma of being Korean.

Yoriko Sugitani, a teacher involved in the minzoku education classes, summarized the importance of using ethnic names as follows:

> For Korean children the use of "real name" is a beginning to reconsider affectionately the ways their ancestors lived, and it is a basis for them to understand the [current] unjust conditions in which they live. The use of "real names" leads to the construction of subjects who fight [against the injustice]. (Sugitani, 1980, p. 35)

The teachers involved in the education of Resident Korean students established a nationwide organization called Zenchokyo—the National Council for the Research on Education—for Koreans in Japan in 1983. The move-ment, supported by many Resident Korean parents, has gradually spread to other geographical areas.

Presently, while the minzoku education movement in Japanese schools is still progressing, some critics raise fundamental questions concerning the practice. It has frequently been the case that, at least initially, Resident Korean students reject the very teachers who attempt to evoke their Korean con-sciousness and encourage them to use their Korean names. In fact, teachers' reports on the practice of minzoku education have often addressed this initial rejection and the ways to overcome it. The rejection seems to occur more often when the teacher is Japanese, suggesting the importance of having Resident Korean teachers as role models in minzoku education (e.g., Inatomi, 1988).

Perhaps the fundamental issue here is the power relations that Resident Korean students have with their Japanese teachers, who are mem-bers of the dominant group. Kim Tae-young (1999) discusses the case of Song Sun-ja. Sun-ja was living in an area with a high concentration of Resident Koreans, and when she entered junior high school she began to use a Korean name. She was regarded as the "model case" by teachers, and at the beginning of every school year, she was asked by the teachers to tell her Japanese classmates her feelings as a Resident Korean. In the teachers' views, it was a good experience for Sun-ja because her classmates would understand her, and she would be able to maintain her Korean identity. But for Sun-ja, it became a burden. As she put it:

> No matter how hard I tried to speak, some were sleeping, some were not listening seriously. Some were thinking that they did not want to listen—I was able to tell by the air. In front of those kids, I did not want to speak, but I was made to talk over the same thing every year. (Kim, 1999, p. 181)

The teachers' good will became another form of oppression, and as soon as she entered high school, Sun-ja decided to use her Japanese name.

Another problem is a type of essentialism that lurks under the notion of the Korean name as "real name." Educators need to recognize that by now the history and character of Resident Koreans as a group is different from that of Koreans in Korea, and that the binary terms "Koreans" and "Japanese," which were used without question in the past, are not quite workable here. Resident Koreans have developed an interethnic culture and lifestyle, and most of them do not plan to return to Korea. Some clearly assert that "I want to be a Resident Korean, rather than Korean," implying that they want to be different from "Koreans" (Inokuchi, 1996, p. 96). The task of teachers would be to ensure an open space in which each Resident Korean student can assert his or her own meaning of being Resident Korean, and decide his or her "real name" by imagining new possibilities in their identity formation.

Apart from these issues, the minzoku education for Resident Koreans in Japanese schools has had some shortcomings. To date, the minzoku education programs have tended to be offered as extracurricular activities, and few Japanese students have really taken part. Also, raising the consciousness of Resident Korean students has been the main purpose, and, thus far, Japanese students, if they participate, have been taught "supportive" roles rather than urged to confront their own prejudice and ethnocentrism. In the following section, we would like to discuss some projects in which teachers at Japanese schools have attempted to change the attitudes and views of the Japanese.

INCLUDING RESIDENT KOREAN PERSPECTIVES IN OFFICIAL CURRICULUM

In Japan, the Ministry of Education has been in charge of developing instructional guidelines (*Shido Yoryo*), and it has been, in principle, mandatory for schools to follow them. Because the instructional guidelines have not addressed the issues of Resident Korean education—meaning that the ministry has not approved a minzoku education as part of official curricula at schools[12]—the development of school curricula that includes Resident Korean perspectives has been limited in its scope. However, this does not mean that there were no such attempts in local schools.

In the 1970s, a few projects were developed to include Resident Korean perspectives in school curricula. One project was set forth in the 1970s at Osaka's Tajima Elementary School, where in 1979, Resident Korean students accounted for about 40 percent of the student population. When a group of social studies teachers began a project called "Teaching about Korea," they found that existing teaching materials contained little information regarding the reasons for the presence of Resident Koreans in the region. They decided to collect teaching materials on their own. Some read history books, while others conducted interviews with Resident Korean elders. The teachers developed their own social studies curriculum and used it for teaching all of the students. Soon the project was expanded into other curriculum areas such as reading, music, and moral education. The teachers also began to have regular meetings with Resident Korean parents. After a few years, many of the Japanese students involved in the project came to state that it was their fault if Resident Korean students did not feel safe enough to use their Korean names (Kishino, 1985).

Another project set forth in the mid-1970s involved Imamiya High School of Industrial Arts—a school located close to the Resident Korean community in central Osaka. A Korean language class was started as an extracurricular activity because some Resident Korean students wanted to study Korean. To the school's surprise, the class attracted not only Resident Korean students, but Japanese students as well. Not only that, but the students wished to make it part of the regular curriculum so that they could use it to meet the foreign language requirements. (At that time only English met the requirement.) The school requested that the Osaka Prefectural Education Board provide funding for a full-time Korean language teacher. The request was granted, and the school began to offer a Korean language class as a part of the regular foreign language curriculum in 1978. One-fourth of the students chose Korean instead of English (Kishino, 1985).

There was also an effort at the level of the Osaka City Education Board. In 1972, after receiving public criticism (as discussed above), the Osaka City Research Council for the Problem of Foreign Children Education was reorganized and came to include many teachers active in the minzoku education movement (Nakayama, 1995; see also Hester, 2000). It began to inform teachers on the issues of education for Resident Koreans. In the mid-1970s, it worked for the development of teaching materials. Following the publication of a brochure entitled *The Great Kanto Earthquake and the Massacre of Koreans* (Kanto Daishinsai to Chosenjin Gyakusatsu) in 1975, it edited a series of supplementary reading materials titled *Saram* ("human being" in Korean). The *Saram* series was intended to develop a positive understanding of Korean culture among Japanese students. The series included Korean folktales, music, picture stories, dramas, and contemporary social issues concerning Resident Koreans. These supplementary reading materials were widely used in Osaka schools, and well received in several other prefectures as well (Kishino, 1985).

Unfortunately, projects like these have not become common practice in other Japanese schools (and in other prefectures), especially where the school population is predominantly Japanese. Beginning in the 1980s, the Japanese government began to declare the importance of the "internationalization of education." It has remained, however, silent about the education of Resident Korean youth, who are the children of the largest "international" population in Japan.

The lack of initiative by the Japanese government is, perhaps, not the only source of the problem, however. History teachers, in teaching about Japan's oppression of Koreans, have tended to focus on its colonization of the Korean peninsula and stop at the point of Japan's defeat in World War II, when Korea regained its independence. As a result, neither the oppression of Koreans residing in Japan during the pre-surrender period nor the struggles of Resident Koreans in the postwar years have been adequately addressed (Oh, 1996). The fact that teachers themselves were never taught, and perhaps never studied, the history from the standpoint of Resident Koreans helps perpetuate the problem. We also suspect that most teachers, being Japanese (i.e., members of the dominant group) are comfortable teaching about the problems of discrimination and prejudice as if these were past and externally over, rather than still present and internally ongoing.

In any case, the lack of historical knowledge and understanding regarding the issue of Resident Koreans has produced a degree of miseducation among students (and adults). For example, Japanese students sometimes respond to Resident Koreans' criticisms of Japanese society with abusive language such as, "Go home [to Korea], if you don't like it here in Japan." The situation suggests a need to examine the meanings students of the dominant group tend to attach to concepts such as nation, state, nationality, citizenship, and identity. This would be timely, since transnational (im)migration has increasingly become common the world over, requiring a complementary change in the way social and political communities are organized, constituted, imagined, and taught (Jacobson, 1996).

Conclusion: Power, Differences, and Curriculum

Power constructs a ground of difference upon which a particular identity can be constructed and imposed, so that particular power relations can be constructed and maintained. The Japanese government, in its attempt to control Resident Koreans, has constructed a ground of difference by designating them as "noncitizens." This legally constructed ground of difference enabled the government to exercise its force to violently repress Korean minzoku schools of the early postwar period and to deprive Resident Koreans of their right to an education in which their difference(s) were recognized and respected.

The ground of difference can also become the ground for opposition. Those who defined themselves as "North Korean overseas nationals in Japan" used the term to challenge the Japanese government. They were able to protect their rights and difference—though as citizens of a foreign country—and positively maintained, or reconstructed, their Korean identity. They successfully revived the Korean minzoku schools, even in the face of explicit institutional discrimination by the Japanese government and society.

Difference in the experience of Resident Korean youth attending Japanese schools was also a key to the reconstruction of their identity. The choice of simply being assimilated into the dominant structure did not solve the real problems of discrimination and prejudice against them. It was crucial for Resident Korean youth to assert their difference and to become "Korean" (in opposition to "Japanese") by using their Korean names. Without becoming such political subjects—which, ironically or not, was constructed on the ground of difference—there would have been no challenge to the exercise of power and as a result, no social change (see also Inokuchi, 1996).

We should note, however, that some Resident Korean youth attending Japanese schools have felt reservations when encouraged to use their Korean names by progressive educators. Those students are quite right in sensing the operation of power—the power to impose a fixed identity—even here. Regardless of how important the practice of using Korean names has been in rendering the invisible power visible and in constructing political subjects (i.e., the Korean students), the terms (Japanese [citizens] vs. Koreans [aliens]) remain the very terms the dominant power wanted to establish and maintain.

Recent declines in the enrollment at GFKR schools also suggests that the North Korea-centric curricula approach and its promotion of North Korean identity became somewhat disconnected from the realities and desires of Resident Koreans living and surviving in contemporary Japanese society. The difference, or the identity, constructed by GFKR schools appears to have met a challenge from differences arising within contemporary Resident Koreans.

The struggles of Resident Koreans seem to have entered a new phase, one in which binary categories such as "Japanese (citizens)" vs. "Koreans (aliens)" need to be challenged and destabilized. This is not to argue that persons of one category are the same as those of the other, but to insist on their differences—"differences that confound, disrupt, and render ambiguous the meaning of any fixed binary oppositions" that exist within any single category (Scott, 1988, p. 177). This new phase perhaps requires a reconceptualization of Korean minzoku education—what is to be taught, who should be taught, and what kind of consciousness should be raised (I. Park, 1995).

At any rate, a new curriculum for Japanese students is long overdue, and it is one that needs to advance the lessons of history and experiences of minority groups, and the perspectives necessary for imagining a nation and national identity that is internally diverse. In the context of community-based democracy, people who are legal aliens in terms of nationality are nonetheless "local citizens" (e.g., Raskin, 1993). In the new curriculum and teaching, the binary categories (e.g., "citizen" vs. "noncitizen") that have been taken for granted for decades need to be scrutinized and deconstructed. The nineteenth-century idea of *nation* as an entity with a common origin, language, and way of life is erroneous. All nations have been built upon differences, whether recognized as such or not. The differences within a nation arise because of the heterogeneous origins, cultures, and histories the nation carries. An important role of education is to help students understand this point and develop a sense of nation—and their identity—that is both multifarious and fluid.

NOTES

I am grateful to Judith Perkins, Sylvan Esh, Yusaku Ozawa, Hiroshi Tanaka, and Tom Burkman for their comments and assistance. A part of this material appeared in Nozaki, Y., & Inokuchi, H. (2001). Ethnic minority students and social studies education: Learning from resident Korean education in Japan. *Delta: Policy and Practice in Education, 53* (1&2), 139–152.

1. In this chapter, the term "Resident Koreans" is used to designate those Koreans who have resided in Japan in the last fifty years.

2. For example, Korean males living in Japan had voting rights after 1931, and several Koreans were elected to the Japanese Diet. See Inokuchi (1996) for further discussion.

3. Japan has basically adopted the *jus sanguinis* principle, so that second- and third-generation Japanese-born Resident Koreans are not granted Japanese citizenship at birth. For further discussion of various citizenship principles, see Hammar (1990).

4. The Ministry of Education has not allowed minzoku schools in the formal school system.

5. In addition to these GFKR schools, there are four schools that operate under the sponsorship of Mindan, the Association of Korean Residents in Japan (AKR), which is affiliated with South Korea. The AKR schools offer varying portions of the K–12 grade range. One of these was established as an accredited school and did not associate itself with either South or North Korea until the 1960s. The other three schools (one of these is an accredited school) have been managed by the AKR. The educational practices of these schools are very similar to those of South Korea. In recent years, the South Korean government has regarded these schools as the means to solving the problem of educating children of Korean businessmen residing in Japan for a short period of time. As the aim of the schools shifts in that direction, ethnic education for Korean Resident children has slowed. Most of the Korean resident youth who align themselves with South Korea have attended Japanese schools. For further discussion, see Umakoshi (1991).

6. *Chogori* is a Korean traditional female attire, which has been used as the female uniform of Korean minzoku schools. When relations between Japan and North Korea became strained in 1994, some Japanese assaulted Korean minzoku school students in *chogori* uniform and ripped their *chogori*.

7. The required consent continued until 1965. The admission list came to include the Resident South Korean children in 1965 and all Resident Korean children in 1991.

8. In 1966, 159,440 Resident Koreans lived in Osaka. This equated to approximately 27.2 percent of Japan's Korean population, which made Osaka the area of highest concentration (Morita, 1996).

9. Although some minzoku education classes served as extracurricular activities and were initially established after the closing of minzoku schools in 1949 as a response to the strong demand by Resident Korean parents, the number increased dramatically after the Japanese teachers' minzoku education movement in 1970s. As of 1999, in Osaka Prefecture, these minzoku education classes were in operation at 140 schools (Minzoku Kyoiku Network, 1999).

10. These Japanese teachers were active in the Buraku liberation movement. Buraku was Japan's outcast group, and, in the Buraku liberation movement, claiming oneself as a Buraku person was regarded as the first step in raising Buraku consciousness and thus fighting against the discrimination. The teachers saw a similarity between the situation faced by

Buraku people and that faced by Resident Koreans, because Buraku people tended to hide their identity as Buraku.

11. A survey in the 1990s showed that more than 80 percent of Resident Korean students hid their ethnic origin (I. Park, 1995).

12. Again, the minzoku education for Resident Korean students has usually been an extracurricular activity.

REFERENCES

Apple, M. W. (1982). *Education and power*. London: Routledge and Kegan Paul.

Apple, M. W. (1999). *Power, meaning, and identity: Essays in critical educational studies*. New York: Peter Lang.

Fukuoka, Y. (1993). *Zainichi Kankoku/Chosenjin* [Korean residents in Japan]. Tokyo: Chuokoronsha.

Fukuoka, Y. (2000). *Lives of young Koreans in Japan*. (T. Gill, Trans.). Melbourne: Trans Pacific Press.

Hester, J. T. (2000). Kids between nations: Ethnic classes in the construction of Korean identities in Japanese public schools. In S. Ryang (Ed.), *Koreans in Japan: Critical voices from the margin* (pp. 175–196). New York: Routledge.

Hammar, T. (1990). *Democracy and the nation-state: Aliens, denizens and citizens in a world of international migration*. Aldershot: Avebury.

Inatomi, S. (Ed.). (1988). *Mugunfa no kaori: Zenkoku zainichi Chosenjin kyoiku kenkyu kyogikai no kiseki to tenbo* [The scent of Althea: The trajectory and perspective of the all Japan conference for the study of Korean resident education]. Tokyo: Yojisha.

Inokuchi, H. (1986). *Zainichi Chosenjin: hisabetsu to aidentiti keisei* [Koreans in Japan: oppression and identity development]. Unpublished master's thesis, Sophia University, Tokyo.

Inokuchi, H. (1996). The finger-printing rejection movement reconsidered. *Japanese Society, 1*, 77–105.

Inokuchi, H. (2000). Korean ethnic schools in occupied Japan, 1945–1952. In S. Ryang, (Ed.), *Koreans in Japan: Critical voices from the margin* (pp. 140–156). New York: Routledge.

Jacobson, D. (1996). *Rights across borders: Immigration and the decline of citizenship*. Baltimore: Johns Hopkins University Press.

Kashiwazaki, C. (2000). The politics of legal status: The equation of nationality with ethnonational identity. In S. Ryang (Ed.), *Koreans in Japan: Critical voices from the margin* (pp. 13–31). New York: Routledge.

Kim, T. (1999). *Aidentiti Porittikusu o Koete: Zainichi Chosenjin no Esunisiti* [Beyond identity politics: Ethnicity of Resident Koreans]. Kyoto: Sekaisisosha.

Kishino, J. (1985). *Jiritsu to kyozon no kyoiku: Chosen-jin ni narukoto, Nihon-jin ni narukoto* [Education for autonomy and co-existence: Becoming Korean and becoming Japanese]. Tokyo: Hakujusha.

Lee, C. (1981). The period of repatriation, 1945–1949. In C. Lee and G. De Vos (Eds.), *Koreans in Japan: Ethnic conflict and accommodation* (pp. 58–72). Berkeley: University of California Press.

Lee, C. & De Vos, G. (Eds.). (1981). *Koreans in Japan: Ethnic conflict and accommodation.* Berkeley: University of California Press.

Li, D. (1956). *Nihon ni iru chosen no kodomo* [Korean Children in Japan]. Tokyo: Shunjusha.

Minzoku Kyoiku Network (1999). *Kyoiku kaikaku to minzoku kyoiku* [Educational reform and Minzoku education]. Tokyo: Yojisha.

Morita, Y. (1996). *Suuji ga kataru Zainichi Kankoku/Chosenjin no rekishi* [Quantitative data regarding the history of Koreans in Japan]. Tokyo: Akashi Shoten.

Nakayama, H. (Ed.). (1995). *Zainichi chosenjin kyoikukankei shiryoshu* (Collected documents on the education of Koreans in Japan). Tokyo: Akashi shoten.

Ogbu, J. U. (1987). Variability in minority school performance: A problem in search of an explanation. *Anthropology and Education Quarterly, 18* (4), 312–334.

Oh, Y. (1996). Intabyu Oh Yunbyong san ni kiku: Zainichi Kankoku/Chosenjin no rekishi o do tsutaeruka [An Interview with Oh Yun-byong: How to teach about the history of Korean residents in Japan]. In K. Kimijima, and T. Sakai, (Eds.), *Chosen/Kankoku wa Nihon no kyokasho ni do kakareteiruka: Sogorikai no tameno Nihon karano hokoku to Kankoku karano hatsugen* (pp. 220–222). Tokyo: Nashinokisha.

Ozawa, Y. (1973). *Zainichi Chosenjin kyoikuron* [On the education of Korean residents]. Tokyo: Akishobo.

Ozawa, Y. (1997). Sengo goju-nen to Chosen gakko [Fifty years after the war and Korean schools]. *Kaikyo, 18,* 16–58.

Park, I. (1995). Minzoku kyoiku-tte nanda? [What is ethnic education?]. *Horumon bunka, 5,* 40–53.

Park, S. (1992). *Towareru Chosen gakko shogu* [Measures for Korean schools questioned]. Tokyo: Chosen seinensha.

Raskin, J. B. (1993). Legal aliens, local citizens: The historical, constitutional and theoretical meanings of alien suffrage. *University of Pennsylvania Law Review, 141,* 1391–1470.

Ryang, S. (1997). *North Koreans in Japan: Language, ideology, and identity.* Boulder: Westview Press.

Ryang, S. (Ed.). (2000). *Koreans in Japan: Critical voices from the margin.* New York: Routledge.

Scott, J. W. (1988). *Gender and the politics of history.* New York: Columbia University Press.

Sugitani, Y. (1981). "Kangaeru kai" no ayumi [History of the study group]. In Nihon no gakko ni zaisekisuru Chosenjin jido/seito no Kyoiku o kangaerukai (Ed.) *Mukuge (Fukkokuban)* (pp. 15–42). Tokyo: Aki Shobo.

Umakoshi, T. (1991). The role of education in preserving the ethnic identity of Korean residents in Japan. In E. R. Beauchamp (Ed.), *Windows on Japanese education* (pp. 281–290). New York: Greenwood Press.

Weiner, M. (Ed.). (1997). *Japan's minorities: The illusion of homogeneity.* London: Routledge.

Yang, C. (1995). Saredo "Urihakkyo" [Nevertheless it is "our school"]. *Horumon Bunka, 5,* 126–132.

Chapter 13

History, Postmodern Discourse, and the Japanese Textbook Controversy Over "Comfort Women"

Yoshiko Nozaki

INTRODUCTION

Postwar Japan has been the setting of a hard-fought struggle over national narratives, especially concerning the official history of World War II as represented in school textbooks (see Nozaki & Inokuchi, 2000). In particular, the issue of "comfort women" ushered in a new phase of that struggle in the 1990s. While there has been little dispute over the fact that so-called "comfort women" (*ianfu*) existed during the Asia-Pacific War (1931–1945), a considerable controversy has arisen over how to interpret and teach about this. In the old interpretation, it was an episode of "love/sex affairs" by Japanese men in service, who were "comforted" by the women. Although the episode never had a place in the official history of the war, it was told and retold privately, and used as a side story in memoirs and novels. Feminist movements inside and outside of Japan, not to mention the victims who broke silence and began to speak out, have challenged the old interpretation and delivered a new one—an interpretation that portrays the women as enslaved by the state and its military and subjected to forced prostitution and systematic rape.[1]

This chapter examines some Japanese scholarly debates on the issue of comfort women and its inclusion in school textbooks.[2] The Japanese controversy over comfort women has involved charged debates among intellectuals of different disciplinary and ideological backgrounds: Progressive and feminist historians have advanced empirical research; right-wing nationalist critics have launched a series of attacks upon the new, critical understandings of the historical facts; "poststructuralist" feminist theories have been brought into the dispute; and some right-wing scholars have employed postmodern discourses to promote their agenda. An examination of these debates helps us understand the problem(s) of historical research and education in a contemporary "politics of history" (Scott, 1988).

The Eruption of Controversy over the Issue of Comfort Women in the 1990s

The feminist interpretation of the history of comfort women was not built in one day. One of the first feminist approaches dates back to the mid-1970s, when Japanese journalist Matsui Yayori (who was very active in Asian women's issues) became interested in the topic.[3] However, it was only after the successes of South Korean democracy and feminist movements in the 1980s that the issue became internationalized. Yun Chung-ok, a professor at Ewha Womans University, was an important catalyst in this development. In the late 1980s, she met with Matsui to exchange critical information about the comfort women in general, the Korean comfort women in particular, and in 1990, she wrote a series of reports on the issue Japanese colonialism and Korean comfort women for a South Korean newspaper. Her reports ignited the South Korean public, which insisted on clear forms of redress.

When the Japanese government responded by denying the involvement of the wartime state and its military in the matter, this further enraged the South Koreans. Among them was former comfort woman Kim Haksoon, whose anger was so deep that in 1991 she "came out" in order to force the Japanese government to confront the issue. In Japan, the effects of her coming forward were palpable. Among other things, Kim's testimonial interviews gave Japanese historian Yoshimi Yoshiaki, a scholar in contemporary wartime social history, a feminist perspective for (re)examining the sources he had seen before (Yoshimi was a progressive historian critical of Japanese wartime wrongdoings). In early 1992, Yoshimi provided the first piece of evidence, clearly demonstrating the Japanese Imperial Army's involvement in the matter (though the extent of its involvement, including its use of force, was still in need of further study). The Japanese government had no choice but to admit to military involvement, and so Prime Minister Miyazawa Kiichi officially apologized to South Korea.

In 1993, the Japanese government conducted a hearing with fifteen former comfort women in Seoul, yielding evidence that many women had been taken and made to work in the system involuntarily. In August 1993, in a statement made by Kono Yohei, then chief secretary of the Cabinet, the government essentially admitted to the direct and indirect involvement of the (Imperial) Japanese force in the establishment and administration of comfort facilities. The government also admitted that various kinds of coercive measures were used in the recruitment and retention of the women, and called for historical research and education aimed at remembering the incident. Kono's statement provided a foundation upon which the issue of comfort women could be addressed in education, so that by 1997, almost all school history textbooks and those in related subject areas included a reference to comfort women (for further discussion, see Nozaki, 2001).

Right-wing nationalists objected strongly to both the government's admission of state involvement in the matter of comfort women and the inclusion of the comfort women issue in school textbooks. They began to attack not only the politicians who supported the government's apologies, but the historians' findings about, and school textbook references to, comfort women by disseminating misleading information. Countering the nationalist offensive, some progressive and feminist historians have made concerted efforts to advance empirical studies on the issue of comfort women, while other feminists have raised epistemological questions for such historical inquiry and education. Interestingly, the nationalist strategies have also included the use of postmodern discourses, which aim at discrediting historical research and argue for a national history that serves "national" interests.

Empirical Debates between the Nationalists and the Progressive and Feminist Historians

Making and keeping the issue of comfort women controversial has been one of the most effective strategies taken up by right-wing nationalists. Namely, they have focused on the minor details of the "facts" presented by historical research, pointing out errors and the impossibility of verification of such events (though, due to their lack of expert knowledge, their points have sometimes turned out to be their errors). The progressive and feminist historians have countered the nationalists by responding to and refuting their arguments one by one with empirical studies. However, the nationalists have continued to make the same arguments, even in cases where they have been completely refuted. Unfortunately, as a result, the dispute has become confusing for the public, and for many educators.[4]

For example, in the early 1990s, some textbooks used the terms *teishin-tai* (volunteer corps) and *jugun-ianfu* (war comfort women) to refer to the women, because these were the most popular terms circulating at the time. The nationalists have argued that the use of *teishin-tai* to designate the women is incorrect and that *jugun-ianfu* is not the "historical term" (meaning that it is not the exact term that was used during the war). Therefore, they have argued, these terms should be removed from school textbooks. There is a fraction of truth to the nationalist claim: research so far has found only a few cases in which the *teishin-tai* women were forced to become comfort women, even though women of various ages who were mobilized under the name of *teishin-tai* during the war assumed various occupations and professions, including factory work and war nursing. Also, the term *jugun-ianfu* was created during the postwar years. During the war, the women were often simply placed into categories such as *shugyofu* (women of indecent occupation) and *ianfu* (comfort women), which included both the women forced to work in the facilities set up by the military and those in private brothels.

Beyond that arguably legitimate semantic issue, however, right-wing nationalist efforts to undermine the history of the comfort women and erase it from school textbooks seem manipulative at best. They argue, for example, that the term *jugun*, as part of a compound noun (e.g., *jugun-kisha*, the term for war correspondents; and *jugun-kangofu*, the term for war nurses), indicates the status of *gunzoku,* or "civilian war worker" (those officially on the payroll of the army and/or navy). The comfort women, they insist, were not in that category. Historians such as Yoshimi have refuted this argument as follows: the term *jugun* literally means "going to the front with the military," and was not used in exactly the same way as *gunzoku.* Most war correspondents, for example, were not employed by the Japanese military (only the army had its own correspondents, and only after 1942). Also, while the term *jugun-kangofu* has been commonplace, the official name for war nurses (of the Japanese Red Cross) was *kyugo-kangofu* (relief nurses), and they became military employees only after 1939. In addition, Yoshimi and others have pointed out that terms used in historical research (and education) are often not the exact terms used during the period under study. In their view, using the term *jugun-ianfu* in school textbooks poses little problem; rather, the real problem is that it is euphemistic—"comfort" (*ian*) is hardly an adequate term for a situation that was, in fact, enslavement (Yoshimi & Kawada, 1997, pp. 9–10).

Another point of dispute has been over the types, agents, and extent of coercion. Right-wing nationalists have taken issue with the term *kyosei-renko* (taken by force). They have defined the term somewhat narrowly as "taken by force by the military and/or government authorities" and argue that no such cases have been found. Therefore, they assert, school textbooks should not use the term when referring to comfort women. More specifically, nationalists argue that the grounds for their objections lie in the testimonies of former comfort women, which, they insist, contain errors and exaggerations; the nationalists also contend that no (Japanese) official documents have been found showing the use of direct force, military or otherwise, in the recruitment of the women. Moreover, they argue, the official documents found so far indicate that the military and police instructed traffickers to follow the law and regulations in their recruitment of comfort women (trading women for prostitution was legal, but regulated).

They also insist that the testimony of Yoshida Seiji, the only person who publicly admitted to the violent means he and his coworkers used to round up and send Korean women to comfort facilities, lacks credibility in several key issues such as dates and places.[5]

While nationalist arguments may sound coherent on the surface, they are misleading in many ways. First, no school textbooks to date have used the exact term *kyosei-renko* (taken by force) in their description of comfort women. The term has often been used to describe the way in which many Korean and Chinese men were gathered and sent into forced labor in places such as coal mines. While references to comfort women usually appear in sections of the texts where the major topic is the forced labor of Korean and Chinese men, it is somewhat inaccurate to charge that these textbooks describe comfort women as *kyosei-renko* (in its narrow nationalist definition).

Second, Yoshimi and others have argued that it is a basic logical error to argue that the absence of official documents ordering the *kyosei-renko* proves that no direct state force was used in the recruitment of the women. While admitting that no official documents have been found ordering the use of military and police force in the recruitment of women—in particular, in colonized regions such as Korea and Taiwan—they have pointed out that many wartime official records were destroyed at Japan's surrender. Besides, it is questionable whether any government would give such an order— "use force to round up women and send them to comfort facilities"—so directly and explicitly.

More importantly, progressive and feminist historians argue that such an absence of official documents does not mean that the military and government authorities were not involved. There has been other evidence showing that the state and military were complicit in many ways, including knowing about, but not stopping the traffickers' use of violence and deceptive tactics in the recruitment of comfort women. Such inaction de facto meant giving tacit approval to such activities. Moreover, some Japanese laws and regulations constraining the recruitment of comfort women were not applied to the colonies, such as Korea and Taiwan, and evidence shows that colonial authorities saw no problem with the fact that very young girls were traded, even though the same act would have been illegal in Japan. In addition, the testimonies given by former comfort women demonstrate that there were cases in occupied territories, such as China and Southeast Asia, where government and military authorities themselves took women by force. Furthermore, the use of force was common not only in the recruitment of women, but also in making them stay and work in the comfort facilities (Yoshimi & Kawada, 1997, pp. 20–31). Yoshimi and others suggest that the nationalist focus on the phrase "taken by force" is, in fact, a strategy being used to digress from the main issue concerning the coercive nature of the entire operation of the military comfort women system.

As matters stand, progressive and feminist historians are winning the empirical debate. Nevertheless, they face several problems: Even though the nationalists have lost battles throughout the debate, they are not withdrawing their arguments; they continue to circulate their discourse not only through that part of the media that is exclusively right wing, but also through the mass media, which has a more general readership. Because of the television coverage (as well as coverage in other media outlets), the controversy has attracted a greater audience than one could have ever predicted. The nationalist strategy of making and keeping the issue controversial seems to have been effective, if not by getting the wider audience to agree with them, then by allowing the public to feel that the arguments of the other side (progressives and feminists) are only as good (or bad) as those of the right-wing nationalists. In addition, because of the nationalist focus on minor details, teaching about comfort women now seems to require more technical knowledge than many teachers would prefer.

A "Poststructuralist" Feminist Critique of "Positivism" in History

Some critics have begun to suggest that new, postmodern approaches ought to replace the current empirical approaches. In a provocative essay, Ueno Chizuko (1997), a noted Japanese feminist sociologist, criticizes as "positivist" (*jissho-shugi*) the arguments of both the nationalists and the progressive/feminist historians involved in the debate.[6] She cites "poststructuralist" theories—though whether her argument is truly (or consistently) poststructuralist is another matter—and maintains that the issue of comfort women links up with the fundamental question concerning the methods and methodology of historical studies. As she puts it,

> [I]s a historical "fact" such a simple thing that it looks the same whoever looks at it? ... Any social science with "a linguistic turn" begins with a serious epistemological question of what "objective fact" is. The study of history is no exception. (Ueno, 1997, p. 159)

According to Ueno, while right-wing nationalists and progressive and feminist historians have argued against each other, both have made their arguments within the positivist paradigm of history. The positivist approach, Ueno argues, regards written historical material as the first and only source for the study of history (*bunshoshiryo shijo-shugi*), and has allowed the nationalists to discredit the testimonies of former comfort women on the grounds that no official documents have been found showing that the women were taken by force. She proceeds to argue that progressive and feminist historians have committed an error, or been "caught in a trap," when refuting the nationalists by advancing the positivist study of history.

Ueno's critique is targeted not so much at the nationalists, but at the progressive and feminist historians.[7] In giving her impression of a televised debate, she states:

> In "Live TV till Morning," Yoshimi Yoshiaki, a conscientious historian who has contributed most vigorously in discovering the historical materials concerning the issue of comfort women, was driven into a corner by the questioning of [nationalists such as] Kobayashi Yoshinori, and [Yoshimi] finally admitted that no written historical materials exist that properly prove the involvement of the Japanese military.[8] If [one] stands on the doctrine of the written historical material as the first and only source, [one] has no choice but to admit "no." It became more or less a shared understanding that the documents Yoshimi found [and reported in 1992] can be indirect evidence for "taken-by-force," but not the historical source that substantiates it as a fact. (Ueno, 1997, p. 159)

Ueno's interpretation is not without its problems. She does not seem to fully understand the point of this particular dispute, as she is unable to distinguish between proof of military involvement and that of being "taken by force" (e.g., Yoshimi, 1998b). Her description of Yoshimi as being "driven into a corner," or her assessment that the nationalists won the argument, may not necessarily represent the views of others. (The viewers' response to the whole debate was, for example, more favorable to the progressives and feminists. The show conducted a viewers' poll by telephone and fax: 57.5 percent of those who faxed in agreed that the issue of the comfort women should be covered in school textbooks, while 37.4 percent disagreed; 50.6 percent of those who called agreed, and 41.3 percent disagreed.[9]) Her conclusion that historians are silent before the logic of "verifiability" ignores the successful efforts of historians to refute nationalist claims.

However, at the heart of her criticism is an important suggestion, a suggestion that empirical history—"positivism" in her word—is at the root of the problem, and that progressive and feminist historians who adhere to it are part of the problem. As she sees it, positivism "denies the 'evidentiary power' of the victims' testimonies," and, thus, discredits "the 'reality' [experienced and told by] the victims" (Ueno, 1997, p. 159). Ueno argues that it is "arrogan[t] of the positivist historians … to think that a given historical fact can be 'judged' [verified] as it 'existed' from the position of a third party, apart from the reality of the persons involved" (p. 161).[10]

What, then, is the alternative that Ueno offers to the positivist approach to history? She suggests the "oral history" approach, but it is difficult to pin down her concrete ideas on how to conduct oral history projects (and how to teach history based on oral history). She states that to negate the testimonies of the former comfort women is to trample their dignity underfoot, and makes a recommendation similar to that of some Western feminists known as feminist standpoint theorists (see, for example, Dorothy Smith [1987]). She states, "Our premise is that, when the victims venture to speak up, we have no choice but to begin with their overwhelming 'reality' " (Ueno, 1997, p. 167); however, she does not suggest what should follow that beginning.

Instead, Ueno goes on to question the power dynamics involved in interviewing the victims. She maintains that a narrative of the victims is, in fact, the "collaborative work" of both the interviewee and the interviewer, and that an exercise of power is always involved in producing such a work. She argues that the interviewers tend to obtain what they want to hear, and that this amounts to "violence distorting the formula of narrative." She suggests that positivist historians "pretending" neutrality and/or persons supporting the former comfort women with good intentions may commit such violence without even realizing it. Again, however, she does not go on to discuss ways for dealing with these problems. Ueno also argues that it is important to recognize "a variety of histories"—a "pluralistic history"—which represent histories from viewpoints other than one's own, because different people live different realities. This variety undermines the foundation upon which the official history establishes itself, and to choose one from the variety becomes unnecessary (Ueno, 1998, p. 30).

The idea of a pluralistic history is fine, and "not to choose" can be an answer in certain contexts. It seems, though, that a common understanding of historical events among different people may still be possible, and it is one of the most important roles of historical research and education to ensure that different people can participate in this common process of understanding the past. In this sense, there is a serious question concerning the viability of Ueno's approach to history (in reference to the controversy over comfort women), since right-wing forces have been using their political power to urge people to choose their version of history and to eliminate others'.

PROGRESSIVE HISTORIANS REPLY TO UENO

There is no doubt that Ueno's argument has caused a stir within the circle of progressive and feminist historians; since the appearance of her remarks, an ongoing, heated discussion has been taking place within the camp. In replying to Ueno, for example, Yoshimi cites the difference between two versions of one former comfort woman's life history (a Resident Korean woman living in Okinawa). That difference, he suggests, is based on the interviewers' social locations and positions—one a Japanese feminist, the other, a Korean support group. Yoshimi notes that "the picture of history is not unitary even in cases where [one] addresses the same object. This is a matter held [by historians] as the common sense of historical studies." This does not mean that verification is not necessary, however. As Yoshimi puts it,

> [T]he picture of history reconstructed will be questioned in such terms as the ways it closes in on the "facts," the degree of persuasive power, and how much logically and persuasively the historical picture as a whole is constructed by the documents, records, testimonies, and other materials. (Yoshimi, 1998b, p. 130)

Yoshimi maintains that the theories and methods of history are tools for analyzing and reconstructing "the actuality called history," where, he argues, verification plays an important role (Yoshimi, 1998b, p. 130). Yoshimi questions if Ueno's position that there are no "facts" or "truths" in history, only "realities reconstructed from given perspectives," ultimately suggests that one's viewpoint is the only thing that matters in studies of history, and he sees such a position as problematic. As he puts it,

> If so, ... which "reality" to choose would be decided by determining which [viewpoint] to choose from the [various] "viewpoints" that construct it [history]. This would result in either agnosticism, or the situation of beliefs and tastes, i.e., which viewpoint one believes or prefers. ... (Yoshimi, 1998b, p. 131)

"At least, if it's scholarship," Yoshimi continues to argue, "it should be questioned which reality, from among various 'realities' reconstructed, has persuasive power, and which has no basis" (p. 131). To ask these questions is to ask for their verification.

In Yoshimi's view, Ueno's belief that pointing out exaggerations and mistakes in the victims' testimonies is denying the power of testimonial evidence is misplaced. There are, in fact, cases in which victims have made mistakes. For example, a former comfort woman gave testimony in which she stated that she had been forced to work in a comfort facility in Japan, but since no military comfort facilities had existed inside Japan, Yoshimi suggests that it is rather difficult to believe her testimony at face value. In another example, a former comfort woman gave contradictory accounts on different occasions. On one occasion, she stated that she had been taken by force, but on another occasion, she stated that she had agreed to the job to earn money (1998b, p. 133). Yoshimi reminds us, however, that even though this particular woman had given her consent to go to the front lines (which turned out to be in Burma), it does not mean that the military had no responsibility for her life in the comfort women system, since because of excessive hardship, she attempted to commit suicide by drowning herself. Yoshimi states, "I would like [Ueno] to consider this kind of effort involved in the reconstruction of the reality" (1998b, p. 133).

Yoshimi's point highlights the fact that an oral history project is not a simple task—it requires careful handling and piecing together of information taken from the testimonies. While Yoshimi admits that another type of research (such as an examination of testimonies as contemporary discursive practices and an exploration of their social and historical meanings in particular contexts), he argues that the controversy over comfort women remains centered around the historical facts, and so his efforts have been geared towards the reconstruction of those facts.

Some historians who have not necessarily been specialists in the comfort women issue have also begun to join the discussion. For example, Yasumaru Yoshio, a well-respected historian, has commented on Ueno's criticism. While Yasumaru (1998) sees some value in Ueno's argument, he disagrees with her assessment of Yoshimi as a positivist historian. Yasumaru argues that Yoshimi began his study because he was deeply moved by the voice of Kim Hak-soon (a former comfort woman), meaning that at the bottom of his study are his empathy and ethics. Since then, Yoshimi has been committed to the issue through his skills and efforts as an historian.

Yasumaru also disagrees with Ueno on how to handle the testimonies. He infers (since she does not clearly state her position) that Ueno believes the idea of Korean and Taiwanese women being taken by force by the military is factual because the women have testified so. He wonders if Ueno's approach could result in preventing researchers from understanding the complexity of the events; in his words, "a number of issues are coming into sight" as researchers accept that there have been no cases of women being "taken by force" by the military in colonized Korea and Taiwan in the literal sense of the phrase (Yasumaru, 1998, p. 206).

One important issue to Yasumaru is a dimension of widespread violence in the everyday lives of people in a given society at a given time. For example, he is concerned with the activities of the traffickers—those who were active agents and mediators between the women and the military—who perhaps played a major role in the everyday, immediate violence against the women, including "taking women by force" or "kidnapping" them. Without their existence and systematic operations, Yasumaru argues, it would have been impossible for the state to collect such a large number of women (some estimate more than one hundred thousand women). If we take Yasumaru's arguments even further, it becomes clear that historians and educators need to link the issue of comfort women to the Japanese colonialism responsible for maintaining multiple oppressions (including race, class, and gender) at different levels of society. Along with the involvement of the state and its military, the colonial relations of ruling that allowed traffickers to commit everyday violence in their activities and operations needs to be examined critically.

The Nationalist Appropriation of Postmodern Vocabulary

While the debate over an appropriate paradigm for historical research has continued within the progressive/feminist camp, some nationalists have begun to speak a specific kind of postmodern discourse, or at least employ its vocabulary. This new element is worth a closer look, especially since the nationalists tend to use postmodern vocabularies with their own particular twists—in this case, to argue for the construction of a Japanese history from "the Japanese view," stressing unity and coherence.

In the fall of 1996, for example, Sakurai Yoshiko (1996), a former TV news anchorwoman and current freelance journalist, gave a lecture at one of the in-service teacher training programs for international education held by the Yokohama City Education Board, Kanagawa Prefecture. (It is not clear whether Sakurai is a true right-wing nationalist, as she has sometimes been involved in some progressive causes, but in relation to the controversy over comfort women, she appears to be one.) Sakurai spoke at length about her views on the comfort women issue, beginning with the critique of school textbook descriptions: "all the textbooks are written, assuming 'taken-by-force' as a major premise; however, … it is my conviction that [the women] were not 'taken by force'" (Sakurai, 1996).

The problem was, in her view, the "structure of the Japanese psyche," which was "self-tormenting." She then proceeded to argue for the concept of history as a story (*monogatari*) of a nation.

> What I'd like to say is that history is a story. … It is a story of individuals, and at the same time it should be a story of their respective nation. Therefore, … it has to be natural that Japan has its own way of viewing [history]. It is natural that China has its own view and Korea has its own view, and it is a reason of nature that all three are separate [and different]. (Sakurai, 1996, p. 13)

According to Sakurai, Japan's (hi)story needed to be told from the Japanese perspective. She suggested that individual teachers educate their students from that perspective, even though the Ministry of Education would not instruct them to do so (at this point, the ministry's official policy was to take into account international perspectives).

Sakurai's ideas echo those held by some right-wing nationalist scholars. For example, Sakamoto Takao (1997), a historian of Japanese political thought, has argued that no education is value-neutral, and that the purpose of education, in particular history education, is to foster "national consciousness." In his view, "history is a story," and the Japanese history taught in schools should be "a story of the formation of a nation, a people," which aims at the construction of a sense of national unity. As he puts it,

> It is necessary to establish in the mind of people a stratum of consciousness that sees "we" as equaling "nation," and the very thing that identifies "us" has to be the "history of nation." ... A "nation" [people] ... recognizes the appearance of its Self in the "story" of "ourselves," and by sharing such "story" it can be a "nation." (Sakamoto, 1997, p. 50)

The discourse Sakamoto employs speaks of a national history, one that is not necessarily based on verified facts from studies of history, but based on facts that may have been "fittingly woven into the story" in order to enhance its reality. In Sakamoto's view, concepts such as "state" and "nation" are, in some sense, "fictions." "However," he contends, human beings are "those who cannot live without fictions," and the "efforts" by human beings "to maintain the fictions" are needed. The vocabulary used here may have been borrowed from recent postmodern literature, but it curiously serves modernist ends (i.e., the construction of a national unity by [re]instituting national history) that have been argued against by postmodernist discourse (see also Iwasaki, 1998).

The new postmodern line put forth by the nationalists also seems to attempt to blur the line between "fact" and "fiction." For example, Fujioka Nobukatsu, a professor of education at the University of Tokyo and the central figure in the latest nationalist attack on history textbooks, has argued that the inclusion of "lies" in history books (and, by implication, textbooks) is acceptable for certain purposes, such as making the story "colorful." Fujioka has disclosed that in the 1990s, when he was involved in authoring *Takasugi Shinsaku*, a series of history books for children (intended to aid their understanding of history lessons in schools),[11] he included some fictitious stories:

> To write [a history] based only on verified historical truths makes [the descriptions] indefinitely close to those appearing in the full-size dictionary of persons, makes it insipid and dry. I changed my policy for the lack of an alternative—I had no choice but to write

the imagination of my own convenience to a great extent.[12] (Fujioka, 1997, pp. 112–113)

The nationalists appear to be in the process of reformulating their discursive strategy, and the key to this strategy is the incorporation of postmodern vocabulary, such as "history as story." As discussed above, one of the major strategies of the nationalists on the empirical side of the debate has been to focus on the details of comfort women research and point out errors or the impossibility of verification, thereby allowing nationalists to extend their argument to suggest the impossibility of verification of *any* part of history regarding comfort women. In this way, they can relativize the epistemological status of any claim concerning the historical facts, and argue for a choice of story from any number of possible—"equally valid"—stories. The notion of "history as story" serves as a license to construct any kind of story as history, including fictive stories with real names. This could be a clever move, since the nationalists are losing the battle on the grounds of empirical history.

To be sure, progressive and feminist historians have put forward their counterargument against this kind of nationalist discourse. For example, Yoshimi points out that the concept of Japanese history as a (hi)story of a "coherent nation" ignores the histories of the excluded and marginalized within the nation. As he puts it:

> [M]any of the major issues that would be left out [from the history the nationalists advocate] would be, for example, [the history] of class and ordinary people, and the histories of local residents, women, the socially less powerful, and minorities [such as Ainu and Okinawans]. (Yoshimi, 1998a, p. 35)

Yoshimi's critique makes good sense, yet there still seems to be a need to go beyond his position—to refute the nationalist discourse from positions that are more explicitly postmodernist. The postmodern debate between Ueno and progressive/feminist historians suggests that they, as a collective, may not yet have fully worked out their part of the postmodern debate(s), and doing so may be essential to countering the new nationalist postmodern discourse.[13]

CONCLUSION

The Japanese controversy over comfort women highlights a range of challenges historical research and education encounter in a contemporary society where meanings of the past are increasingly contested. The testimonies of former comfort women that appeared in a particular national and international political context in the early 1990s changed the interpretive framework for research on the issue and for what counts as truth. Since then, historical research has uncovered disturbing details about the comfort women system, forcing the Japanese government to admit to state/military involvement and to issue apologies to neighboring Asian countries. History as research and education has played an important role in this development.

Right-wing nationalists have countered the Japanese government's apologies and attempted to discredit the recent scholarship on comfort women with resistance and backlash. By focusing on minor details, these nationalists have effectively made and kept controversial the historians' findings concerning comfort women. Progressive and feminist historians have fought back and have won a number of empirical debates on the basis of expert knowledge, but a great deal of technical (and often seemingly trivial) knowledge has been brought into play, making it difficult for public audiences, including many schoolteachers, to understand and assess specific points of the dispute.

The empirical approach to history (as it is conceived and practiced traditionally) has met with limited success in settling a controversy that has been more political in nature than scholarly. Moreover, even with historians' best efforts, some matters remain extremely difficult or practically impossible to verify (for a number of reasons, including the lack of witnesses and the destruction of key official documents at Japan's defeat). At this juncture, where the empirical approach has been disabled, postmodern discourses have entered the controversy. For example, the Japanese feminist Ueno has raised some important questions regarding the epistemology, methods, and methodology of historical studies (and thereby, of education). Her argument suffers, however, from a lack of knowledge (concerning the precise points made during a dispute over the historical facts of comfort women), from her ambiguity concerning where she herself stands on methodological and theoretical questions, and from her seemingly unfair designation of progressive and feminist historians as positivists. Ueno's argument would have been more effective had she acquired a better understanding of the specific disputes surrounding the controversy as well as that surrounding the state of historical research on the topic.

In any case, the limits of an empirical study of history do not mean an end to historical inquiry and education; rather, they suggest the need to conduct historical research and education with theoretical understandings (i.e., epistemology and methodology). Indeed, the postmodern debate in the progressive/feminist camp, if conducted in productive ways, ought to benefit schoolteachers, who tend to embrace classic, commonsensical notions of historical objectivity and stress teaching about "the facts" (Nozaki, 2001).

Teachers can, in turn, join the debate by bringing to attention the questions they face when teaching about "the fact" or "(hi)story" from postmodern perspectives. Such an expansion of the debate will certainly make teachers (and therefore students) less vulnerable to nationalist attacks featuring postmodern discourses such as "history as story." This is not to suggest that schools and teachers must rely solely on academia: Japanese teachers have been relatively autonomous, dictating their own possibilities and constraints. The point here is that an important space for educational discourse and practice can be opened in which theories can inform teaching practices, and where the everyday struggles of teachers can fuel theoretical debates.

NOTES

This article is part of a larger study supported by a 2001–2002 (U.S.) National Academy of Education/Spencer Postdoctoral Fellowship. I would like to thank Sylvan Esh and Hiro Inokuchi for their assistance. A different version of this material appeared in Nozaki, Y. (2003). "I'm here alive": History, testimony, and the Japanese controversy over "comfort women." *World History Connected*, 1 (1), 46 pars. <http://worldhistoryconnected.press.uiuc.edu/1.1/nozaki.html>.

1. In this chapter, I employ the term "comfort women" (hereafter without quotation marks) because it is the term that has been most often used. A number of volumes and articles on the topic (written in Japanese, Korean, and English) have been published since the early 1990s, and this chapter can only discuss a part of that literature. For historical research on comfort women, see Yoshimi (2000) and Tanaka (2002).

2. For a discussion of other aspects of the controversy, such as the play of social forces in the spheres of politics and education, see Nozaki (2001). See also the two introductions in Yoshimi (2000) (one by the translator and the other by Yoshimi).

3. Japanese and Korean names in this essay follow Japanese and Korean name orders.

4. There have been numerous publications (e.g., C. Uesugi, 1996) on the comfort women issue by right-wing nationalists in the 1990s.

5. Yoshida published several volumes on the topic, including *Watashi no Senso Hanzai* [My war crimes] (1983). Yoshida's books created a sensation within and outside of Japan, and were followed by volumes and articles which were written based on, or implicitly citing, his account of "rounding up" Korean women. However, right-wing scholars conducted research to check his account and reported that they found no evidence to support it. Yoshida has not responded to the charges brought against him.

6. In Japan, *jissho-shugi* is a historical research paradigm that asks for verification by empirical evidence (historical sources), which may not be exactly the same thing as positivism in Western historical studies. Although in subsequent publications on the same topic Ueno has revised her description of the progressive and feminist historians slightly to represent them in a more positive light, her basic "poststructuralist" argument remains the same (e.g., Ueno, 1998).

7. In fact, in her later articles, Ueno makes it clear that it is not her intention to dispute with the nationalists.

8. To be sure, Yoshimi's research proved "the military involvement." It seems that Ueno misunderstood the dispute in this segment of the televised debate, or lacked the precise knowledge needed to understand it. In any case, Ueno's confusion indicates that the nationalist strategy of making the issue controversial worked well.

9. Uesugi Satoshi (1997) speculates that the fax users are probably younger than the telephone users.

10. Here Ueno discusses the problem in terms of the victims' testimonies, but her point seems more general, especially since in a later publication, she criticizes both the nationalists and the progressive/feminist historians for their dismissal of Yoshida's "testimony" in his confessional volume (1983).

11. The book is named after a Japanese samurai hero who lived during the time of the Meiji Restoration of 1968.

12. Fujioka argues that the "lies" should fall within a limit of "common sense." It follows that the real question might be: What kinds of "lies" are actually inserted? Interestingly, one lie he included was very much phallocentric. The (hi)story narrates that when the hero was born, his parents and grandparents were extremely happy to see the baby was a boy—a successor of the family—and included the line that "[his father] made really sure that the baby in bathing water ... had penis with it" (cited in Fujioka, 1997, p. 113). For a discussion of the masculine tendency of Fujioka and his followers, see also Hein (1999, pp. 360–364).

13. Among the progressives, Sato Manabu (1998) most successfully rearticulates the approach to history education from postmodern perspectives.

References

Fujioka, N. (1997). Ronso kingendaishi kyoiku no kaikaku, 21: Rekishi jinbutsu shirizu 'Takasugi Shinsaku' o kaite, Meiji-ishin to buhsi 2 [The debate on the reform of the education of modern and contemporary history, no. 21: On writing about "Takasugi Shinsaku" for the historical figure series, the Meiji Restoration and samurai, no. 2]. *Gendai Kyoiku Kagaku, 494,* 112–113.

Hein, L. (1999). Savage irony: The imaginative power of the "military comfort women" in the 1990s. *Gender and History, 11* (2), 336–372.

Iwasaki, M. (1998). Bokyaku no tameno "kokumin no monogatari": "Rairekiron" no raireki o kangaeru ["A story for nation" for the purpose of oblivion: Thoughts on the origin of the "origin"]. In Y. Komori and T. Takahashi (Eds.), *Nashonaru Hisutori o Koete* (pp. 175–193). Tokyo: Tokyo Daigaku Shuppankai.

Nozaki, Y. (2001). Feminism, nationalism, and the Japanese textbook controversy over "comfort women." In F. W. Twine & K. M. Blee (Eds.), *Feminism and antiracism: International struggles for justice* (pp. 170–189). New York: New York University Press.

Nozaki, Y., & Inokuchi, H. (2000). Japanese education, nationalism, and Ienaga Saburo's textbook lawsuits. In L. Hein and M. Selden (Eds.), *Censoring history: Citizenship and memory in Japan, Germany, and the United States* (pp. 96–126). Armonk: M. E. Sharpe.

Sakamoto, T. (1997). Rekishi kyokasho wa ikani kakarerubekika [How should history textbooks be written?]. *Seiron 297,* 46–60.

Sakurai, Y. (1996 October 3). Janarisuto Sakurai Yoshiko ga mita nihon, gakko, kodomo [Japan, schools and children from journalist Yoshiko Sakurai's view]. Lecture presented at the Heisei 8-nendo Kyoiku Kadai Kenshukai, the Yokohama City Education Board.

Sato, M. (1998). Ko no shintai no kioku karano shuppatsu: Sengo no rekishi kyoiku heno hansei" [A departure from the memory of individuals: Critical reflection on the postwar history education]. In Y. Komori and T. Takahashi (Eds.), *Nashonaru Hisutori o Koete* (pp. 305–318). Tokyo: Tokyo Daigaku Shuppankai.

Scott, J. (1988). *Gender and the politics of history.* New York: Columbia University Press.

Smith, D. (1987). *The everyday world as problematic: A feminist sociology.* Boston: Northeastern University Press.

Tanaka, Y. (2002). *Japan's comfort women: Sexual slavery and prostitution during World War II and the U.S. occupation.* London: Routledge.

Ueno, C. (1997). Kioku no seijigaku: Kokumin, kojin, watashi [The politics of memory: Nation, individuals, and I]. *Impaction 103,* 154–174.

Ueno, C. (1998). Jenda-shi to rekishigaku no hoho [Gender history and the methods of history]. In Nihon no Senso Sekinin Shiryo Senta (Ed.), *Simpozium Nashonarizumu to "Ianfu" Mondai* (pp. 21–31). Tokyo: Aoki Shoten.

Uesugi, C. (1996). *Kensho "jugun inanfu": Jugun ianfu mondai nyumon* [The verification of the "comfort women": An introduction to the issue of comfort women]. (rev. and enl. ed.). Tokyo: Zenbosha.

Uesugi, S. (1997). "Kioku no ansatsushatachi" to toron shite: "Asamade nama terebi" to "sande projekuto" [The debate against "assassins of memory": "Live TV till morning" and "Sunday project"]. *Senso Sekinin Kenkyu, 15,* 34–41.

Yasumaru, Y. (1998). "Ianfu" mondai to rekishigaku: Yasumaru Yoshio ni kiku" [The issue of "comfort" women and the studies of history: Interview with Yoshio Yasumaru]. In Nihon no Senso Sekinin Shiryo Senta (Ed.), *Simpozium Nashonarizumu to "Ianfu" Mondai* (pp. 203–214). Tokyo: Aoki Shoten.

Yoshida, S. (1983). *Watashi no senso hanzai: Chosenjin kyosei-renko* [My war crimes: Taking Koreans by force]. Tokyo: San'ichi Shobo.

Yoshimi, Y. (1998a). "Ianfu" mondai to kingendaishi no shiten [The issue of "comfort" women and the perspective of the modern/contemporary history]. In Nihon no Senso Sekinin Shiryo Senta (Ed.), *Simpozium Nashonarizumu to "Ianfu" Mondai* (pp. 32–47). Tokyo: Aoki Shoten.

Yoshimi, Y. (1998b) "Jyugun ianfu" mondai to rekishizo: Ueno Chizuko-shi ni kotaeru [The issue of "comfort women" and the image of history: Reply to Chizuko Ueno]. In Nihon no Senso Sekinin Shiryo Senta (Ed.), *Simpozium Nashonarizumu to "Ianfu" Mondai* (pp. 123–142). Tokyo: Aoki Shoten.

Yoshimi, Y. (2000). *Comfort women: Sexual slavery in the Japanese military during World War II* (S. O'Brien, Trans.) New York: Columbia University Press. (Original work published 1995)

Yoshimi, Y., and Kawada, F. (1997). Eds., *"Jugun ianfu" o meguru sanju no uso to shinjitsu* [Thirty lies and truths surrounding "war comfort women"]. Tokyo: Otsuki Shoten.

Contributors

Jyh-Jia Chen is Assistant Professor, Institute of Education, National Chiao-Tung University, Taiwan. With experience as an elementary school teacher and legislative assistant, she has developed her research interest in the relationships between state formation and education, critical sociology, and the educational reform movement.

Gay Garland Reed is Associate Professor of Educational Foundations. Her research and teaching focus on cultural diversity and education and cultural values and education. She has published on education in North and South Korea and the People's Republic of China and is currently serving as Interim Special Assistant to the Chancellor at the University of Hawai'i.

Hiromitsu Inokuchi is Associate Professor of Sociology at the University of East Asia, Shimonoseki, Japan. His major area of interest is Japanese cultural politics, especially concerning educational policies and minority issues. He is currently conducting a project on the transformation of Japanese views on the Asia-Pacific War.

Cushla Kapitzke is Lecturer at the School of Education, University of Queensland. She has published in the areas of community and virtual literacies, and is currently researching the literacies of libraries.

Misook Kim earned her Ph.D. at the University of Wisconsin at Madison, and currently she is a researcher at the (South) Korean Educational Development Institute. She has been interested in gender and class relations in schooling, and has recently been involved in a project of school evaluation in South Korea.

Dong Bae (Isaac) Lee is currently teaching Korean Popular Culture, Applied Linguistics, and Korean Language in the Department of Asian Languages and Studies, School of Languages and Comparative Cultural Studies, the University of Queensland. His major research areas are language education, postcolonial studies, critical discourse analysis, and cultural studies.

Yongbing Liu is currently a research associate at the Center for Research in Pedagogy and Practice, National Institute of Education, Nanyang Technological University, Singapore. He earned his Ph.D. at the University of Queensland, Australia. Prior to attending the University of Queensland, Yongbin worked at Jilin University of Technology in China as a Lecturer of Applied Linguistics for nearly twenty years. He has also worked as a Lecturer of Chinese Language and Culture at the University of Tasmania. His research interests are in applied linguistics, language education, and comparative cultural studies.

Allan Luke is Professor and Dean of the Center for Research in Pedagogy and Practice, National Institute of Education, Nanyang Technological University, Singapore. He is author and editor of numerous books, and his work has appeared in *Harvard Educational Review, Teachers College Record, The American Journal of Education, The Canadian Journal of Education, Educational Theory*, and *Linguistics and Education*. He is co-editor of the *Journal of Adolescent and Adult Literacy, Discourse,* and *Teaching Education*. He is currently Educational Advisor to the government of Kiribati, and Language Benchmarking Consultant to the Hong Kong government.

Yoshiko Nozaki is Assistant Professor at the Department of Educational Leadership and Policy, State University of New York at Buffalo. She earned her Ph.D. at the University of Wisconsin at Madison, where she studied curriculum history, educational anthropology, cultural studies, and critical and feminist theories. She was a social studies teacher in Japan in the 1980s, and has also had teaching experience in the United States, Australia, and New Zealand.

Darren M. O'Hern is a Ph.D. candidate in the Department of Educational Leadership and Policy, State University of New York at Buffalo. He earned a master's degree in International Development and Social Change from Clark University in 2001, and served as a U.S. Peace Corps volunteer in Kenya from 1996 to 1998, where he taught in local schools. His research interests include environmental education in developing countries, the effects of international development schemes on educational policies and practice, and rural-urban differences in educational provision and content in the developing world.

Roger Openshaw is Professor in the Department of Social and Policy Studies in Education at the Massey University College of Education. He taught in primary and intermediate schools (elementary and junior high school equivalents) in New Zealand prior to becoming an academic. Roger is a historian of education, who has published widely in curriculum history, especially in regard to social studies.

Michael Singh is Professor in the School of Education and Early Childhood Studies, University of Western Sydney. He is currently completing a research project on White Australia politics and the conversion strategies used to reproduce "White Australians." Professor Singh has been responsible for the conceptualization of innovative projects that focus on the policy and practice of local engagements with the problems and possibilities of globalization.

Noparat Suaysuwan is Assistant Professor in the Department of English, Rajabhat Institute Rajanagarinda, Chachoengsao, Thailand. She has extensive experience teaching English in the Thai context and is currently completing her Ph.D. at the University of Queensland.

Ting-Hong Wong is Assistant Researcher in the Institute of Sociology at Academia Sinica, Taiwan. His book, *Hegemonies Compared: State Formation and Chinese School Politics in Postwar Singapore and Hong Kong*, was published by Routledge. He is currently developing a research project on nationalism and education in postcolonial Taiwan.

Index

Adkins, E.C.S., 44, 54*n1*

Affirmative action, 2

Alexander, D., 22

Alexander, J.C., 13, 23

Altbach, P.G., 80

Althusser, L., 148

Anderson, B., 22

Anderson, W., 169, 172

Ang, I., 168

Apple, M.W., 61, 79, 147, 200

Arboleda, A., 80

Archer, E., 26

Ash, J., 136

Asia-Pacific. *See also* specific countries: comparitive views from Western perspective, 1; decolonization in, 4; educational policies in, 2; foreign context of education studies of, 1; multiperipheral/multicentered geopolitics in, 5, 6; struggles over difference in, 7; treatment of curriculum as exceptional, 2

Australia: amelioration function of education in, 21, 22; Anglo-fundamentalism in, 164, 165, 169, 171, 173, 174; asylum-seekers in, 166; attraction function of education in, 21; British colonization of, 163, 164; challenges to biological assimilation project in, 169; colonial legacy in, 8; conversion strategies in, 164–167; cosmopolitics in, 9, 165, 166, 170, 175–179; curriculum development in, 11–23; disavowal of indigenous rights by White Australia, 167, 168, 172; exclusive entitlement to land by Whites, 168; immigration programs in, 165; immigration/refugee debate in, 15; Indigenous-Asian Australians issues, 163–180; Indigenous Land Rights struggles in, 163; indigenous peoples in, 3, 163–180; lack of constitution in, 166; Mabo Native Title decision, 173, 175; misrecognition of hybridity in, 14; multiculturalism and, 169, 172; national identity issues, 23, 165, 166; nation-building in, 14, 166; non-European presence in, 165; postcolonial history, 23; Queensland New Basics reform in, 15; racialized caste system in, 174; reappropriation of resources in, 173; Reconciliation and Reparations Movement in, 9, 164, 171, 173; reconciliation of indigenous and Asian Australians, 167–179; relegation of indigenous Australians to lowest caste, 174–179; removal of indigenous peoples from land, 163; rights to Native Title in, 163; role of social studies education in, 163–180; "solidarity" of Asian Australians with White Australia policies, 167, 174; Stolen Generation in, 170, 175; *terra nullius* policy in, 163, 171, 172; "Welcome to Country" ceremony in, 172; "White blanket" histories in, 175–176, 177; White Nation

239

Movement in, 164, 169, 178; Whites-only federation of, 163
Awaya, A., 192

Baker, C.D., 94, 126–127, 128
Banister, J., 132, 133
Baxter, Mrs. J., 33
Beck, U., 122
Bell, J.F., 33, 34
Benhabib, S., 12, 16
Berkovits, A., 138
Bernstein, B., 160
Biculturalism, 36
Bilingualism: in Taiwan, 63
Binney, J., 29
Bourdieu, P., 160, 163, 164, 165, 174, 178
Bowles, S., 160
Brah, A., 188
Bray, M., 80
Brookes, B., 32
Budby, J., 22
Burbules, N.C., 90
Burrow, H.C., 81, 83, 84
Butler, J., 148, 150

Cambodia, 17–18; effects of genocide in, 18
Campbell, A.E., 33
Capital: accumulation, 63; cultural, 22, 165; destructive forces of, 23; distribution of, 21, 23; economic, 14, 22, 164; educational, 18; expansion, 6; global distribution of, 18; human, 6, 12, 15, 17, 21, 117; investment, 21; multicultural, 164; social, 164; symbolic, 22; transnational flows, 5
Carstens, S.A., 47
Castells, M., 22
Catron, G., 48, 55n7
Chafy, R., 136, 142
Chapman-Taylor, R., 28, 29, 31
Cheah, B.K., 43
Cheah, P., 14
Chen, J.-H., 7
Chen, J.-J., 59–74, 66
Cheng, T.C., 49
Chiang Ching-kuo, 63
Chiang Kai-shek, 48
China: capitalist features of, 7; centralization of curriculum in, 139;

closed system of cultural knowledge in, 111–113; commodification of labor in, 100; constraints on education in, 8; construction of cultural knowledge in, 99–133; consumerism in, 100; cultural values/beliefs in textbooks, 103, 103tab, 106–109; culture knowledge in, 7; curriculum content driven by textbook selection in, 102; curriculum emphasis on technological superiority in, 8; development experiences in, 102; discourse of dominant values in, 99–113; downsizing of work force, 101; economic reform in, 100; economic/sociocultural context, 100–102; education reform in, 102; environmental degradation in, 131, 132–134; environmental education/development in, 8, 131–145; "expert" phase of development in environmental education, 137; extracurricular activities in, 143; fear of "Russian disaster" in, 102; features of capitalist society in, 7, 100–102; "four modernizations" in, 141; globalization and, 134–137; Great Leap Forward in, 133; income disparities in, 100, 101; industrialization in, 132–134; investment in, 100, 135; justification of rule by present government, 102; lack of adequate materials/resources in environmental education, 139; lack of support for environmental education, 138–139; lack of teacher training in environmental education, 140; language textbooks in, 7; managerial view of education in, 8; marginalization of environmental education, 138; multinationals in, 100; National Environmental Protection Bureau in, 137; national testing in, 139, 142; nongovernmental organizations in, 136; organizational barriers to environmental education, 139; patriotism in textbooks, 103, 103tab, 104–106; political changes in, 101; privatization in, 100; pro-environment education for, 144–145; pro-science/technology views in textbooks, 103, 103*tab,* 109–111; "red" phase of development in environmental education, 137; role of education in sustainable economic growth/development, 141–143; rural-urban disparities in development, 143; "share holdings" in, 100; social issues in, 101; structural inequalities in, 7; "sustainability" phase of development in environmental education, 137; teacher-centered instruction in, 8; Three Gorges Dam in, 135–136; transmission of moral code to students, 102; urbanization in, 132; vocational/technical schools in, 142; in World Trade Organization, 100

Chinese Communist Party (CCP), 47–48, 50, 53; in Hong Kong, 42

Chinese School Certificate Examination (CSCE), 49, 51

Christian-Smith, L.K., 79

Clientelism, 60

Cold War, 117

Colonialism, 4, 117; aftermath of, 19; education as disciplinary instrument of, 19; relations with indigenous peoples and, 8

Comfort women, 9; controversy over textbook portrayal of, 217–231; feminist movements and, 217, 218, 219–222; human rights violations and, 9; poststructuralist theory and, 222–224

Committee on Syllabi and Textbooks (CST), 46

Communication: democracy and, 48; transcultural/intercultural, 22

Conflict: cultural, 5; development and environment, 8; political, 119; sources of, 12

Consumerism, 7, 8, 90, 100, 123–127

Corral-Verdugo, B., 140

Corral-Verdugo, V., 140

Cosmopolitanism, 166; Australian, 165, 170; defining, 165

Creamer, B., 187

Creech, W., 35

Cultural: action, 12; affiliation, 195; appropriateness, 2, 13, 19, 20, 23*n1*; capital, 22, 165; change, 11; circulation, 64; conflict, 5; crisis, 54, 101; development, 117; differences, 4–5, 188; dominance, 186; elites, 102; formations, 87; hegemony, 7, 68; heritage, 44; identity, 8, 9, 32, 118, 184; imperialism, 19; incorporation, 41; knowledge, 141; pluralism, 20; production, 64, 173; relativism, 6, 13; renaissance, 101; resources, 147; rights, 3; sensitivity, 19; tradition, 54; traditional anthropological version of, 20; values, 81, 102, 103, 106–109

Culture, 1; capitalist, 5, 117; consumer, 5; dominant, 41; ethnic, 7; hybrid, 3; knowledge, 7; local, 186; Maori, 6; of narcissism, 14; native, 66; plantation, 186; popularity of Western, 5; preservation of, 66; of progress, 142; of the subordinated, 41

Curriculum: assumptions on, 2–3; colonial, 19; core, 11; decisionmaking on, 60; denationalization of, 47–52; de-Sinicization of, 43–47, 44–46; development, 15, 66; economic/cultural change and, 11–23; essentialism and, 6; fragmentation, 17; governmental, 6; grand narratives in, 11–23; hegemonic, 7; hierarchical forms of knowledge in, 160; in Hong Kong, 7, 47–52; indigenization of, 64, 65; making, 11, 12, 17; narratives, 11–23; narrowing of, 13; national identity and, 12; nationalistic, 62; neo-Tylerism and, 15; in New Zealand, 25–37; organization, 150; Pinar reconceptualist perspective and, 15, 17; policymaking, 7; post-September 11, 11–23; quantifiable outcomes and, 15; realignment, 15; reform, 46; responses to changing realities, 3; in Singapore, 7, 43–47; social studies, 6, 25–37; specification, 22; theory, 12, 99; totalization and, 6; uncritical adherence to, 6; Western, 2

Curtis, B., 53

Davis, S.G., 50

Deculturalization, 54

Democracy: citizenship education for, 26; communication and, 48; textbooks deregulation and, 59; Western, 2

Democratic Progressive Party (Taiwan), 63, 66, 67, 69

Denationalization, 47–52

Deng Xiaoping, 135, 141

Development: cultural, 117; curriculum, 15, 59, 66; discourses of, 1; educational, 20; environment issues in, 8, 134–137; infrastructure, 21; neoliberalism and, 20; outsourced, 20; rural-urban disparities in, 143; social, 117

De Vos, G., 199

Difference: cultural, 4–5; within difference, 13; ethnicity and, 6; globalization and, 3–6; linguistic, 4–5; living together in, 22, 23; portrayals of, 37; recognition of, 5; silence around, 12; struggles over, 7; symmetrization of, 13

"Diploma Disease," 139

Discourse: of aid, 1; constructed, 59; construction, 15; counter-hegemonic, 50–52, 62; critical analysis and, 7; democratization, 62; of development, 1; helping, 20; hybrid, 3; Judeo-Christian, 19; of liberation, 20; nativization, 67; neoliberal, 1; normative, 23; pedagogic, 50–52, 64; postmodern, 217–231; of "quality assurance," 20; of technicality, 16; of textbook reform, 7

Diversity: in education, 22; enabling, 12; encouraging, 12; engaging, 13; trans-cultural strategies for addressing, 11

Dore, R., 139

Earth Summit (1992), 137

Economic: capital, 14, 22, 164; change, 11; formations, 1; globalization, 13, 18; policies, 2, 16; rationalization, 1; reform, 100; restructuring, 141

Economy: cross-border influence, 117; global, 22, 117; information-based, 117; intervention in, 60; political, 20

Education: of the Other, 22; challenging metanarratives of, 6; citizenship, 26–27; colonial, 19; "developing" contexts, 18; dissection of key learning areas into outcomes, 21, 22; diversity in, 22; environmental, 8, 131–145; ethnic, 9; ethnic constructions in, 6; indigenization of, 63, 64, 67–70;

international, 18; language, 64; managerial view of, 8; minority communities and, 3; moral/civic purposes of, 20; multilingual, 64, 68; narrative and, 11–23; nativization of, 60; piecemeal visions of, 20, 21; reform, 66, 70, 102; shifts in provision of services, 19; short-term goals in, 21; social studies, 25–37; struggle for identity and, 8; teacher, 72; technocratic, 19; upward mobility through, 66

Educational systems: challenges to, 1; continuities in, 5; recognition of differences by, 5; responses to changing realities, 3

Education and Culture Committee of the Legislative Yuan (Taiwan), 66

Elson, R., 167

English as a Second Language (ESL), 18

English for Academic Purposes (EAP), 18

English for Special Purposes (ESP), 18

Environment: conflict with development, 8; crisis in, 8; shared responsibility for, 144

Environmental Educators' Initiative for China, 143

Essentialism: curriculum and, 6, 16

Estep, G.A., 188

Ethics: of care, 22; of empathy, 22

Ethnic: culture, 7; education, 9; harmony, 6; identity, 9, 43, 184; labels, 9; marketing strategies, 6

Ethnicity: Maori, 25–37; in New Zealand, 6; portrayals of, 37

Ethnonationalism, 4

Ewing, J.L., 30

Existentialism: philosophic/literary, 23

Fairclough, N., 99, 120

Farrell, J., 80

Featherstone, M., 123

Federation of Malaya: mistrust of Singapore by, 43

Feinberg, W., 167, 168, 170

Feminism, 118; comfort women and, 217–222; international, 5

Fenn-Wu Committee, 44

Fitzgerald, F., 22

Foley, D., 20

Foucault, M., 23

Frankenberg, R., 190
Frankfurt School, 23
Freebody, P., 94, 126–127, 128
Frias-Armenta, M., 140
Fukuoka, Y., 199
Furman, G., 188

Gabriel, J., 166
Gender, 1; identity, 85, 85*tab*, 87–88, 184; misrepresentation, 59; portrayal in textbooks, 80; structural inequalities of, 8; vocational education and, 8
General Federation of Korean Residents (GFKR), 127
Genocide, 18
Gibbons, P.J., 30
Gilroy, P., 167, 172, 176
Gintis, H., 160
Glick, C.E., 191
Globalization: acceleration of Western values and, 117; aspects of, 135; critical analysis and, 3; cultural, 1; difference and, 3–6; economic, 13, 18, 22; effects of, 117; ethics of, 3–6; impact on societies, 89; intensifying practices of, 169; marginalization of local culture and, 117; resistance to, 117; schooling and, 6; textbooks in period of, 89–94
Goodman, S., 89
Goodson, I.F., 37
Gopinathan, S., 42, 80
Gorrie, A.M., 31
Graddol, D., 89
Graham, P., 13, 16
Gramsci, A., 41, 53, 60
Green, A., 41, 53
Guo Wei-fan, 66, 67, 69
Gupta, A.F., 80

Hahm, C.B., 117
Hall, S., 60
Hammer, R., 22
Hannum, E., 136, 143
Hanson, P., 164, 170
Hao, D.Y., 113
Harris, W.B., 28, 29, 30
Harrison, K., 35
Hawai'i: cultural dominance in, 186; ethnic makeup of, 184; *haole* identity

in, 9, 183, 188, 189, 190; *hapa* identity in, 9, 184, 190–194; heterogeneity of student population in, 3; identity fastening in, 183–197; identity filters for separation of local/nonlocal, 186–190; identity negotiation in, 9; immigration into, 186; individualism v. communitarianism in, 187–188; language use in, 187, 188; local culture in, 186; local identity in, 183, 184, 185–190, 189; mixed-race identity in, 190–194; negotiating identity in, 183–197; patterns of intermarriage in, 191, 192, 192*tab*; repositioning of Whiteness in, 9; significance of personal names in, 194–196; social stratification in, 186; stigma of being *haole*, 189, 190; suppression of language and culture in, 195
Hayneman, S., 80
He, Q.L., 101
He, X., 102
Hegemony, 1; building, 53; cultural, 7, 68; curricular, 7; defining, 41, 60; state formation and, 41–54; strategies of, 54; Western, 188
Henliques, J., 148
Herring, R.D., 190
Heta, Mrs. J., 33
Holloway, W., 148
Hong Kong: adoption of curriculum/textbooks from mainland China, 42; articulation of denationalization principle in, 48–50; change in regard for China as motherland, 49; Chinese Communist Party in, 42, 47–48, 50; Chinese School Certificate Examination in, 49; Chinese school curriculum in, 41–54; Chinese studies as means of cultivating East-West relations in, 49; counter-hegemonic discourse in, 50–52; curriculum in, 7; decolonization of, 42; denationalization of Chinese school curriculum, 43, 47–52; encouragement for local publishers to produce texts, 50; hegemony and, 41–54; human capital rationale in educational policy in, 118; influence

of Taiwan on, 42; Kuomintang in, 49; monoracial society in, 42; pro-Chinese schools in, 55*n7*; pro-KMT schools in, 52; racial politics in, 43; state formation and curriculum policy-making in, 7, 41–54; struggles over difference in, 7; Taiwanese activities in, 48; ultra-nationalistic schools in, 51, 52; unwillingness of leftist schools to participate in CSCE curriculum, 51

Howard, J., 164, 166, 170, 177

Hu, A.G., 101, 102

Huang, Z.-C., 59

Hurtig, J., 20

Hutchinson, S.M., 143

Hybridity, 14

Identity, 1; ambiguous, 193; children's, 95; classed, 8; collective, 195; commercial student, 150, 152; construction, 7, 9, 15, 183; as contested issue, 32; conversion, 163–180; cosmopolitan, 12; cultural, 8, 9, 32, 118, 184; cultural context and, 185–190; ethnic, 9, 43, 184, 193; ethnonational, 12; fastening/unfastening, 183–197; filters, 187; formation, 5, 6, 8, 64, 65; gender, 5, 8, 85, 85*tab,* 184; group, 186; immobile concepts of, 23; local, 9, 12, 41, 52, 183; middle-class, 89; misrecognition of, 14; national, 9, 12, 23, 41, 163, 165, 166; native, 63; negotiating, 9, 183–197; plantation, 189; politics, 12; postcolonial, 5; poststructuralist view of, 183; raced, 8; reductionist categories of, 183; shared, 12; social, 87; solidarity and, 12; struggle over, 8; youth, 5

Imperialism, 49

Inatomi, S., 208

Indigenous peoples: in Australia, 163–180; cultural rights of, 3; of New Zealand, 25–37; postcolonial relations and, 8

Indonesia: mistrust of Singapore by, 43

Industrialization. *See also* individual countries: air quality and, 132–133; decreasing biodiversity and, 132; disposal of toxic waste and, 132; health issues, 133; in Korea, 119;

in New Zealand, 27; pressure on rural agriculture sectors and, 132; in Thailand, 7, 81, 85–89

Infante, E., 187

Inokuchi, H., 9, 36, 199–212, 202

Institutions: access to, 60; cultural, 59; formation on continuum, 2; postwar technocratic, 20; Western, 101

International Monetary Fund, 134; structural adjustment policies of, 11, 20

Intervention: state, 71

Investment: attracting, 21; capital, 21; multinational, 100

Ip, D., 22

Iraq, 4

Japan: Alien Registration Law in, 200, 202; assimilationist educational policy in, 206; Buraku liberation movement in, 213*n10*; closure of Korean education schools in, 203; colonialism and, 200; colonization of Korea, 200–202; comfort women issues, 9, 217–231; General Federation of Korean Residents in, 203–206; heterogeneity of student population in, 3; inclusion of Korean perspective in official curriculum, 209–211; involvement in comfort women issue, 217–231; issues of identity/difference for Resident Koreans in, 199–212; *jus singuinis* principle in, 202, 213*n3*; League of Koreans in Japan and, 200; migration of Koreans to, 200–202; Mindan in, 213*n5*; minzoku education in Japanese schools, 206–209; minzoku programs as extracurricular activity, 207; minzoku schools in, 200–206; nationalist efforts to refute testimony of comfort women, 219–222, 227–229; North Korea-centric education in, 203–206; oppressive social policies in, 199, 200; recategorization of Koreans in, 202; Resident Korean education in, 9, 199–212; "Teaching About Korea" program in, 209–211; transfer of power in Taiwan by, 61; use of Japanese names by Resident Koreans, 206–209

Jessop, B., 60

Ju Young Jung, 119

Kadohata, C., 195
Kapitzke, C., 7, 79–95
Kashiwazaki, C., 200, 202
Kawada, F., 221
Ke, Z.-Z., 59
Keesing, R.M., 36
Kellner, D., 13
Kim, M., 8, 147–161
Kim Dae Jung, 119
Kinsella, A.E., 33
Kishino, J., 207, 209, 210
Knights, D., 148
Knowledge: commercial, 154; construction of, 99–113; content, 79; control over, 60, 61; cultural, 7, 99–113, 141; hierarchical, 160; indigenous, 16; legitimate, 61, 147, 159; official, 42, 60, 61, 99; organization of, 61; processing, 147; school, 60, 147–161, 159; struggle over, 61
Korea: *chaebols* in, 119; commercial/vocational education in, 147–161; consumerism in, 117, 118, 123–127; contemporary ideologies in texts in, 7, 8, 117–129; emergence of Western lifestyle in, 8, 117, 118; environmental issues in, 8, 119, 120–123; evaluation in commercial schools, 153; export-oriented development strategy, 118; feminist movement in, 118; *Following Father* narrative, 124–125; gendered/classed subjectivities in commercial schools in, 147–161; gender inequality in, 8, 118; general subject teachers' opinions of commercial students, 156–159; global change effect on textbooks, 118; heterogeneity of student population in, 3; human capital rationale in educational policy in, 118; income disparity in, 118; industrialization in, 119; introduction of children to new social "realities" in, 118; language textbooks in, 117–129; lowering of teaching levels for commercial students, 156–159; marginalization of vocational education in, 147; media in, 119; middle class in, 118, 123, 129; Mt. Kumgang Tourism in, 119; multinational destruction of environment in, 120–123; *My Daily Life* narrative, 126; new local cultural forms in, 118; omission of Korean cultural ideologies from textbooks in, 80; in Organization for Economic Cooperation and Development, 118; pollution in, 119; portrayal of everyday life in textbooks, 117–129; regulation of students in, 147; request for reform of commercial school curriculum, 161n3; reunification issues in, 8, 119, 126–127; *The Reunification Train Runs* narrative, 127, 128; service-based economy in, 123; six-three-three-four educational system in, 149; *The Song of Insects* narrative, 120–123, 128; *A Story of Balloons* narrative, 126–127, 128; student practice for skills not utilized in workplaces, 153; students in commercial schools, 149–155; *Summer Holiday Plans* narrative, 123–124; *Sunday Morning* narrative, 125–126; technical qualifications for commercial students, 151–155; testing in commercial/vocational schools, 150, 151; textbook gender bias in, 126, 128; textbooks in, 7, 117–129; transfer of blame for pollution from industry to citizens in, 120–123; undeveloped rural sector in, 118; views on quality of students in commercial schools, 155–156; worker alienation in, 119
Kramsch, C., 20
Kress, G., 80
Krongkaew, M., 81
Kuhn, A., 160
Kuomintang, 42, 49; authoritarian regime of, 62; corporatist structure of, 62; legitimacy of, 61–63; Taiwanization policy by, 62
Kurusapa Press, 81, 89
Kwan, T., 138
Kwok-Chun, T., 80

Lakoff, R., 176
Land, R., 22
Language(s): education, 64; education as means of transmitting ideology, 99; of instruction, 64; as medium of cultural production, 64; native, 75n8

Lee, C., 199, 200
Lee, D.B., 7, 80, 117–129
Lee, J., 131, 137, 138, 139, 143
Lee Kuan Yew, 46
Lee Teng-hui, 63, 64, 70
Lemke, J., 99
Levinson, B.A., 20
Li, X.D., 133
Lidstone, J., 138
Lind, A.W., 186
Lingard, R., 22
Liu, F., 102, 113
Liu, G., 135
Liu, X., 135
Liu, Y., 7, 99–113
Loh, P.F.S., 42, 47
Louie, K., 22
Luke, A., 1–10, 11–23, 79, 89, 94, 99, 120
Luke, C., 13, 22, 95
Lum, D., 187
Lyotard, J.F., 16

Mabo, E., 163, 173
Macdonald, D.S., 119, 121, 125
Maori Educational Foundation, 33
Maori peoples: community life of, 26, 27; confiscation of lands, 25, 29; controversy over Washday at the Pa, 32–35; cultural contributions of, 26, 27; cultural identity issues and, 32; culture, 6; exclusion from suburbia, 32; government dependence on support from, 29; Hauhau by, 29; idealization of lifestyles of, 32; image of "difference" of, 25–37; Land Wars and, 25; meaning of culture of, 25; middle class, 6, 36; modern, 31–32; portrayal in textbooks, 28–31; racism and, 32, 34; resistance to settlement by, 30; in Ringatu church, 29, 30; stereotyping of, 32, 33; superficial treatment in curriculum, 30–31; "upmarket" image for, 36
Maori Women's Welfare League, 32, 33, 34, 36
Mao Zedong, 133
Marginson, S., 135
Materialism, 27
May Fourth Movement, 49, 55n5
McGee, J., 26

McIntyre, A., 197
McLaren, P., 167, 169, 171
Meaning: hierarchical, 157; locally contested, 148; making, 8; preconstituted, 150; selectively mobilized, 153; systems, 154; temporarily fixed, 148
Media: emergence of new, 5; in Korea, 119; modes of, 13; recognition of differences by, 5; role in forming Whiteness, 167; stereotyping of the Other by, 167; in Taiwan, 62
Mills, M., 22
Milojevic, I., 22
Min, Y.S., 133
Miyoshi, M., 4
Moeran, B., 36
Mohanty, C.T., 4
Morita, Y., 200
Mother Tongue Article (Taiwan), 64
Mouffe, C., 60
Movements: feminist, 217, 218, 219–222; historical, 20; May Fourth, 49, 55n5; opposition, 62, 66; population, 21; Reconciliation and Reparations, 9, 164, 171, 173; social, 5, 9; White Nation Movement, 164, 169, 178; women's, 3–4
Multiculturalism, 2, 169, 172
Multinational corporations: recognition of differences by, 5
Murdoch, J.H., 26, 27

Nairn, T., 165, 166, 174, 178
Nakaso, D., 184
Nakayama, H., 207
Narrative(s): analysis of, 16; education and, 11–23; ethno-nationalist, 16; grand, 16; inequality of, 16; racist, 16; sexist, 16; skepticism of, 16, 20
Nash, R., 27
Nationalism, 12, 22
Naughton, B., 100
Neocolonialism, 4, 117
Neoliberalism, 15; development and, 20
New Party (Taiwan), 64, 65, 75n9
New Zealand: biculturalism in, 25, 36; Committee on Social Studies in, 28; conceptions of Maori culture in, 27; concern for political rather than educational issues, 25–37; controversy

over depiction of Maori life, 32–35; curriculum making in, 11; debate on ethnicity in, 25; "difference" in, 25–37; establishment of European dominance in, 29; ethnicity and difference in, 6, 25–37; government dependence on Maori support in, 29; indigenous rights in, 3; introduction of social studies in, 26; Land Wars in, 25, 29; Man A Course of Study program in, 37n4; official curriculum in, 28–31; Official Information Act in, 35; Ratana Labour Pact, 29; reorientation of method and content in social studies in, 28; social demographic changes in, 32; social studies curriculum in, 25–37; superficial treatment of Maori peoples in curriculum, 30–31; "Syllabus of Social Studies in History and Geography" in, 28; Syllabus Revision Committee in, 30–31; textbook issues, 28–31; Thomas Report, 26, 37n2; Treaty of Waitangi, 25; use of British system of school classes, 37n1; views of equality in, 26

Ng Lun, N.H., 47

Nolan, P., 135

Nongovernmental organizations, 20, 136, 144

Nozaki, Y., 1–10, 36, 199–212, 217–231

Oakes, T., 101

Ogbu, J.U., 200

Oh, Y., 210

O'Hern, D., 8

Okamura, J., 186

Oksenberg, M., 102

Ong, K., 168

Openshaw, R., 25–37, 110

Ou, Y.-S., 59

Owens, J.M.R., 25

The Oxford English Course for Thailand (Burrow), 81–85

Ozawa, Y., 204

Palmer, P., 183, 195

Park, I., 205

Park, S., 204

Parliamentarianism, 60

Partington, G., 35

Passeron, J., 160

Patriotism, 103, 103*tab*, 104–106

Payne, E.M., 44, 45

Pedagogy: grand narratives in, 11–23; responses to changing realities, 3; second language, 23n1

Pennycook, A., 18, 19

People's Action Party (PAP), 43, 46

Petty, E.J., 101

Philippines: heterogeneity of student population in, 3

Pluralism, 60; theoretical, 13

Policy: comparitive views, 1; decentralized, 66; economic, 16; formation, 11; making, 66; neoliberal economic, 2; social, 2, 16; state, 6, 135; structural adjustment, 11, 20; textbook, 6; textbook deregulation, 59–74

Political: conflict, 119; economy, 20; ideology, 7; opposition, 7, 62; pragmatism, 6; violence, 21

Politics: of autonomy, 63; ethnic, 65; identity, 12; nationalistic, 67; one-dimensional, 22; racial, 43; resentment, 174; of textbook deregulation in Taiwan, 59–74

Postmodernism: engaging diversity and, 13

Poststructuralism, 148, 183

Poverty, 8; amelioration, 1

Power: discursive, 148; relations, 60, 99, 113; state, 70; state distribution, 60; symbolic, 63

Privatization, 100; in Taiwan, 64, 65

Qi, S.H., 133

Ratana Labour Pact, 29

Reality: constructions of in textbooks, 61; social, 113, 118, 128

Reed, G.G., 9, 183–197

Reform: curriculum, 43, 46, 53, 69; economic, 100; education, 20, 62, 66, 70, 102; political economy of, 20; textbook, 7, 44, 59, 60, 72

Refugees: treatment of, 15

Relativism, 12; feminist critique of, 16

Rendel Report, 42

Reproduction theory, 160–161

Resident Koreans: considered "different," 9; ethnic education and, 9; identity formations by, 9; in Japan, 9, 199–212

Ringatu church, 29, 30
Robbins, B., 165
Rohrer, J., 183, 190
"Rooted in Taiwan, Mindful of the
    Mainland, Looking out to the World,"
    64, 67
Ruddock, P., 177
Ryan, A.B., 31
Ryang, S., 199

Sabhasri, S., 20, 136
Sakamoto, T., 228
Sakurai, Y., 227, 228
San Francisco Peace Treaty (1951), 202
Sarday, Z., 117
Saunders, E., 31
Schafer, H.J., 132
Science Across Asia-Pacific Project, 136
Scott, J.W., 148, 200
Shi, C., 143
Shu, W.-D., 69
Singapore: adoption of
    curriculum/textbooks from mainland
    China, 42; British preference for de-
    Sinicization, 44; capability for
    hegemonization of Chinese culture,
    43; Chinese school curriculum in,
    41–54; Committee on Syllabi and
    Textbooks in, 46; concept of
    "proximity" in, 45; creation of local
    consciousness in, 42; curriculum in, 7;
    decolonization of, 42; de-Sinicization
    of Chinese curriculum in, 42, 43–47;
    encouragement of Malayanization of
    teaching materials in, 46; Fenn-Wu
    Committee in, 44; gap in state-
    promulgated syllabi and textbooks
    used, 46–47; General Textbook
    Committee (GTC), 44, 45; hegemony
    and, 41–54; human capital rationale
    in educational policy in, 118; Japanese
    occupation, 43; limits on curriculum
    space for Chinese history, 46;
    multiracial society in, 42; People's
    Action Party in, 43, 46; proposal for
    localization of curriculum, 44; Rendel
    Report and, 42; resistance from
    Chinese to de-Sinicization, 44–46;
    Singapore Chinese School Conference
    in, 45; state building objectives in, 42;
    state formation and curriculum

policymaking in, 7, 41–54; struggles
    over difference in, 7; suggestion for
    common Malayan culture for, 44;
    Teachers Advisory Committee (TAC),
    44, 45; United Chinese School
    Teachers' Association in, 44; United
    Publishing House Limited and, 44, 45
Singapore Chinese School Conference
    (SCSC), 45
Singh, M., 8, 163–180
Sitglitz, J.E., 1
Smith, B., 175
Smith, D., 224
Smith, L.T., 3
Social: action, 12; capital, 164;
    cartography, 186; class, 36, 129, 184;
    cohesiveness, 13; development, 117;
    differentiation, 8; engineering, 31;
    equity, 11; formations, 1; identities,
    87; integration, 7, 41; movements,
    3–4, 5, 9; opposition, 62;
    organization, 148; policy, 2, 16;
    problems, 101; reality, 113, 118, 128;
    stratification, 186; transitions, 7
Social studies: in Australia, 163–180;
    citizenship education and, 26–27,
    163–180; curriculum, 6; enrichment
    of, 167; identity conversion and,
    163–180; innovatory materials
    challenging prevailing values, 36;
    liberal social engineering in, 31; Man
    A Course of Study program, 37n4; in
    New Zealand, 25–37
Society: civil, 60; integration with
    consent of subordinated, 41;
    multiracial, 41; regulation of, 60
Sorrenson, M.P.K., 25, 29
State: building, 42; capacity for cultural
    incorporation, 41; formation, 2, 6, 7,
    41–54, 53, 54; gendered identity of,
    4; internal articulation of, 60;
    intervention, 71; official educational
    policies of, 4; policies, 6, 135; political
    ideology in, 7; power, 41, 61, 70;
    power distribution in, 60; realization
    of hegemonic projects by, 60;
    representation systems, 60;
    transformation, 7, 59
Statism, 22
Stevenson, R., 140, 141
Stimpson, P., 131, 134, 139, 143, 144

Stone, R.C.J., 31
Structural adjustment programs, 11, 20
Students: appearance as factor in
employment, 161*n2*;
commercial/vocational school,
149–161; concerns about
employment, 157; crossing borders by,
3; "pure," 154; sense of self in relation
to school, 147
Suaysuwan, N., 7, 79–95
Sugitani, Y., 207
Supriya, K.E., 183
Sweeting, A., 47

Taiwan: activities in Hong Kong, 48;
bilingualism in, 63; capital
accumulation in, 63; centralized
educational administrative system in,
62; Chinese Communist Party in, 61;
Coalition for Educational and Cultural
Reform in, 72; Commission on
Educational Reform (CER), 69, 71;
community education in, 70;
Compulsory Education Law in, 72;
cultural institutions in, 59; cultural
reconstruction in, 62; curricular
decentralization in, 63; Curricular
Standards Revision Committees
(CSRCs), 68; curriculum development
in, 59, 66; curriculum reform in, 69;
Democratic Progressive Party in, 63,
66, 67, 69; democratization discourse
in, 62; demographic composition,
75*n3*; depoliticized ethnic politics in,
65; Directing Commission on
Humanities and Social Sciences
Education in, 68; Diverse High School
Entrance Program in, 69; Education
and Culture Committee of the
Legislative Yuan (ECCLY), 66;
education reform groups in, 63;
elementary school textbooks, 63–67;
ethnic-related self-identification on,
75*n3*; first wave of deregulation,
61–63; Getting to Know Taiwan
subject, 64, 65, 67; hegemonic
approach to textbooks reform, 60–61;
high school textbooks, 67–70; identity
formation in, 64, 65; indigenization of
curriculum in, 63, 64, 65, 67–70;
indigenous rights in, 3; influence on

Hong Kong, 42; introduction of
Sinicization education policy in, 61;
junior high school textbooks, 71–72;
Kuomintang in, 61–63, 75*n3*;
languages of instruction in, 63;
"life/experience-centered curricula" in,
71, 72; localized curriculum making in,
63; martial law in, 61, 62; media in,
62; Mother Tongue Article, 64;
National Curricular Guidelines in, 71;
National Curricular Standards in, 62,
63, 64, 65, 70, 71; National Education
Conferences by Civic Organizations in,
63; national entrance exams in, 66, 69;
National Institute for Compilation and
Translation (NICT), 62, 68, 70, 72;
nationalist politics in, 67; native
identity in, 63; nativist curriculum
supplementary to existing curriculum
in, 64, 67; nativization in, 61, 67,
75*n7*; New Party in, 64, 65, 75*n9*;
official reform discourse in, 70;
opposition movements in, 62; political
parties in, 62; private publishers in, 64,
65; privatization in, 64, 65; pro-
independence forces in, 68; "ROC on
Taiwan," 63; "Rooted in Taiwan,
Mindful of the Mainland, Looking out
to the World," 64, 67; second wave of
deregulation, 63–72; standardization of
textbooks in, 7; state building in, 59,
61, 63; state transformation in, 59;
student-centered instruction in, 72;
symbolic power in, 63; "Taiwan first"
stance in, 60, 69; Taiwanization
Education Coalition, 68; Taiwanization
policy on, 75*n5*; textbook deregulation
in, 59–74; textbook production in, 64,
65, 70; Textbook Reform Coalition in,
68; Three Principles of the People
in, 70; transfer of power from Japan,
61; Xiangtu Art Activity subject,
64; Xiangtu Instructional Activity
subject, 64
Taylor, N., 31
Teaching: assumptions on, 2–3;
fragmentation in, 19; fragmentation of
work of, 13; language, 18, 19
Technology, 109–111; information, 5;
textbooks as, 5
Te Kooti Arikirangi Te Turiki, 29, 30

Testing: high-stakes, 142; national, 142; national entrance exams, 66; standardized, 20

Textbooks: Chinese education in Singapore and, 44–47; Chinese language, 99–113; as constant in colonial/postcolonia education, 5; constructions of reality in, 61; control of content, 61; as cultural artifacts, 61, 95; decontrol of market for, 63; deregulation in Taiwan, 59–74; deregulation of standardized, 7; diversified, 64, 65; as economic commodities, 61; economies of production, 5; as form of educational technology, 5; gendered identity in, 4; gender portrayal in, 80; ideal child portrayal in, 84–85, 87–89; ideological messages in, 80; introduction to cultural knowledge through, 99; issues in New Zealand, 28–31; language, 7, 99–113; legitimation of governmental version of events, 113; liberalization of, 62, 63, 64, 65; localization of in Hong Kong, 50; as major mode of information, 5; marketization of production, 60, 61; neocolonial pedagogies in, 80; official approval procedures, 28, 29; policies, 6; politics and, 6; portrayal of Maori peoples in, 28–31; private publication of, 62, 64, 65; production, 60, 64, 65, 66, 70, 80; readers and, 5, 6; reading positions in, 80; reform, 59, 60; as regulated products controlled by states, 61; representation of knowledge in, 80; selection of, 59; as sites of ideological/cultural hegemony, 7, 79; standardized, 7, 59, 62, 64, 65, 66; subject positions in, 80; United Publishing House Limited and, 44, 45

Thailand: adoption of Western practices in, 7; agricultural economy presented in texts in, 82–83; British colonialism portrayed in textbooks in, 81–82; communitarian values in, 93; dependence on textbooks as main pedagogical technology in, 79; *English is Fun* series, 85–89; English-language textbooks in, 79–95; English texts in period of globalization, 89–94; English texts in postwar industrializing period, 81–85; gender portrayal in textbooks in, 85, 85*tab*, 87–88, 92; heterogeneity of student population in, 3; ideal child portrayal, 84–85, 87–89, 91–93; industrialization in, 7, 81, 85–89; language/identity construction in, 93; middle class life in, 83–84, 86–87; presentation of Western values in texts, 89–94; social transition in, 7; spiritual beliefs in, 7; *On the Springboard* series in, 89–94; teacher education in, 79; textbooks in, 7; traditional life in, 7, 82–83; uncritical adoption of Western ideas from textbooks in, 79–95; us of *The Oxford English Course for Thailand* in, 81–85

the Center, 5

the Other: de-authorized, 148; education of, 22; marginalization of, 16; stereotyping by media, 167; treatment of, 15; Western studies of, 1

Therborn, G., 148

Thomas Report, 26, 37*n*2

Three Principles of the People (Taiwan), 51, 70

Tilbury, D., 131, 137, 138, 139, 143

Tirikatene, E., 34

Torres, C.A., 90

Totalitarianism, 101

Treaty of Versailles, 55*n*5

Treaty of Waitangi, 25, 35

Ubduvudyakusn, 36

Ueno, C., 222, 223, 224–227

United Chinese School Teachers' Association (UCSTA), 44, 45

United Kingdom: annexation of New Zealand by, 25; anti-Chinese predisposition of, 54*n*1; curriculum making in, 11; desire to reproduce nation's past, 165; in Hong Kong, 48, 50

United Nations: Food and Agriculture Organization, 133

United Publishing House Limited (UPHL), 44, 45

United States: curriculum making in, 11; inclusion of different ethnic groups into Whiteness category in, 166

Urbanization. *See also* specific countries: in China, 132; in New Zealand, 27
Urwin, C., 148

Van Loon, B., 117
Venn, C., 148
Vurdubakis, T., 148

Wah Kiu Yat Poh (newspaper), 50
Walker, A., 177
Walkerdine, V., 148
Wang, L., 135
Wang, X.Y., 100, 101
Wasserstrom, J.N., 101
Weedon, C., 148
Weiner, M., 199
Wen Wei Pao (newspaper), 50
West, C., 166, 167, 168, 169, 170, 171
Westra, A., 32
Whittaker, E., 190
Wibulswas, P., 20, 136
Wilden, A., 13
Wilson, B., 129
Wolpe, A.M., 160
Women. *See also* Feminisn: social/intellectual movements of, 3–4

Wong, S.C., 133
Wong, T.H., 41–54
Wong, Ting-Hong, 7
Woo, W., 135
World Bank, 134
World Bookstore, 47
Wu Jing, 70

Xenophobia, 165
Xiao, G.Q., 102
Xie, Q.-D., 59

Yan, Y.X., 100
Yasamaru, Y., 226
Yayori, M., 218
Yeo, K.W., 42
Yoshida, S., 221
Yoshimi, Y., 220, 221, 223, 224–227
Yu, L., 143

Zerubaval, E., 187
Zhang, G., 133
Zhang, Q.-L., 59
Zhu, H., 139
Zhu, Z., 132
Zhu H., 144